For Grandpa John, in loving memory.
Now you are gone, no one laughs at my jokes.

We Fight Fascists

We Fight Fascists

*The 43 Group and Their Forgotten
Battle for Post-war Britain*

Daniel Sonabend

VERSO

First published by Verso 2019
© Daniel Sonabend 2019

All rights reserved

The moral rights of the author have been asserted

1 3 5 7 9 10 8 6 4 2

Verso
UK: 6 Meard Street, London W1F 0EG
US: 20 Jay Street, Suite 1010, Brooklyn, NY 11201
versobooks.com

Verso is the imprint of New Left Books

ISBN-13: 978-1-78873-324-3
ISBN-13: 978-1-78873-326-7 (UK EBK)
ISBN-13: 978-1-78873-327-4 (US EBK)

British Library Cataloguing in Publication Data
A catalogue record for this book is available from the British Library

Library of Congress Cataloging-in-Publication Data
Library of Congress Control Number: t2019947010

Typeset in Sabon by Biblichor Ltd, Edinburgh
Printed and bound by CPI Group (UK) Ltd, Croydon CR0 4YY

Oh, we
Who wanted to prepare the ground for friendliness
Could not ourselves be friendly.

Bertolt Brecht, 'To Those Born Later' (1940)

Contents

Introduction

Morris Beckman was getting a kicking. It was two against one, and though the former Merchant Navy radio operator 'could have a fight', he was no *shtarker* (the Yiddish word for a strong man who can really throw a punch). The fascist heavies he was grappling with had his measure, and his pals were a bit busy with brawls of their own. Beckman managed to get himself loose and sprinted towards the low wall just behind the cinema not far away. He clambered up and threw himself over. Before his feet touched the ground, Beckman had realised his catastrophic error. Half a dozen Mosleyites watched him land and, recognising him for a 43 Group Jew, pounced. Beckman cried out as he fell under their blows.

'And suddenly,' recalled Morris Beckman over sixty years later, 'I heard the roar that was Gerry Flamberg shouting, "You silly bastard, you silly bastard." He vaulted the wall and started attacking the fascists who were attacking me, in fact he was kicking out as he was still falling. He landed and yelled at me to stand next to him, which I did. "Down here! Quick!" he yelled, and two more 43 Group members jumped over the wall. Together we fought them off.'

It was in March 2012 that Morris Beckman told me that story, and of all the wonderful anecdotes he shared that is the one to impress itself most deeply on my mind. It's not hard to see why. The image of the six-foot-tall 'flat-faced, pug-nosed, browned-off' (his words) twenty-something ex-paratrooper Gerald Flamberg leaping over a wall into a mass of fascists, limbs going out in every direction as he calls his friend a silly bastard, is one that's hard to forget. But more than that, it's a perfect distillation of the anti-fascist organisation he founded; an organisation which arrived in my life very much like a large man leaping over a wall. One moment I'd never heard of it, and the next it had completely taken over my life.

My story begins four months earlier, when my very old friend Luke Brandon Field got into his bath to watch a documentary about Vidal Sassoon. When he got out, he immediately called me. As a somewhat follicularly challenged individual, I am not the most obvious person to call after one has just watched a documentary about the world's most famous hairdresser (confession – before Luke's call I am not entirely sure I knew who Vidal Sassoon was), but Luke was not calling to talk about hair.

'Have you ever heard of the 43 Group?' he asked.

'The what?'

'The 43 Group. Jewish soldiers who fought fascists after the Second World War?'

'Don't you mean after the First World War.'

'No, Second I think.'

'That doesn't make any sense, there weren't any fascists after the Second World War. There was Mosley before it, but not after.'

'Yeah they were fighting Mosley.'

'I think you've got your facts mixed up, mate.'

'I was just watching a documentary about Vidal Sassoon, and he was apparently in it.'

'Oh . . . right. Err . . . The poet?'

'The hairdresser.'

'Oh yeah . . . of course.'

'Just look up the 43 Group, and give me a call back.'

Returning to the reading room of the British Library I had quickly walked out of to answer Luke's call, I looked up the 43 Group and realised I owed my friend an apology. But feelings of contrition were quickly replaced by those of confusion. Here was a story about an organisation predominantly consisting of young British Jewish men and women who from 1946–50 fought fascists on the streets of Britain. Surely an organisation like that would have a legendary status within the Anglo-Jewish community? I'm a member of that community, and yet I'd never even heard of the 43 Group. Over the ensuing months I would come to realise that I was not the exception but the norm; friends of mine who were either far more involved in the community or knew more about its history had also never heard of the Group. Jews fighting back and beating up fascists – these are some of our favourite stories, so why had the community forgotten?

Digging further into the details, I realised that the epicentre of the fighting between the Group and Oswald Mosley's fascists was around Ridley Road, Dalston, in the north-east London Borough of Hackney. Well known for its market, Ridley Road was also for decades the location of M. Joseph's, the grocery store set up by my great-grandparents. Not only did this realisation give me a personal connection to the events, it also gave me a lead, and I called up my grandmother Pat, who for a time had lived above her parents' shop, to ask if she recalled the weekly fights that happened on Ridley Road. Unfortunately, she did not, as by that time the family had moved to west London, and she was never around Dalston on Sunday evenings, when the fights and riots occurred. Also a teenager in London around that time was my grandfather John, who I decided to question as I was driving him to my parents' house for dinner one Friday in early 2012.

'Have you ever heard of the 43 Group?'

'Heard of it,' he said with jocular indignation, 'I was in it!'

'What!' I exclaimed, whipping my head round while just about maintaining a straight driving line. 'You were in it!'

'Yes,' he said with a big smile on his face, clearly delighted by my shocked expression.

Dozens of questions and much research later I came to understand that this was a statement that needed to be qualified. When my grandfather was seventeen, he was heavily involved in a Zionist organisation through which he learnt of a group that needed some volunteers to attend fascist street meetings and report back on all they had observed. My grandfather volunteered, but his involvement never went beyond that. The 43 Group was known for its street fighting and my grandfather was by his own admission a coward in a fight, and so there was only so far he was willing to go with the Group. Even so, he had never mentioned to any member of our family that as a young man he had spied on fascist meetings for a militant Jewish anti-fascist organisation.

While I had been asking my family members about the Group, Luke had been doing the same and had come up with similar results: rumours, potentially revealing anecdotes, advice on who might know a little bit more. We also both got our hands on copies of the only book ever written about the 43 Group, which was first published in 1993 as *The 43 Group: The Untold Story of Their Fight against Fascism* by one of the founding members, Morris Beckman.[1] After devouring the book within a few days we both agreed that this was a story that needed to be told, and we wanted to be the people to tell it.

Both of us had recently left university and shared ambitions of making a go of it in film or television, me as a writer and Luke as an actor, and we thought the 43 Group could be our meal ticket. I mean, what could be simpler. Find a great idea, check it out, write a killer film script (hubris? – Never heard of it . . .), and hey presto – the Oscars! This did not happen. Which is not to say we were completely delusional. After several people suggested that it was a story that would be better told on TV, a couple of production companies came on board and we received some interest from broadcasters. Knowing that Luke and I were not the only ones who believed the story of the 43 Group needed to be told, I hit the books and dived into the archives, while Luke went on the hunt for any veterans of the Group who were still around and were open to talking to us.

Only a few months after we first discovered the Group and a long time before we started working on developing the TV show, Luke's superior investigative skills led him to discover that Jeanette Beckman, a prominent New York–based punk photographer, was probably related to Morris Beckman. He reached out to her and discovered he was right on the money, and a few weeks later we were standing in Morris's flat, literally a thirty-second walk away from Luke's old house in West Hampstead. There, laid out on the table, Morris had arranged photos and memorabilia from both the 43 Group and his time as a merchant seaman during the Second World War. For the next three hours Luke, my sister Gabriella, who was filming the interview, and I listened transfixed to the story of the 43 Group. Morris shared many wonderful anecdotes that had us in fits of laughter, including the story of his rescue by Gerry Flamberg.

For me, interviewing Morris and reading his books was just the beginning; over the next few years I spent countless hours in archives and interviewed around a dozen Group members, together with the families of some of those who had passed away. Through this research I learned that the current historical knowledge of the Group was deeply inadequate; it deserved to be the subject of a new historical account.

As Beckman's book has been the only one published on the 43 Group, subsequent historians writing about the subject have leaned heavily on his *Untold Story*. The problem is, most of the Group veterans thought it was a load of tosh. Some felt Beckman had overstated the Group's influence, while others believed that by focusing on the big events he had sensationalised the Group and failed to convey the mundane drudgery that was so much of its existence. Others derided Beckman's use of the term 'commandos' and stressed that the Group was not a team of crack troops, but a bunch of young men and women doing their best and making mistakes along the way.

For the majority, the journey to becoming militant anti-fascists began in the schoolyard, where Jewishness sometimes meant they received unwelcome attention from their fellow students. At its mildest, regularly being called a Jew boy or girl was common, but others got it far worse. Mildred Levy, who grew up in Balham, South London, was frequently attacked by other schoolchildren; hair-pulling was frequent and, on one occasion, she had a lit match thrown down her dress. She got no comfort from her teachers, who could themselves be deeply anti-Semitic. Away from school things were hardly better. Her parents' shop was often targeted, and dog shit was once posted through their letterbox.[2] Mildred's anger and desire to fight and stand up for herself was forged in these early years, as was Morris Beckman's. After he was attacked by some bullies at school, he learned to fight from his older cousin Nat. 'It's a hard world,' Nat told him, 'and being Jewish makes it that much harder. You've got to make yourself so able to fight that you'll never fear a one-to-one confrontation. Not with anyone.'[3] It's no wonder that so many of Britain's best boxers in the early twentieth century were Jewish; young Jews had to grow up fighting in one of the toughest and poorest areas of the country.

In 1934, the situation grew far worse with the arrival into the East End of the British Union of Fascists (BUF). Formed two years earlier by Sir Oswald Mosley, a former member of both the Labour and Conservative parties, the BUF had seen its membership soar to 50,000 and had attracted some prominent and influential figures. Among them was the newspaper proprietor Viscount Rothermere, who proclaimed in his *Daily Mail*, 'Hurrah for the Blackshirts!' – the nickname of Mosley's followers, derived from their all-black uniforms.

Support for Mosley transcended class divides, and he had devout followers among the aristocracy, as well as the middle and working classes. In 1934, the BUF membership converged for a series of huge meetings, the most famous of which was held at Kensington Olympia in June 1934. Around 12,000 Blackshirts were in attendance, as were numerous anti-fascists whose heckles and jeers were swiftly dealt with by Blackshirt stewards. Over fifty people needed treatment following the beatings meted out by the stewards, and one witness said it was a wonder no one had been killed.[4] For the first time the brutality of fascism was laid bare. When a few weeks later reporters relayed the news of a Nazi massacre in Germany that has become known as the Night of the Long Knives, the public recoiled from the dark heart of fascism. The BUF's membership plummeted, and the *Daily Mail* withdrew its support.

The BUF had always given voice to anti-Semitic positions, but following Kensington Olympia deeply pro-Nazi and anti-Semitic men such as William Joyce came to the fore, advocating strongly for anti-Semitic actions, especially in areas with large Jewish communities, in particular the East End. BUF street meetings in the neighbourhood attracted large working-class non-Jewish audiences, and Jews had to give these events a wide berth. Fascist provocations took many forms. Homes, shops, and places of worship were vandalised; individuals were harassed or even physically attacked.

The Jewish community was not willing to take these attacks lying down, and many different defence organisations rose up to counter the BUF threat. The most prominent anti-fascist organisation was, of course, the Communist Party of Great Britain (CPGB), and its willingness to actively attack the fascists led to a huge surge in its Jewish membership. Like the BUF, the CPGB also held frequent meetings throughout the East End, sometimes within a few metres of where the fascists were gathering. The resultant clashes scarred the East End for years, and helped popularise the notion, promulgated by newspapers, politicians and the police, that the fight between communists and fascists was nothing more than political gang warfare, in which both sides were equally at fault.

Those Jews who wished to fight fascism but did not want to join the CPGB would have been forgiven for turning for help to the Board of Deputies. The main establishment body for Anglo-Jewry, the Board should have been the organisation most willing and able to defend the Jewish community. However, it was hamstrung by a fear of controversy, worried that any violent response to provocation would stir up greater anti-Semitism. So determined was it to stay above the fray that the Board stated: 'We cannot declare ourselves against Fascism per se' – a position that seems beyond apathetic in retrospect. In truth, the Board was not completely inactive in the fight against fascism; it just preferred to do its work behind the scenes, and in 1938 created the Jewish Defence Counsel (JDC) specifically to carry out this work.[5]

There was deep resentment among the East End Jewish community towards the Board, especially among the youth, and other Jewish organisations tried to fill the gap left by the Board's inaction. In 1936 representatives from numerous political and communal organisations formed the Jewish People's Council Against Fascism and Anti-Semitism (JPC). Not long after, news arrived of Mosley's plans to march his Blackshirts through the East End on 4 October. The JPC resolved to rally the East End in protest. What followed was the famous Battle of Cable Street, when Jews, communists, East End locals, and Irish dockworkers came together to blockade the streets of the East End and prevent the Blackshirts from marching. Most of the violence that day was between the anti-fascists and the police who tried unsuccessfully to try and clear the way for the Blackshirts. Eventually the commissioner of the Metropolitan Police, Sir Philip Game, instructed Mosley to abandon his plans. That evening the words 'They Did Not Pass' were scrawled all over the East End.

The Battle of Cable Street was a great victory, inspiring generations of anti-fascists, including the founders of the 43 Group. Many of them witnessed the battle first-hand but were too young to take part in the action. However, Cable Street was by no means the end of the BUF's East End campaign, which only got worse in its wake as the Blackshirts sought their revenge and subjected the Jewish community to a reign of terror. One night a carefree fifteen-year-old, Morris Beckman, took a short cut home through Hackney Downs and, lost in his own happy thoughts, failed to spot four young Blackshirts 'on a high, smelling of beer' until it was too late. 'That's as far as you go, Jewboy,' said one, pushing Beckman in the chest.

Then . . . the adrenalin of shock and fear galvanised me into swinging round and hitting the one on my left on his face and, at the same time, jumping from a standing start clean over the four-foot-high railing . . . Scrambling frantically to my feet I hared it back the way I'd come through the long grass.[6]

Lennie Rolnick was only twelve when he came face-to-face with three Blackshirt boys for the first time. He had not yet learnt when to run and when to fight:

They sauntered towards me with an air of menace. They blocked my path and taunted me: 'Hey, Jew-boy! How does it feel being rubbish?' In spite of my youth I felt more anger than fear. I stood my ground . . . I shouted, 'I'm proud to be a Jew!' That remark enraged them and they charged at me. 'We'll give you something to be proud of,' they roared. That day I got the first beating of my life! One of them looked at me as I lay on the ground, nose bleeding and with a rapidly swelling eye, and commented, 'See that? Well he ain't proud no more. Rubbish!'[7]

Rolnick opened his unpublished memoirs, entitled *That's What's in It for Me,* with this story, going on to explain that this moment was his political awakening, engendering in him a life-long commitment to anti-fascism. He was not alone. Instead of demoralising the young Jews who came of age during the BUF's East End campaign, the fascists created the next generation of resolute antagonists. Ten years later, as members of the 43 Group, they would make the fascists' lives hell.

In 1938, Mosley purged his most anti-Semitic lieutenants from the BUF and reoriented the party's activities towards opposing the coming war. Renaming his organisation the British Union (BU), Mosley recast his politics as pacifist, arguing for a strong alliance with Hitler and Germany, and rejecting the warnings of 'warmongers' like Churchill. When war broke out in September 1939, the BU redoubled its efforts and continued to advocate for a peaceful settlement, campaigning for an immediate cessation of hostilities.

However, the new focus of the BU did not mean London's Jewish community was any safer. In 1939, nine-year-old Jules Konopinski arrived with his mother from Germany and moved into a house in Bethnal Green. Sadly for Jules, the neighbourhood was home to an organisation possibly even worse than the BUF. The Imperial Fascist League (IFL) had been set up by veterinarian and camel expert Arnold Leese, a man so vehement in his anti-Semitism he considered Mosley and the BUF 'kosher fascists'. Leese gathered around him a gang of thugs who turned Bethnal Green into a hotbed of anti-Semitism, and Jules recalled having bricks hurled at him on his way to school and regular fights in Victoria Park.

The BU and IFL were the main street-based fascist and pro-Nazi organisations, but they were by no means the only ones operating in Britain at the start of the war. Other notable groups included the Link, headed by Admiral Sir Barry Domville, which sought to foster Anglo-German friendship, and the Nordic League, which was connected to all the various far-right organisations operating at the time. The slogan of the Nordic League, 'Perish Judah', would become a notorious fascist toast and greeting, and 'PJ' was often scrawled on Jewish properties. One prominent member of the Nordic League was Captain Archibald Henry Maule Ramsay, Conservative MP for Peebles, who in May 1939 founded the Right Club, which would seek to 'oppose and expose the activities of organised Jewry'.

In 1941 it was revealed that Ramsay kept a padlocked ledger, later referred to as the Red Book, in which he wrote down the names of the 135 members of the Right Club. While this might seem like a paltry number, Ramsay was only interested in recruiting members of the aristocracy and other high-ranking individuals and several peers of the realm were among the club's members. The revelation of the Red Book's existence caused a stir: it confirmed the suspicions of many anti-fascists who were convinced that there existed a deeply anti-Semitic and pro-Nazi cabal operating in the highest echelons of British power.[8]

The Red Book had been discovered by MI5 in 1940 following the conclusion of an intelligence operation focusing on the Right Club and the threat its members posed to the war effort. Among the Right Club's members were Anna Wolkoff, the daughter of a Russian admiral, and Tyler Kent, an American cipher clerk working in the US Embassy in London. Kent had for years been copying messages from the US embassy which he hid in his apartment. When Kent told Wolkoff and Captain Ramsay that among these were communications between Churchill and Roosevelt, which, if made public, could lead to Roosevelt pulling his plans for supporting the Allies, Wolkoff said she wanted to use a connection at the Italian Embassy to get these documents to William Joyce, who was now broadcasting from Germany as the infamous Lord Haw-Haw.

Unfortunately for Wolkoff, the Right Club was full of agents of MI5's Maxwell Knight, who swooped into action. On 20 May 1940, having convinced the US embassy to waive Kent's diplomatic immunity, Knight ordered police to raid Kent's flat and arrest him and Wolkoff. In Kent's flat, Knight discovered the Red Book, along with boxes and boxes of stolen documents which Ramsey had asked Kent to keep, trusting in the American's diplomatic immunity. The Kent–Wolkoff affair gave Knight and others in the British security services the proof they needed that, as they'd long suspected, British fascists posed a serious fifth column threat and would actively seek to hinder the war effort, and aid and abet the enemy.

On 1 September 1939, Defence Regulation 18B had come into effect, enabling the arrest and internment of anyone who might engage in 'acts prejudicial to the public safety or the defence of the realm'. At first it was only used on hardcore Nazis, with only fourteen people being arrested.[9] But following the Kent–Wolkoff case the new prime minister Winston Churchill agreed that 18B should be expanded to include all prominent British fascists, and on 23 May, Oswald Mosley, Sir Barry Domville and other fascist and pro-Nazi leaders were arrested. Later that month the BU was banned and proscribed.

By the end of 1940 over 1,000 fascist men and women had been arrested and were being held in prison camps, often converted holiday resorts or race courses – the largest was on the Isle of Man. This might have seemed like a drastic move, considering most of these men and women had committed no crime and were being held without trial, but in 1940 the situation looked desperate. The retreat by the British at Dunkirk meant Hitler's armies were now just across the Channel and invasion seemed imminent. Allowing any potential fifth columnists their freedom was seen as just too big a risk. And while it was the British Isles that were under threat from invasion in 1940, the Nazis' ambitions were global and so all known fascists needed to be rounded up, even if they were in the most far-flung corners of the Empire.

1

Dipping a Toe in the Water

Floating out in the harbour of Port Stanley, the capital of the Falkland Islands, was a derelict ship, which in June 1940 the powers-that-be determined would make a suitable prison for certain undesirables. The ship had four occupants: two guards who occupied the wheelhouse, and two prisoners who were left to languish down in the hold. The first prisoner was a sea cook of German extraction from the Sudetenland, the second was a tall, thin, pale young man of Welsh origin named Jeffrey Hamm, who just a few days earlier was leading a peaceful existence teaching in remote farmhouses across the islands. While no one had given Hamm any explanation for his sudden arrest and detainment, he had some idea, and surely marvelled at the absurdity of the situation.

After a week down in the hold, Hamm was brought back to Port Stanley and put in front of a tribunal which accused him of being in sympathy 'with a Government with which his Majesty is at war'. Hamm strongly denied the charges, but he was ignored and was returned to his floating prison. Certainly, a strong case could be made that in a war between the Allies and the Nazis, the young man might favour the latter. Born in 1915 in the small Welsh town of Ebbw Vale, Hamm was the son of a lower-middle-class Englishman who discouraged his son's dreams of higher education, deeming it a pointless indulgence for those who should be at work. For Hamm, who had a certain regard for his own intelligence and high hopes of attending university, this was a major disappointment and a source of bitterness throughout his life. It was just such a bitterness that made Hamm particularly susceptible to the pull of fascism, which declares that hard-working, deserving, Christian men are often deprived of their dues by a corrupted system.

Hamm first encountered these ideas in the summer of 1934 when he was on holiday in London. Walking past a street meeting in Kilburn, Hamm wondered why the crowd seemed so determined to drown out the speaker. He put this question to one of the disrupters and was told that they had come not to listen to the meeting, but 'to smash it!' When the meeting finished, Hamm fell in line behind the speaker and his allies, all of whom were wearing black shirts, and followed them back to their headquarters.

Back home in Pontypool, Wales, where he was now working as a teacher, Hamm subscribed to all the BUF's publications and the following March became a member. He longed, however, to be in London at the heart of BUF activities, and in 1936 he finally left Wales for London. Unfortunately, the only teaching post he could find was in Lewes, East Sussex, some fifty miles from the capital. Seeking to assuage his feelings of isolation, Hamm began a correspondence with a Fraulein Gertrud Fritz after he responded to an advert in the BUF paper *Blackshirt*, and the following summer he was the honoured guest of the ardently Nazi Fritz family of Heidelberg. These would be the happiest weeks of Hamm's life, beginning with a blissful train ride during which he was struck not only by 'the beauty of the German countryside' but also by how 'every available square inch of land was cultivated along the railway embankments almost up to the rails, in Germany's effort to be self-sufficient, and so independent of international finance.'[1] As for the obvious and overt signs of the Nazis' persecution of the Jews, Hamm later wrote:

In retrospect I certainly would not praise, or even condone everything, such as the notices over the doors of restaurants and places of entertainment . . . Jews not wanted here. Or the more stark . . . Jews strictly forbidden here . . . Let me display an honesty often sadly lacking in many who admired Germany in that era, but now pretend that they had always opposed it. I saw it all, and most of what I saw I liked.[2]

The Hamm who returned to Britain was a self-confessed political zealot, and one who could now contribute to his party, having finally secured a teaching post in London. Even better, the school was in Harrow, Oswald Mosley's former parliamentary seat and a hive of BUF activity that Hamm threw himself into with gusto. If Hamm was never more than a foot soldier, frequently marching within the ranks of Blackshirts, he regarded the BUF's senior leaders as 'Olympian Gods' and Mosley as the 'greatest orator of this century', and he could not believe his luck when after a meeting the great man Mosley shook his hand and exchanged a few words.

It would, however, be a conversation with Mosley's number two, Neil Francis-Hawkins, which would set Hamm off on his strange new path. Hamm had just been accepted for the position of travelling teacher on the Falklands, which he had applied for on a whim; and although he wanted to go, he felt guilty about abandoning his fellow fascists and their peace campaign. Hamm was so conflicted that he sought a meeting with Francis-Hawkins, who advised him to take the post; Hamm sailed for the Falklands in the first week of 1940.

Hamm's role in the Falklands was to ride to remote farmhouses and give a week's teaching to the farmers' children. He had been doing this for some five months when he learnt from the BBC's Overseas Service of Mosley's arrest on 23 May 1940 and the extension of Defence Regulation 18B. Hamm feared he too would be arrested, but as the days passed, 'I began to think it unlikely that any attention would be paid to a rank-and-file member of British Union now going about his routine duties in a tiny island eight thousand miles from the European centre of war.'[3] This reasoning had some logic to it: after all it was hard to see how Hamm could greatly assist the Führer's military plans from the Falkland Islands. So Hamm was shocked to discover that eleven days after Mosley's arrest, the three men who had turned up at the shepherd's cottage where he was staying were members of the Falkland Islands Defence Force with instructions for his arrest.

After four months held on board the prison ship in Port Stanley harbour, Hamm's fellow inmate went stir-crazy and threatened to set it on fire. The authorities decided to bring the two men back to land and hold them in a remote cottage while their fates were decided. It took several weeks for a decision to be made, but eventually they were put on a ship that was destined, Hamm learnt during the journey, for South Africa. Hamm was sent to an internment camp near Johannesburg, which mostly consisted of Germans split into Nazi and non-Nazi sections.[4] Placed in the latter, Hamm's request to be transferred away from the 'simply appalling Jews, murderers, perverts and sub-men' was granted; in the Nazi section he quickly proved just how much he belonged there and received an enthusiastic welcome. Imprisonment with fellow fascists and Nazis only further entrenched and hardened Hamm's own politics, consequently his situation provides an excellent illustration of the major problem with 18B internment.

The purpose of 18B was to remove the threat posed by a potential fifth column in Britain and her colonies in the event of a German invasion. This was particularly critical on mainland Britain where, following Dunkirk, invasion seemed inevitable. Regulation 18B was never designed to cure the fascists of their politics, indeed for the majority it had the precise opposite effect.

The government decided that fascist 18B detainees should be held together in camps such as the massive one that was set up on the Isle of Man. There, locked up with only their political brethren, the fascists engaged in a mutual stoking of each other's fires and their convictions only grew more fervid. It was a mark of how little internment did to dent such beliefs, that in post-war fascist circles 18B detainment was seen as a badge of honour.[5] And if a staunch fascist was not a rabid anti-Semite before he or she went into the internment camps, they certainly would have been by the time they left, as the fascists fed each other's hate. All concluded that on top of the Jews' past sins they were now due a reckoning for both their history with Germany and the fascists' present incarceration.[6] For the already deeply anti-Semitic Hamm, now surrounded by German Nazis stuffed full of Goebbels's propaganda, this radicalisation occurred in extremis.

In April 1941 Hamm learnt that his petition for release had been granted,[7] and two months after his Nazi friends saw him off with the German military song of farewell, he disembarked in Glasgow. One of the reasons why internment so angered the British fascists was because, first and foremost, they considered themselves to be patriots who would never take the side of another country against their own. Mosley had in fact gone out of his way to say to his followers, 'I ask you to do nothing to injure our country, or to help any other Power.'[8] Hamm, like a number of other fascists, went one step further and applied to enlist in the armed services, but quickly discovered his 18B status was a serious obstacle. His application to the RAF was rejected and although he was subsequently accepted into the Royal Armoured Corps he was never deployed, and he spent the duration of his army career being sent to different camps around the country, before being eventually discharged without explanation in 1944. Throughout his time in the army Hamm had little to do with fascist politics, which during the war years was publicly centred around a charitable organisation, the leader of which did the utmost to deny any political affiliation.[9]

George Dunlop was a former BUF organiser in East London who, having managed to avoid internment, established the 18B Detainees' (British) Aid Fund,[10] to raise money for the wives and children of internees. A decentralised organisation, the Fund relied on local organisers to collect money from sympathetic individuals which was passed on to struggling families. In 1941 the government began releasing the lesser fascists and many of these subsequently worked for the Fund, which became an effective and entirely legal means of keeping the fascists connected and perpetuating their network.[11] For Norah Elam, a former suffragette who was a key member of the BUF's women's movement,[12] the Fund enabled 'a complete organisation of B.U. to be carried on legally', and meant 'every worthwhile member can be contacted'.[13] Mosley let it be known that the Fund had his blessing.

What enabled the Fund to survive was its apolitical facade, with Dunlop keenly stressing that it was there to support detainees and their families and had nothing to do with fascism. When he learned of a beneficiary who had never belonged to the BUF, he trumpeted the fact. Not that he was fooling anyone. As an MI5 report noted, the Fund was 'capable of being used either directly or indirectly as a basis for the resuscitation of the BU'. As the war progressed, more and more fascists joined the Fund. It flourished, and Dunlop became one of the most important and influential wartime fascists. However, by 1946 he was a nobody, mocked and derided by his old friends. His story makes an interesting counterpoint to Hamm's, who rose to the top from nowhere. And the reason why one man would rise and the other would fall was because one of the men was foolish enough to put his future in the hands of a certain Oswald Mosley.

The Devil Priest and Prophet

I was warned years ago, and correctly, that I had a physique well constituted to endure exceptional strain and fatigue but, conversely, particularly and adversely affected by inactivity . . . It is suggested that I feel a great sense of injustice at my imprisonment, and that the necessity to repress this feeling has psychologically and therefore physically affected me. It is true that I think our treatment is a disgraceful and disgusting business but I never worry about something that I can do nothing about.[14]

So wrote Oswald Mosley to his mother on 1 October 1943, but while Mosley could do little about his situation, he had well-connected relations who could, including his mother-in-law, Lady Redesdale, who constantly pestered her former bridesmaid, Clementine Churchill, with news of Mosley's deteriorating condition, in the hope that she would relay the news to her husband, the prime minister.[15]

In the summer of 1943 Mosley's personal physician noted that 'confinement and isolation are breaking Sir Oswald's nerve'. King George VI's private doctor concurred, warning that if there were no improvement in Mosley's condition there was a 'substantial risk' of his phlebitis 'producing permanent damage to health and even to life'. Following an appeal from Mosley's solicitor for his client's release, Home Secretary Herbert Morrison asked for an assessment from the prison's medical officer, who found Mosley to be substantially underweight and suffering from 'a deep sense of frustration and consequent depression'. This was clearly not serious enough for Morrison, and he turned down the appeal.[16] However, as 1943 wore on a feeling grew that another winter behind bars would finish Mosley off. 'I think no good of him,' Churchill told the *Manchester Guardian* on 22 October, 'but he's been in prison all this time and he's likely to die in prison this winter and he has never been accused and never tried – a frightful thing to anyone concerned about English liberties.'

The fear of imminent Nazi invasion, which had warranted the introduction of Defence Regulation 18B, had by this point mostly passed and with the Allies turning the tide against the Nazis on every front, the government no longer felt they could fully justify the continued suspension of habeas corpus. On top of that, Churchill had no intention of turning Mosley into a martyr. Whereas the prime minister might have had no personal problem with the fascist leader dying in prison, he was aware of the political capital Mosley's supporters could make out of such an event; far better to let him out and, with luck, have him fade away in obscurity.

Six days after Mosley's friend Lady Metcalfe wrote to Churchill informing him that 'today he looked like a dying man', a conference of prominent physicians was convened on the matter of Mosley's health and all agreed the man should be released. However, these physicians did not have to consider the political concerns which plagued Morrison. Yes, on the one hand, not releasing Mosley ran the risk of making him a martyr, but releasing him would likely trigger a furore, especially from the left.

On 17 November Morrison announced to cabinet that Mosley was to be released on 'humanitarian grounds'. When the decision was made public shortly afterwards, it was the medical grounds for the release which were most heavily stressed.[17] No such reasons were given for Diana Mosley, though, who was to be released with her husband. Public outrage was swift and furious, with the socialist *Daily Worker* leading the charge:

> Mosley is the personification in this country of everything we are fighting against. He represents in all its foulness the fascism which the best sons of Britain are determined to destroy. They are fighting and dying in this fight while Hitler's wealthy ape is being offered his freedom.[18]

In the following days the *Worker*'s calls for nationwide protests were gamely answered. On 19 November, the day before Mosley's release, vast crowds gathered in Whitehall to protest, the Communist Party organised strikes on factory floors, and a deluge of letters descended on the Home Office. The Board of Deputies, by contrast, said nothing; its silence did not go unnoticed in the Jewish community.[19]

On the day of Mosley's release, the press gathered outside the gates of Holloway Prison to witness Mosley's re-emergence and see for themselves just how sickly he was. They were to be disappointed: the prison authorities had let the Mosleys slip away unnoticed at 7 a.m. via the side entrance known as the Murderess's Gate.

Their first stop was Rignell House, near Banbury, the estate of Diana's sister Pamela and her husband Derek Jackson,[20] a close friend and sympathiser with Mosley. The Mosleys were welcomed with a lavish feast and within a few days Mosley's health was already starting to recover. It did not take long for the press to get wise to Mosley's whereabouts, and their siege of Rignell House brought Morrison to his senses. After all, despite his political beliefs Jackson was a prominent research scientist at the Air Ministry privy to state secrets, so was hardly the ideal person to be hosting Mosley.

On 7 December, the occupants of Rignell House were woken by the sound of police dogs, and the Mosleys were bundled away to a disused hotel in Oxfordshire. A tipped-off press were lying in wait, but again failed to notice the Mosleys entering via a rear entrance. In the days that followed there was a strange standoff between the Mosleys, confined to the private apartments of the hotel, and the press, camped out in the bar. When a photo of Mosley, finally snapped by a patient photographer, was published in the Sunday papers confirming the fascist leader's whereabouts, it caused much agitation and protests, with the local Communist Party demanding 'CLEAR MOSLEY OUT OF OXFORDSHIRE'.

Meanwhile in London, a major rally protesting Mosley's release was held in Trafalgar Square and several unions organised strikes and walkouts, and an entire day of parliamentary debate was given over to the matter, with plenty of MPs sharing the view of Dr Haden Guest, the member for Islington North, that now 'when we are fighting the foul evil of Fascism' was not the time to release its 'devil priest and prophet', who could 'only encourage the forces fighting against us'.[21] Meanwhile Morrison's office began receiving bottles labelled 'Rat Poison' and 'Cure for Phlebitis'.[22] He was not the only one to receive mail with unwelcome content: in her correspondence with her recently freed sister, Jessica Mitford was kind enough to enclose some 'Put MOSLEY back in GAOL!' stickers. Still, this was hardly surprising from the staunch communist who told the *San Francisco Chronicle* that Mosley's release was 'a slap in the face of anti-fascists in every country . . . They should be kept in jail where they belong.'

Not that being out of prison made Mosley a free man, and the conditions of his release were strict. Mosley had to report his whereabouts to the police at all times, was not permitted to travel outside of a seven-mile radius of his current residence, and was also forbidden from communicating with any former members of the BUF, and engaging in any political activity, including publishing materials, making speeches or giving interviews to journalists. Furthermore, Mosley was well aware that he was under constant surveillance, with phones tapped and letters read.[23] Besieged in the Oxford hotel, Mosley's only interest was in finding a farmhouse where he and his family might more comfortably enjoy their house arrest. In early 1944 he purchased a farm near Crux Easton in Hampshire and the family moved to their new home, where Mosley farmed while waiting out the war.

For the most part, Mosley adhered to the numerous restrictions placed upon him. But in February 1945, a Secret Service source revealed that Mosley had been spotted in Potters Bar, a town on the outskirts of London and almost seventy miles away from his Crux Easton farm. Apparently in the backroom of the White Horse pub Mosley had met with three other men: the first unknown, the second a prominent fascist journalist called G. F. Green, and the third George Dunlop, whose desire to solidify his position at the heart of British fascism had precipitated the meeting.

Dunlop had a problem. He was one of the most important fascists in wartime Britain, but he had achieved this position as the head of an organisation that would clearly have no purpose once the war had ended and 18B been rescinded. Without his position as head of the charitable fund Dunlop had nothing, so he was unlikely to come out on top in the inevitable scramble for position that would occur among Mosley's lieutenants at war's end. Dunlop's only option was to be the first out of the gate. Of course, he could have turned the 18B Detainees' Aid Fund into a political party, but this would have required the support of the Fund's other leading figures, and that would have meant diluting his influence, which he was not willing to do.

So instead Dunlop decided to draw up plans for a new party, one he hoped would be a replacement for the BUF; but that would require Mosley's backing and Mosley was out of reach. Under the terms of Mosley's release he was forbidden from any contact with former members of the BUF; but there were those who, although never members of his organisation, were sympathetic with Mosley. One such person was Enid Riddell, a vehement anti-Semite. She had been a member of the Nordic League and the Right Club, and interned under 18B, but she had never been a member of the BUF. Consequently her infrequent visits to Crux Easton were permissible and meant she could act as a go-between for Mosley and his lieutenants. It was through her that Dunlop learnt that the leader supported his venture.

While Dunlop clearly had some skills as an organiser, he was no intellectual and so, armed with the knowledge of Mosley's backing, Dunlop approached the journalist Green and asked him if he would help draw up plans for a new fascist party. Green agreed and since he had already done this for an organisation he had called the 'British Comrades', he merely changed some of the aims and policies, and renamed it the 'Independent Nationalists' (IN).

On 21 February 1945 Dunlop drove Green to the White Horse pub where Mosley and the unrecognised fourth man were waiting in the back room, where they conversed. Mosley later spoke with Green alone outside and told him that while he broadly approved of his proposal, if they wanted Mosley's support the principal staff would have to consist of individuals without political records who would be controlled by dedicated fascists behind the scenes. Green agreed, and he and Dunlop left, convinced that their plans had Mosley's full support.

Special Branch, on the other hand, were sceptical, and thought Mosley was just planning to use Dunlop and Green to test the waters; which begs the question, why did he even take the risk of meeting them? In doing so he had broken numerous terms of his release and given Special Branch plenty of grounds for throwing him back in prison; only a desire to protect their valuable source kept them from doing so.[24] It was decided that the best bet was to maintain their current policy of Masterly Inactivity.[25] Clearly Mosley saw some obvious advantage in taking the risk to offer Dunlop and Green his support, and the two men went to work ensuring that the Independent Nationalists was ready to launch as soon as the war ended, confidently assuming that Mosley would keep to his word and declare his support for them. After all, none of Mosley's other followers were making moves, excluding two upstarts stomping the pavements of west London.

Blah-Blahs and Petty Jealousies

With his ex-18B status, getting a position as a teacher was always going to be out of the question for Hamm when he returned to London in mid-1944, but at the Park Royal Coachworks he was able to find work as a clerk. Around this time, Hamm also met his future wife Sally. Hamm was something of a womaniser, and although he soon married Sally, who not long after became pregnant, he never let this get in the way of his favourite pastime. With his life in London falling into place, Hamm finally felt he was able to satiate the political cravings that had been gnawing at him for years, and so on his first free Sunday Hamm went down to Speakers' Corner to, as he put it, see what was going on. It was a happy decision for while cheering enthusiastically for an ex-BUF man who was condemning the injustice of 18B to a mostly antagonistic crowd, he encountered fellow fascist Victor Cecil Burgess, who had a most interesting idea.[26]

Burgess, like Hamm, was another young fascist with aspirations to lead. Olive-skinned with a head of thick black hair (he was rumoured to be a gypsy's son), Burgess cultivated a distinctly Bohemian manner. He was popular among fellow fascists, and even the 43 Group would later acknowledge his 'engaging personality as a public speaker'. They also noted he was 'vain and sadistic'. Like Hamm, Burgess was a womaniser. Small fry in the BUF, Burgess was detained under 18B after he refused to wear the uniform of the Middlesex Regiment in which he served for eight months.[28] Released in 1942, Burgess moved to Edgware in north London where he opened the Corporate Utilities print shop which would over the ensuing years become one of the main publishers of fascist literature and a clearing house for foreign anti-Semitica. To provoke the area's growing Jewish population, Burgess often displayed this literature in his shop window – a major risk in wartime, and he was lucky not to be prosecuted for seditious libel.[29] By 1944, however, Burgess clearly had aspirations to run more than the print shop and its associated Corporate Book Club. He wanted his own political party and, as he explained to Hamm, he had found a way of getting around the government's ban on fascist parties.

Burgess told Hamm of a Birmingham man called James Taylor who he had met during his internment. In 1938 Taylor founded the British League of Ex-Servicemen, after falling out with the British Legion over his disability pension. He subsequently got mixed up with his local branch of the BU, although he might have never been a member, and was consequently interned for a very brief period.[30] Burgess suggested to Hamm that they join the League to advocate for the rights and pensions of soldiers, while at the same time they would use the League as a platform for disseminating fascist views and reviving Mosley's reputation on the streets.

Hamm joined Burgess and the two men spent the next few weeks attracting other kindred spirits and discussing how the League would function. As these discussions became increasingly pedantic and mundane, Hamm grew frustrated with his collaborators and decided to take matters into his own hands. Armed with a small stepladder, Hamm went down one evening to a corner of Edgware Road in west London and made his very first outdoor speech. A few mildly curious passers-by gathered, and Hamm was able to collect a few coins. It was a moderate success and Hamm convinced Burgess that this was the way forward, and a few more small street meetings around west London were held.

It was Hamm who suggested adding 'Women' to the League's name, in the hope that doing so would attract the vast numbers of women who would be leaving the services as war drew to a close. Not that one needed to have served to join; all ex-BUF members counted as ex-servicemen, whether they had served or not,[31] and later Hamm would accept pretty much anyone so long as they supported the fascist creed. Recruitment was a principal aim for their street meetings, but west London had never been as fertile a fascist recruiting ground as east London. However, as that area held deep historic significance to the BUF, Hamm felt it should be one of the 'Olympian Gods' of old that returned fascism to that famous stomping ground. He had similar beliefs about Speakers' Corner, and assumed that before long a leading fascist would stand up there and inform the people of London that British fascism was alive and well. The year 1944 wore on and it never came to pass, so Hamm decided that honour would be the League's.

On Sunday, 5 November 1944, Hamm and Burgess took their small platform to Hyde Park and claimed a pitch. It must have taken the crowds at Speakers' Corner a few moments to realise what they were hearing from the organisation that purported to be representing ex-servicemen, but when they realised that the thin young man with the Welsh lilt was ridiculing the war effort and spouting the sort of fascist ideas that had not been uttered there for four years, the booing and heckling began in earnest and easily drowned out Hamm's attempts to make himself heard. Hamm and Burgess were not deterred, though, and the following week they returned, with Burgess speaking first. He hadn't been speaking for long when a majority of the two to three hundred people who had been listening to other speakers rushed over to his platform and started booing and heckling him. Shouts of 'Fascist scum!' and 'Why don't you go and join the Nazis!' were directed at Burgess who found it impossible to make himself heard above the din.[32]

For Hamm this was a setback, but not in the way he imagined. The report of his forays into Hyde Park made the papers, and as a result he lost both his job and his lodgings, and went to live rent free for a while at the home of rabid fascist Leslie Grundy. Grundy's son Trevor recalled how Hamm and his wife, Sally, shared a single room and outdoor toilet, and how Hamm always wore the same jacket and trousers.[33]

By spring 1945 Hamm was back on his feet with new rooms in Arundel Gardens in Notting Hill, and he and Burgess had resumed their street meetings. But Hamm was ambitious and wanted the League all to himself. He went on a fervid recruitment drive at street meetings, which, after April, never featured Burgess, signing up fascists and sympathisers who he believed would be loyal to him. Soon Hamm had grown confident enough in his control of the League to propose to a members' meeting a policy of not admitting Jewish ex-servicemen. What the League's few actual non-fascist ex-servicemen thought of such a move is unclear, but they were the next to leave, with Hamm purging all non-fascists shortly afterwards.[34]

While increasingly the king of his own castle, Hamm struggled to gain an audience on the streets. In Westbourne Grove, Hamm managed to attract a crowd of around 150, which included a small but loud and hostile Jewish contingent, but audiences of forty to fifty were the average. On one evening in Bayswater, Hamm attracted just three people before deciding to end the meeting and cut his losses. This was hardly surprising: these were the heady days of impending victory, and yet Hamm spoke of a nation that had been duped into fighting the wrong war by 'the old gang parties', 'International Financiers', 'American Bankers', aliens and communists, all terms the fascists used when they really meant Jews.[35]

Even if Hamm had yet to make an impact on the streets, his efforts were beginning to make waves in fascist circles. In April, Hamm received a message from Dunlop informing him of his new outfit which would be the 'only genuine National Socialist movement operating in Britain' and instructed Hamm to relinquish control of the League and amalgamate it with Dunlop's group; Hamm refused. Dunlop was furious. He had obeyed Mosley's instruction to stay apolitical, while Hamm had not, and yet despite this transgression the younger man was reaping the rewards.[36] Dunlop was not the only senior fascist who was peeved by Hamm's activities. Since being freed from internment, most of these old leaders had been in a state of inertia, as they fought among themselves and tried to second-guess the intentions of the inaccessible Mosley. As a result, they were infuriated by the gall of the young upstart Hamm, who had jumped the gun and taken it upon himself to lead the Mosleyite resurgence.

Fortunately, the time of confusion, infighting and inertia was coming to an end as on 8 May 1945 VE Day was declared and the Defence Regulations were immediately lifted. The fascists did not share in the wild jubilation of the majority of the population, after all their Nazi brethren had just been defeated by the seditious forces of Jewish Communism, but they could at least do as they pleased once again. Based on the deluge of letters that flooded Crux Easton in the following days, it seems that the first thing most fascists wanted to do was write to their former leader, wish him well, and remember themselves to him.[37] The first responses Mosley sent were to his closest lieutenants, whom he invited to Crux Easton. Among those accorded this honour were Neil Francis-Hawkins, Alexander Raven Thompson and Alf Flockhart.[38]

It was Neil Francis-Hawkins, Mosley's old number two and former Director General of Organisation of the BUF, who originally encouraged Mosley to embrace anti-Semitism. Interned at the same time as Mosley, Francis-Hawkins was not released until 1944. After the war he quickly faded into the background and played an at best advisory role in the post-war fascist movement. By contrast Alexander Raven Thompson, a Scotsman regarded as the leading intellectual luminary of British fascism, was very active both before the war, when he served as the BUF's director of policy, and after it. Interned in Brixton Prison, he fared very poorly and had a nervous breakdown; he too was released in 1944. Alf Flockhart, by contrast, had been a mere BUF district leader in Shoreditch. However, this proved to be a blessing for, in the words of the 43 Group's newspaper *On Guard*, the 'insignificant-looking little man' was released from 18B far sooner than the others.[39] Liberty restored, Flockhart threw himself back into fascist activities and became the social secretary for the 18B Aid Fund, and Mosley's man in the Fund.[40]

On 30 May, they and a fascist called McKechnie, the BUF's London administrator, met Mosley in his Dolphin Square flat in Pimlico. Here, Mosley revealed his much-anticipated master-plan – to wait. The moment, he told them, was not a propitious one for launching a new fascist movement. Far better to let people think they had disappeared into the shadows until such time as the conditions were more suited to their return. This, he assured them, would occur soon enough, for the economy was sure to deteriorate and people would once again seek strong leadership. In the meantime, they should only engage in activities that did not seek the limelight. Cultural societies and book clubs that would help maintain fascist networks and be a useful tool for subtle recruitment were to be encouraged; graffiti, vandalism and activities that brought the attention of the Home Office were not. He also did not object to the publishing of new materials, especially those that warned against alien infiltration, communism, and international finance, but under no circumstance should Jews ever specifically be mentioned. He himself planned to retire to his farm where he would write, but hoped to return in due course with a very different set of instructions.[41]

The following week Mosley met with the leaders of the 18B Aid Fund and shared with them the same news. Dunlop was stunned: this was expected to be the moment when Mosley was to declare his leadership of the Independent Nationalists, and instead he was announcing his retirement. Mosley explained that as they had been planning to launch the party by standing candidates in the next election, the calling of elections so soon after victory 'rendered obsolete much of the painstaking work which had been prepared'. Far better, he suggested, putting the Independent Nationalists on hold for a while. However, it was not all doom and gloom: Mosley wished there to be a party to celebrate the end of 18B and all the Fund's good work, before it shut down; should they organise such an event he assured them he would be in attendance.

The moment Mosley left, Dunlop started berating the others in the room. You have 'all worked against me', Dunlop shouted at Flockhart and two others, Spicer and Franklin. The Independent Nationalists, he continued, 'was killed by publicity and innuendo, and by your blah-blahs and petty jealousies, before it had a chance of survival'.[42] It turned out that Dunlop was correct; unaware that Mosley had given his backing to the new party many other fascists had turned against it, although how far that influenced Mosley's decision is unclear.[43] Despite this setback, Dunlop, led on by mixed messages from Mosley,[44] did not give up hope and remained sure that Mosley's public support of his new party was imminent.

Whereas Mosley's decision stopped Dunlop in his tracks, Hamm, who had never depended on Mosley's direct backing, was unaffected. Seeing his role as paving the way for Mosley, the only thing Hamm wanted was the knowledge that Mosley did not disapprove of his actions. As for the rest of the old guard, Hamm clearly did not give a fig of what they thought of him, which was useful as the more successful he was the more they took against him, derisively referring to him as 'Führer Hamm'.

True Englishmen

Throughout the summer of 1945, Hamm continued to struggle to gain an audience on the street. Sometimes a few onlookers were sympathetic or interested, but more often they were deeply hostile. A transcript from a meeting in Westbourne Grove in April 1945 gives a flavour of a typical Hamm speech in those early days:

> At the last meeting the majority of my hecklers belonged to the good old Communist Party; they poured abuse on me because I happen to be a true Englishman who is anxious to see that my fellow countrymen take their proper place in this country after the war. These communists, through lack of intellect, did not understand my remarks on economic nationalism and they adopted their old game of trying to make me say something which would have brought trouble on to myself . . .
>
> I have been asked repeatedly if anyone can join our organisation. The answer is that we will be pleased to enrol new members who are of British birth and origin. We do bar Chinese, Eskimos, Hottentots and Jews . . .

A woman in the crowd identified herself as Jewish and yelled at Hamm, 'Why don't you get into uniform! You are nothing else but a Blackshirt!' This led to a barrage of heckles over which Hamm repeatedly stated that he had been in the army, before bringing the meeting to a close.[45] Although such hostilities were very common, Hamm continued to slowly gain more members, and in August he received a substantial boost from an unlikely source: Arnold Leese.

During his days as the head of the IFL, Leese had recruited a particularly vicious breed of men, who, now war was over, were keen to return to their Jew-bashing ways. Leese, however, was no longer in the game of running street organisations, preferring to run clandestine networks including the 'Jewish-Interest Information Bureau' and the 'Aryan Action Council', and publish his new newsletter *Gothic Ripples*, which became one of the most virulently anti-Semitic publications of the post-war years.[46] None of these projects though were suitable for Leese's old IFL thugs who had come to him looking for direction. After weighing up the options, Leese recommended his followers join the League, which was just starting to venture into Bethnal Green, where Leese was based. In many ways Hamm, a dyed-in-the-wool Mosleyite, was a strange choice, but Leese figured that with enough of his members in the League he could take it over. Well aware of Leese's intentions, Hamm correctly believed his control of the League was strong enough to resist any challenge to his authority.[47]

The first consequence of this influx of men was that it gave Hamm the manpower he needed to protect himself in the rough-and-tumble world of East End street politics, and consequently the League became an increasingly working-class organisation. For his smattering of middle-class and female members, Hamm held private meetings in his flat, but these were few and far between. So while the League provided a home for working-class fascists, none of Mosley's more middle- and upper-class followers had an organisation they could join.

Non-Mosleyite fascists on the other hand had a home in the British People's Party (BPP). Founded by the Duke of Bedford and run by John Beckett, a former Labour MP who had become a prominent BUF organiser before dramatically falling out with Mosley, the BPP had been established in 1939 as a pro-peace party. Due to his aristocratic status, the Duke avoided internment and the BPP was never proscribed which allowed it to become, according to the Home Office, in 1945 'the most substantial organised Fascist party today'.[48] With several regional branches, a regular bulletin entitled *Facts* and a newspaper called *The People's Post*, both edited by Beckett, the BPP never participated in street politics and was able to attract far more middle- and upper-class fascists, including Aubrey Lees, a former deputy-governor of the Jaffa district in Palestine.[49] While plenty of Mosley's supporters would never have joined an organisation run by his rival, those who did not feel as strongly saw the BPP as an acceptable alternative, and at its first major meeting in December 1945 at Holborn Hall around 1,000 people were in attendance. The meeting proved to be a setback for the BPP, however, when a small antagonistic section of the audience began heckling Bedford's speech, immediately followed by an invasion of around 100 young people who charged into the hall chanting 'Political rats!' and 'We don't want Fascism here!' Bedford and Beckett were forced to abandon the stage.[50]

It was in the wake of this debacle that Beckett began to seriously consider uniting with another nascent fascist outfit, this one run by another former BUF man, A. K. Chesterton. Chesterton had been Mosley's propaganda director, before growing disillusioned with him and leaving the BUF. In 1944 he had been hired as the deputy editor of *Truth,* a right-wing paper with ties to the fringes of the Conservative Party, whose editor Colin Brooks had, at the behest of several prominent industrialists, started planning a post-war anti-communism organisation. Soon Brooks handed over the setting up of the 'National Front after Victory' (NFAV) to Chesterton, who was able to draw on his considerable network among the far right. Chesterton was also a rabid anti-Semite and he insisted that the NFAV had a strong anti-Semitic platform. This made many of his wealthy backers uncomfortable, fully realising that any organisation that took such a stance was doomed to fail in the post-war landscape. Chesterton, however, refused to budge from his position that only those who 'recognised the Jew as the enemy' were worthy members, and as a result all the money and resources that had been promised disappeared. When he first heard that Beckett was interested in joining forces, Chesterton baulked, convinced that he would just try to subsume the NFAV into his own BPP; but a continued inability to recruit new members and replace lost financial support soon made him realise he had no other options.

Chesterton's struggles signalled a clear separation between those fascists who had been interned under 18B and those members of the upper classes who had backed or sympathised with them and shared their prejudices, but who had never themselves been members of fascist organisations or interned. When war was declared, the majority of these individuals swept their admiration for the Führer under the carpet and embraced the required patriotism. Similarly, most understood that the anti-Semitism which had been perfectly acceptable in the pre-war days now carried dangerous connotations, and whatever views might be held in private it was dangerous to continue to subscribe to them in public. For the ex-18Bers who would forever be tarnished with that brush, moving away from their fascist past would be significantly harder, and so many chose to stick with their own. This was apparent soon after war's end, when a series of parties for ex-detainees helped reconnect old friends.

The first of these was a 'Welcome Home' social and dance held by the 18B Aid Fund at St Peter's Hall in Hackney on 21 July. There Neil 'Mick' Clarke, one of Mosley's lieutenants, addressed the sixty-plus crowd and talked nostalgically of the glory days of the BUF and the crowds their marches once attracted. Those days would come again, Clarke assured his audience. But first it was imperative that they retaliate for all the ordeals they had suffered. The following party, a dance at the Royal Hotel in Russell Square held on 6 October, was the one Mosley had assured the Aid Fund he would attend. Five hundred fascists had bought tickets hoping to greet him, but they were to be disappointed. Mosley had instead chosen that day to move from Crux Easton to his new Crowood estate in Ramsbury, Wiltshire, which would become the base for his operations for the rest of the decade.

When Mosley had told Flockhart he would not be attending he gave the excuse that it might seem like he was launching a new political party, which was not the impression he wanted to give. However, Mosley suggested, if a Christmas party were to be arranged that would be a far more suitable and appropriate occasion for his first public appearance.[51] Unwittingly this played into the hands of Dunlop, who was getting increasingly peeved with Mosley and was now happy to plot his petty revenge. At the final meeting of the Fund on 20 October, Alf Flockhart informed members that Mosley wished to hold a Christmas party for the 18B detainees and he hoped to do so under the aegis of the Fund. Dunlop reminded Flockhart that the Fund had already had its last dance, and as this was the Fund's final meeting, it was quite impossible for it to throw such a party and he could take no part in organising it, although, he added, he would certainly attend in order to greet Mosley.

Before he brought the meeting and Fund to a close, Dunlop announced that he would be pushing forward with the Independent Nationalists with or without Mosley's support. Of course, this support never materialised and over the next few weeks Dunlop began to more openly express his grievances with Mosley and his lieutenants, who he was convinced were behind Mosley's betrayal. Although this was probably inaccurate, they certainly were not in his corner – Francis-Hawkins suggested smashing up the Independent Nationalist's east London branch,[52] while Mosley himself said he believed Dunlop to be an MI5 agent. Nevertheless, Dunlop ploughed on, but other than attracting a few ex-BUF members who felt sympathy towards him, he struggled to recruit new members, and his feelings towards Mosley continued to sour. And yet Dunlop remained deluded for as the Christmas party fast approached, he believed there was still a chance Mosley might use his speech to declare his support and leadership of the Independent Nationalists.

The 'Ex-18B Detainees' Christmas party was held at the Royal Hotel on 15 December 1945 with around 1,000 former 18B detainees, their partners and friends in attendance. The Mosleyites were in the majority, but followers of the Duke of Bedford and Arnold Leese were also present as were other fascist notables including Captain Ramsay and Quentin Joyce, the brother of William Joyce, who was currently awaiting execution. There was also good representation from all the classes – the aristocrats, middle and working classes all present and correct.

Some of the attendees were servicemen and wore their uniforms; they had a girl dressed as a 'Hitler maiden' tending to their needs.[53] The party was heavily stewarded, only ticket holders were permitted and journalists and cameras were strictly forbidden. One journalist who did manage to sneak in was spotted and kicked, punched and thrown out for note-taking during Mosley's speech. A Special Branch officer, after failing to gain entry, had to climb a fire escape to the hotel's roof where an open window allowed him to observe the events below.[54]

The affair began at 18.45 and from the outset there was a palpable sense of excitement among the fascists who had not seen their great leader for over five years. When at 20.40 Sir Oswald and Lady Mosley were escorted into the hall by a bodyguard formed of heavies and Mosley's closest lieutenants, the room erupted in hysteria. His name was chanted to the rafters along with yells of 'HEIL WHITE MAN' and 'DOWN WITH THE KANGERS!!!'[55] Mosley stood on the stage gratefully accepting the chanting which went on for several minutes, accompanied by a multitude of raised-arm salutes.

In his speech Mosley told his followers how good it was to be with them all again and to see that they were just the same as before. Although this was not a political gathering, Mosley reminded his audience, he wished to make a prophecy that in the future their treatment would not be forgotten, and nor would their enemies be allowed to forget what had been done to them. Beyond that, Mosley refused to offer his audience any concrete ideas or plans for the future, as he did not want to give the government 'an excuse for suppressing my ideas, for it is these which they fear'. He would, he assured them, be publishing some of his ideas in due course. Mosley concluded his remarks by saying that he was delighted to see them all again as it showed that 'something high and noble still lives in the world'.

As Mosley descended from the stage, he was mobbed by people who wished to have his autograph or shake his hand while the uproarious chanting of his name recommenced.[56] One person who did not join the Mosley love-in was Dunlop. Before

Mosley had delivered his remarks, Dunlop was invited onto the stage along with the other leaders of the Fund; but if he thought this was to be the moment Mosley announced his support for the Independent Nationalists, he was to be sorely disappointed. Instead what Mosley gave him was a clock radio in thanks for all his hard work, and three cheers. This surely must have been the lowest point for Dunlop: being cheered by hundreds of people who, despite the fact he had formed the organisation that had kept them together, had turned on him, and all because he had put his trust and faith in the man in the room they all worshipped. When Mosley did mention Dunlop in his speech it was only to thank him for his efforts; the Independent Nationalists were never mentioned, and all Dunlop's devotion had been for nothing.[57]

Particularly relieved to hear of Dunlop's failure was Jeffrey Hamm. A month earlier Hamm had heard a rumour, most likely put about by Dunlop, that his was the only organisation recognised by Mosley, who looked upon the British League with disfavour. Panicked Hamm went to Francis-Hawkins, who assured him that this was nonsense. Mosley, Francis-Hawkins declared, was watching the League with great interest and was grateful for all Hamm's work.[58] Nevertheless, he would speak well of Hamm next time they met and promised to arrange a meeting. This he did, and a few days after the Christmas party Hamm and Mosley properly met for the first time in an East End pub. Congratulating the young man on his efforts, Mosley expressed his wish that up and down the country others would emulate Hamm's movement.[59]

Hamm had started to rise while Dunlop had fallen. By going out to the streets and taking the initiative, Hamm had built his own following which meant, unlike Dunlop, he was prey to neither the jealousies of Mosley's lieutenants nor the leader's own capricious nature. Moreover, Hamm gave Mosley exactly what he wanted: an apparently completely independent organisation which would beat the drum for Mosley's return to politics. One might think that if Mosley believed in December 1945 that the

British public would be drawn to fascism in the near future, he was living in cloud cuckoo land. And yet perhaps not, for as one leafy middle-class area of north London had shown, anti-Semitism was still alive and well in Britain.

The Hampstead Anti-Alien Petition

Hampstead in north London is a well-to-do area whose extensive Heath has long attracted writers and artists, and as a result is known as a centre of tolerance and progressive politics in London.[60] However, after the war it was like the rest of the city: more focused on rebuilding its homes. The area had undoubtedly borne its fair share of destruction with 13,500 homes seriously damaged, 204 lives lost, and 930 injuries. It was unsurprising then that many natives had chosen to leave the borough during the war for the significantly safer countryside. This option was not, however, open to the area's poorer residents, many of whom were refugees from Nazi persecution and so were mostly Jewish. By 1940, there were approximately 14,000 Jewish refugees spread out across Hampstead and neighbouring Golders Green and Hendon, although of course this number was often greatly exaggerated. The confluence of Jewish incomers and the exodus of those who could afford to move made it appear to many of those who stayed that their neighbourhood had suddenly been overrun by Jewish immigrants. Predictably, many of these remaining locals took against their new neighbours; one letter to the *New Statesman* typified local opinion decrying 'the ill-mannered and unsocial behaviour of a percentage of foreign Jews'.

In October 1945 two residents, Margaret Crabtree and Sylvia Gosse, organised a petition, the text of which stated: 'We the undersigned petition the House of Commons in a request that aliens of Hampstead should be repatriated to assure men and women of the Forces should have accommodation upon their return.'[61] By focusing on accommodation, Crabtree and Gosse were tapping into the wider concerns of the British public over the massive shortage in the national housing stock caused by the Blitz, and consequently they garnered not inconsiderable support from many prominent Hampstead locals. Hampstead's mayor signed, as did four Conservative councillors and the Conservative MP for Hampstead, Flight-Lieutenant Charles Challen, who promised the organisers his unstinting support and asked several questions in parliament on their behalf.

Naturally the organisers denied that the petition's creation was motivated by any form of prejudice or anti-Semitism, with Crabtree insisting that their only desire was to secure housing for 'our dear boys'. As to what should happen to the refugees if they could not be immediately repatriated to make way for the returning servicemen, Crabtree suggested they should be 'housed in Army camps, POW reception camps or empty hotels'.

Although the actual text of the petition was stripped of any overt anti-Jewish content, interviews with Crabtree and Gosse and the campaign around the petition revealed how tied up it was with anti-Jewish prejudice. Signatures for the campaign were in part collected via local shops, where many patrons found themselves bullied into signing by others who were spewing anti-Semitic invective. Meanwhile, letters to newspapers supporting the campaign revealed deep-seated prejudice, with one anonymous letter declaring how refugees had been sent to Britain to subvert its moral, cultural and racial fibre.

Not everyone in the area was on board, however, and the *Ham and High* newspaper received many letters that spoke out against it, including a few that drew attention to the way the petition's sponsors were stooping to 'Nazi methods'. Meanwhile, local soldiers, who were the supposed beneficiaries, were vocal in their condemnation, as were local party groups and various other organisations. In parliament Home Secretary Chuter Ede disputed the very facts of the petition, stating that there were only 9,168 refugees occupying 3,093 homes, half as many people and a third as many homes as the petitioners claimed.

When the Hampstead Town Council voted to repudiate the petition, Crabtree and Gosse, who were becoming distinctly uncomfortable with the negative and now national attention, convened a private meeting with two individuals who were far more willing to bear the brunt of the hostile publicity. The first of these was Eleonora Tennant, chairwoman of the 'Face the Facts Association', an organisation which claimed to be staunchly anti-German but used this as a way to thinly veil its anti-Semitism. Tennant was an Italian woman who had strong sympathies with fascism and whose British husband had been a close friend of Nazi ambassador Ribbentrop in the 1930s. Tennant was also a resident of Chelsea and not of Hampstead. The second person at this clandestine meeting with Crabtree and Gosse was also not a resident of Hampstead, and his name was Jeffrey Hamm.

Hamm and Tennant subsequently became the petition's chief advocates, and, although they had differing agendas, worked well together, at least at first. Shortly after they met, Hamm invited Tennant to one of the League's private meetings in his Notting Hill flat, hiding the photograph of Mosley, which usually sat proud on the mantelpiece. To the around a dozen League members, Tennant explained how there was a German fifth column in the country who were planning Germany's next attempt at world domination. At that a League member called Walsh wondered whether she was in fact talking about Jews, as all good Germans had stayed in Germany. Tennant observed that there was not in fact much difference between their organisations, as she too had spent her political career 'alive to the menace of the Jew', but she avoided dealing with that question from her platform. She then invited Hamm to speak at a meeting she was holding the following week, with the only proscription that he avoid using the word Jew. He could of course say 'alien' as often as he liked.

Held on 30 November at St Peter's Hall in Belsize Park, that meeting could barely progress thanks to the constant interventions of hecklers. The following week Hamm attempted to hold a meeting in the same venue, but when the vicar barred him from doing so, he decided to blame Tennant, and the two promptly fell out.

Not long after, the furore around the petition began to fizzle out, which suited Tennant who was growing increasingly uncomfortable with the ugly mood that surrounded it, believing it hindered her more respectable aims. Hamm, however, welcomed the discord that for the first time was getting his name featured in the papers and allowing him to start building up his profile. The petition's other benefit to Hamm was that it showed him what a fertile recruiting ground Hampstead could be, and he subsequently began holding meetings at Whitestone Pond, which sat atop a hill just above Hampstead and had an excellent view of the whole city.

It was there, on an afternoon in May 1946, that four Jewish ex-servicemen chanced upon Hamm speaking from his platform and decided that their days of fighting fascism were not yet behind them.

2

Who's Going to Stop Them?

Of the four men who were present that day, at least two of them strongly disagree on how it all started. For Morris Beckman it was a completely spontaneous event; Len Sherman insisted it had been planned. However, on the matter of who started it all, they were in complete agreement.

Born in December 1922 in Hackney, Gerry Flamberg was the third of four sons of Jack, an immigrant from Poland, and his wife Miriam who had been born in Stepney. Living in Hackney, the Flambergs were part of the wave of Jews migrating out of the desperately cramped East End ghetto, but the homes in Hackney were often not much better, and the Flambergs struggled to make ends meet. As a result, Gerry left school at fourteen and went to work. He was still only fourteen when he started his second job, at a clothes factory. On his first day he was horrified by the terrible working conditions employees were made to endure. He leapt into action: by lunch he had got all the other workers to unionise and strike for better working conditions, and by dinner he had to look for a new job. For the next five years Gerry worked in numerous jobs, joined his local Boys Club and became an excellent boxer.

In 1941, the nineteen-year-old Gerry received his call-up papers and joined the King's Royal Rifle Regiment. Six months later, a recruiting officer came to Flamberg's garrison to find recruits for the newly formed paratroopers. Upon hearing of the slightly better pay and the possibility of more adventure, Flamberg enthusiastically volunteered. As a private in the 156th

Parachute Battalion, Gerry jumped behind enemy lines on numerous occasions and served in North Africa, Sicily and Italy. Over the years he became an enormously popular figure in his battalion and won acclaim as its middleweight boxing champion.

On 18 September 1944 the 156th Parachute Battalion was dropped into Arnhem during Operation Market Garden. On the second day, Flamberg's squadron was trying to attack an enemy position when they came under fire from another direction. Assuming it was friendly fire, Gerry's CO sent him out with a recognition triangle to inform their unwitting assailants they were on the same side. When Gerry stepped out of their position, he saw that it was not British soldiers that were shooting at them but Germans in a tank. A bullet ripped through his shoulder. Flamberg hit the ground and was able to crawl back to his squadron. Concealing his injury from his CO, Gerry said that he reckoned he could get close enough to take it out with a Gammon Bomb. The CO gave him the go-ahead and Gerry crawled back out and, managing to evade notice, got within ten feet of the tank. Then with his uninjured arm he hurled the bomb onto the tank, which, substantially damaged, withdrew. Gerry cheerfully returned to his squadron and only then mentioned he had been shot.

Later in the battle Gerry was captured by the Germans and taken prisoner; the 156th itself sustained such heavy casualties that it was disbanded shortly after the battle. After being treated for his wounds, Gerry was sent to the Stalag XI-B POW camp, but he would not stay there for long. Flamberg's CO, who had also been captured, worried what might happen to Gerry if his captors realised he was Jewish. He put in a request to have Private Flamberg transferred to his officer's camp, Oflag 79 near Brunswick; the request was accepted. Brunswick, though, was hardly better; conditions at the camp were appalling and for the rest of his life Gerry was always incredibly conscious of cleanliness and had perfectly manicured hands, a legacy of the filthy conditions he was forced to endure.[1]

Oflag 79 was liberated by the Americans on 12 April 1945. Since his capture Gerry's status had been Missing in Action, and so it was only now his family learnt he was still alive. Gerry was brought to Hollymoor Hospital near Birmingham to recuperate, but it was not long before an enterprising aunt with a costume jewellery business in the city coaxed him out of hospital to sell jewellery for her door-to-door. After all, a handsome former POW in uniform made an unbeatable salesman, and Gerry now also had a shiny new Military Medal pinned to his chest, a reward for his bravery at Arnhem.

Finally released from hospital, Gerry returned home to a city and community massively damaged by war. 'Desolation on a Pompeian scale', writes the historian Jerry White of London in 1945.[2] Buildings half-destroyed or completely flattened were strewn across London like the scars on the face of a smallpox victim. The East End was particularly badly hit with housing estates, warehouses, and most of the docks completely obliterated. This landscape, which forms the backdrop to this story, also serves as an apt physical metaphor for the mental landscape with which post-war Jewry was beginning to reckon. For while Britain celebrated the end of war and the freedom peace delivered, the Jewish community was beginning to come to terms with the sheer unadulterated horror of the Holocaust. 'Their sense of a world restored was checked by the sense of a world irretrievably lost,' writes historian Stephan Wendehorst, who goes on to quote Litvin, a Zionist Rabbi: 'While all nations were celebrating peace we Jews were contemplating the inordinate losses we had suffered.'[3]

For many of the returning ex-servicemen, especially those who had been fighting in theatres outside of Europe, it would only have been when they returned home that they first learnt the full extent of what had occurred. 'You've got to be in 1945 where we were,' Stanley Marks told historian Dave Renton. 'It was only when we came back from the war that we saw the pictures. A lot of people that would have been in Burma or wherever didn't know what was going on. It dominated your feelings.'[4] Morris Beckman recalled the mood at Maccabi House, a Jewish sports club in West Hampstead:

> Maccabi's pre-war ebullient friendliness had gone; in its place was a subdued ambience reflecting the weariness and uncertainties of the times. Tolerance levels of the ex-servicemen were low, and an uncomfortable tension existed between them and the teenage members who had missed the war. The ex-servicemen, in their ill-fitting demob suits awkwardly adjusting to the vacuum of peace, had little in common with the extrovert noisy youth dressed in 'zoot suits'.[5]

The headquarters of the Maccabi World Union, an international Jewish sports organisation, Macabbi House was a large town-house boasting a gymnasium, sports hall, cafeteria, and numerous social rooms. At war's end, the Jewish ex-servicemen and women who had been Macabbi members before joining the services headed back there to reconnect with their old friends. For Gerry Flamberg, still working as a door-to-door jewellery salesman, it became a regular hangout.

It was here that the twenty-four-year-old Flamberg came together with three other Maccabi regulars: Morris Beckman, twenty-five; Len Sherman, twenty-seven; and Alec Carson, twenty-two. Of medium height and stocky build, the tousle-haired Beckman was a keen footballer and cricketer, who had served as a radio operator in the Merchant Navy during the war and had the misfortune of being torpedoed twice during the Battle of the Atlantic. Alec Carson had also had a very near miss. He had joined the RAF as a pilot in 1942 but crashed during his training in Nova Scotia. Carson took two years to recuperate, and finally received his wings in 1944. He flew a series of sorties over Germany in Mosquitos towards the end of the war. After he was demobbed, he joined his father in the cabinetry business. Len Sherman was the only one of the four who had been an infantryman, serving in the Welsh Guards. A rare blonde-haired, blue-eyed Jew, Sherman's boyish features belied an often brutal disposition. Into weights and martial arts, Len was Maccabi's judo and wrestling champion, honours he also held in his regiment. Upon his return to London he found work as a pattern cutter for a dressmakers.[6]

According to Morris Beckman, all four were good friends and frequently spent time together at Maccabi. The way Len Sherman tells it, he had never seen Gerry Flamberg before a meeting of the club's leadership. A 'tall fellow with a flat nose and a red beret' who 'looked like a real bastard' stormed in, demanding, 'Who's the Guvnor?' 'Who are you!?' asked Sherman, who was chairing the meeting. Flamberg hurriedly introduced himself before explaining that there was a fascist event underway in Hampstead which he was determined to close down. Sherman and a couple of others agreed to join him, and they all piled into a car and headed up to Hampstead.[7]

Beckman's version begins in the Maccabi canteen where he, Sherman, Flamberg and Carson saw that once again the club was offering the same egg and chips it always did. Flamberg took one look at the fare and declared, 'I can't stand it anymore. If I have any more egg and chips, I'll attack the bloody man by the counter!'[8] He then proposed a trip to Jack Straw's Castle, the large white pub by Whitestone Pond, to which the others agreed.[9]

As Beckman's small Ford Prefect finally pulled itself to the top of Whitestone Pond it drew parallel to the spacious area next to the road where the League were holding a meeting. A small crowd of around sixty were listening to Hamm on his platform, while four heavies stood in front of him, ostensibly selling fascist newspapers but really ensuring Hamm's small audience behaved.

'Aye, aye,' observed Carson. 'The 18B Regulation Fusiliers are here!'

Beckman parked the car and the four boys wandered over to the meeting and listened to Hamm for a few moments.

'Sod the drinks!' muttered Gerry. 'Let's go.' The friends made their way further into the crowd and eyed up the platform and stewards.

'The platform's mine,' said Gerry.

'I'll take the two on the left,' said Len.

Probably not overly enthused with the direction the evening was about to take, Beckman and Carson were hardly going to shirk the fight, and they divided up the remaining two stewards between themselves. With Len in front the four men pushed through the crowd.

Len approached his two stewards and asked to buy a couple of copies of the League's new monthly paper, *British League Review*. Caught off guard by his Aryan looks they gave him the price and as Len fumbled in his pocket for change a couple of coins dropped to the ground. In the half-second in which the falling change caught the attention of the stewards, Len smashed their heads together. They both slumped to the floor. If Hamm caught sight of this lightning-fast action it was unlikely to have distracted him for long, as he was suddenly presented with the hulking figure of Gerry Flamberg, who grabbed his small platform and with a roar lifted it up and sent the former teacher flying. In a moment, Flamberg had pounced on the sprawling Hamm and started beating seven bells out of him. Beckman's steward was wise to the attack. Beckman raised his fists. The steward did the same. Beckman kicked him in the groin.[10] Alec Carson meanwhile was having a tougher time with his steward, and the two men fell to the ground wrestling before the steward was able to break away and flee. Carson got up and chased after him, but the steward was faster. Flamberg, who had finally finished with Hamm, spotted the escaping steward and would have chased him through the heath had the others not managed to call him back.

When the four young men returned to Maccabi and told the other ex-servicemen about what had happened, it was not condemnation they were met with but support. Over the next few months these young Jewish ex-servicemen saw the Whitestone Pond attack not as a one-off but as the template for an anti-fascist organisation.[11] The young men who increasingly thought that this was the way forward were not political radicals or anarchists, they had no desire to take on the state or destroy the status quo. In fact, they would have preferred existing institutions and organisations dealt with Hamm and his ilk, but as 1946 progressed it became increasingly obvious that no one else was willing to do what they felt needed to be done.

Adequate Protection

In April 1946 the government's Committee on Fascism presented its final report to Cabinet.

> We have considered whether an attempt should be made to prohibit the organisation of fascist parties or the propagation of fascist doctrines. We consider that such an attempt would be difficult to defend in principle and ineffective in practice. An attempt to silence a political minority because its views are abhorrent to the majority would be a departure from a valuable tradition.[12]

Formed two days after Mosley's Christmas party, in part as a response to that event, the committee was asked to review all available evidence as to the re-emergence of fascism and 'the case for amending the existing law with a view to checking the growth of such a movement'.[13] For four months the committee met, deliberated and received numerous briefings from the Secret Services, and in the end concluded that:

> We consider that, if it is firmly enforced, the existing law affords adequate protection against the emergence of a strong and dangerous fascist movement in this country.

As for the threat posed by the fascists to the Jewish community, the report declared that it would not be 'desirable' nor 'in the best interests of the Jews themselves to introduce any special measures against anti-Semitic propaganda'. However, in the wake of 'the revelations of Nazi anti-Semitic atrocities' it was understood that the consequences of anti-Semitic propaganda can be 'serious enough to justify proceedings for seditious libel'.[14]

For the next two years the government, and in particular Home Secretary James Chuter Ede, refused to budge from the positions laid out in this report. As a result, Britain became one of only a few European countries that in the post-war years permitted the publication and dissemination of fascist propaganda and views.[15] This was not a popular position, with a Gallup poll showing that 66 per cent of people were in favour of taking action to suppress fascism.[16] So why did Britain's first majority Labour government choose to do nothing?

'There is no immediate threat of the re-emergence of a significant fascist movement in this country,' declared the Cabinet report, and although it acknowledged that the BPP and Mosley loyalists 'contained the germ of such a movement', they doubted these would amount to anything. Yet this was a conclusion which was based on some uncertain assumptions, namely that if the 'Government can make the next five years a period of orderly and relatively prosperous reconstruction, no fascist movement will develop into a serious threat'. In 1946 Britain, this was a risky bet. The continuation of rationing and austerity into peacetime was already beginning to breed discontent, and the government was well aware of upcoming issues that could crash the economy and create the perfect conditions for a fascist resurgence.

Of far greater concern to the Attlee government was the need to swiftly retreat from the authoritarian practices which war had necessitated and to return to peacetime norms and the principles of British democracy. A vital part of this return was the restoration of the rights of assembly and free speech to those who had been stripped of it during the war. Moreover, there was a fear that if the fascists did not have their rights returned to them, this would lead to 'progressively increasing interference with the rights of unpopular minorities' leading to 'the employment of methods indistinguishable from those of fascism'.

There has been much discussion as to why Chuter Ede was so steadfast in his refusal to act against the fascists. The contemporaneous socialist MP, lawyer and vehement anti-fascist D. N. Pritt believed that the Labour government's own staunch anti-communism and a pro-fascist bias at the Home Office both contributed to the inertia. The historian Nigel Copsey has doubted whether Pritt's first point would have made much of a difference, and instead argues that the root cause of the issue was a belief at the Home Office that the 1936 Public Order Act had sufficiently contained the BUF before the war and so was more than suitable after it.[17] Historian Richard Thurlow also lays the blame with the Home Office, which, he argues, was far more concerned 'with safeguarding freedom of speech than with protecting ethnic minorities from racial abuse'.[18]

The one Cabinet member who did not agree with the report's assessment was Minister of Fuel and Power Emmanuel 'Manny' Shinwell, the country's most senior Jewish politician. Shinwell had been a member of the five-man committee and time and again throughout the hearings argued that just because the fascists were weak and disorganised now, that did not mean they would always be. He pointed to the threat posed by a leader like Mosley who could rally all the disparate forces and provide a focal point for like-minded individuals. Shinwell was not alone in believing that responding only to the threat posed by fascism in its present moribund state, and not the potential threat posed by a revived fascist movement, could prove to be a grave error.

In expressing a belief that the fascist threat needed to be taken far more seriously, Shinwell was voicing the beliefs of the Jewish community, which was once again beginning to feel the impact of fascism. By the start of 1946, Hamm had begun his slow incursion into heavily Jewish east London, in particular Bethnal Green. League members were reoccupying old fascists haunts like the

Mitford Tavern in Mare Street, Hackney, and drunkenly harassing Jewish-looking passers-by. Meanwhile, fascist graffiti, including the letters 'PJ' and the flash insignia, began to appear on walls in north and east London. The Jewish theatre in Stepney was vandalised, as were walls throughout Stamford Hill.[19]

For the returning Jewish ex-servicemen this fascist recrudescence made the blood boil. They had risked their lives and endured appalling and traumatic experiences to rid the world of Nazism, so to come back and find the Nazis' British cousins preaching freely on street corners was galling beyond belief. Such feelings of outrage were exacerbated by the increasing awareness of the Nazi genocide of the Jews of Europe, which from the middle of 1945 onwards had started to permeate the public consciousness, as photographs and newsreel from Bergen-Belsen were shown to the British public. Subsequently the Nuremberg Trials made abundantly clear the sheer horror and scale of the Nazis' crimes.

For many in the Jewish community the losses were of course deeply personal, and those future 43 Group members who witnessed the horrors of the camps themselves were often scarred for life. The man who would become the Group's spiritual leader, Rabbi Leslie Hardman, was the first Jewish chaplain to enter Bergen-Belsen where he oversaw the burial of over 20,000 bodies. It was an experience from which he never recovered, and led to his fierce support of the 43 Group in its battle against fascism. When I interviewed Martin Block, an engineer in the RAF, about his time in the war he begged my forgiveness and said he would rather not discuss his wartime experiences. From another source I learnt that Block had worked on transport planes that rescued survivors from the camps. Of course, one did not need to see the horrors to feel the pain and anguish, and this, as Murray Podro explained, was easily transformed into anger.

'Most of the 43 Group members could be, or were, quite violent to say the least and lots of them were people who had terrible tragedies in their families. I did for instance: I had family members in Paris about '45 or thereabouts all of them murdered in Auschwitz.'[20]

These various first- and second-hand experiences of the horrors of Nazism were juxtaposed with the memories of how London's own Jewish community had been targeted by the fascists in the 1930s. In his autobiography, Lennie Ronlick listed the confluence of factors that led to his decision to stride up to the front line in the fight against fascism:

> The beating I received as a boy. Also a cousin of mine, Solly Solomons, who was a most inoffensive young man, was battered to the ground by a Fascist mob and thrown through a shop window ... Finally, I did it because of the horrific pictures we were shown of the devastation caused to human life in the concentration camps throughout Europe by the Nazis and their fellow travellers.[21]

Add to this the increasing presence of League speakers and newspaper sellers who were beginning to appear on street corners, and one can see why the ex-servicemen were beginning to feel an irrepressible drive to action. Morris Beckman shared in the 'sick sense of shame that no action had ever been taken to save the [concentration] camp inmates'. Nor had their suffering ended: many of the survivors were still in displaced persons camps, while those trying to make their way to Palestine had been apprehended by the British and sent to Cyprus. Beckman continued:

> Watching the Royal Navy stop Greek and Turkish bucket ships crammed with the sick and broken survivors of the camps, and the Pathé Gazette and Movietone films of these derelicts being incarcerated behind barbed wire in Cyprus, seemed to plumb the very depths of inhumanity ... We felt useless.[22]

In an attempt to allay these feelings of impotence, some Jewish ex-servicemen turned to the Association of Jewish Ex-Servicemen

(AJEX) to force it into confronting the fascists. Formed with the express purpose of representing and advocating for the needs and beliefs of Jewish ex-servicemen, AJEX had been involved in anti-fascist politics before the war and had been active at the Battle of Cable Street. It therefore should have been the perfect organisation through which the Jewish ex-servicemen could confront fascism, and both senior and junior members pressured the leadership to take action.

In response, one of AJEX's leaders, Major Lionel Rose, proposed a programme of outdoor speaking events in areas where Hamm and other fascists held public meetings. Such a proposal, however, failed to impress many members, who felt that public meetings were an ineffective way of dealing with fascists and demanded a more active approach.

The problem was that AJEX was hamstrung by its loyalties to the Board of Deputies, which even after the war was shackled by its conservative impulses and fear of doing anything that might be controversial or jeopardise the good name of the Anglo-Jewish community. Through its Jewish Defence Committee, a particularly conservative and cautious part of the organisation, the Board controlled what was referred to as the 'official defence structure'. AJEX, one of the organisations within this structure, was consequently constrained by the JDC's insistence that all defence work be law-abiding and in no way bring the community into disrepute. AJEX was also constrained by the JDC's seemingly pathological desire for control. When Rose proposed his Speakers Programme the JDC insisted on a strict series of rules and conditions to be agreed before it gave its final consent; this took six months.

As for its own defence work, the JDC's activities included publishing informative pamphlets and materials about British Jewry, letter writing and putting on lecture series. Following an intense lobbying campaign, a deputation from the JDC was received by Chuter Ede in May 1946 and they told him of the fascists' return and the anxieties and concerns this triggered within the Jewish community. Ede was sympathetic but informed the gentlemen of the government's position on the sufficiency of the current law for dealing with the fascist threat. The envoys of the JDC left with the sense that the meeting had been a mere formality.[23]

For the ex-servicemen, the JDC epitomised the older generation of Jews who seemed to want only to talk and debate, to jaw-jaw, and who ran for cover the moment danger reared its head. What made it even worse was the thought that this was the mentality of the German Jews whose docility, compliance, and fear of rocking the boat had led them straight to the gas chambers. That the representatives of Anglo-Jewry seemed incapable of learning from the tragic deaths of their European cousins infuriated the younger generation. As Morris Beckman put it, this younger generation saw themselves as 'of a different metal to the community of the pre-war days. The keep-your-head and get-indoors-quickly mentality had gone for good.'[24]

However, the JDC were not quite the wet blankets these men took them for. It was thanks to their work that in March 1946 one fascist plot was dealt a devastating blow. John Beckett and A. K. Chesterton had been in talks to merge their organisations, the British People's Party and the National Front after Victory, for several months, with Chesterton entrusting the nitty-gritty negotiations to a three-man team, two of whom were spies of Sidney Salomon, the JDC's head of intelligence.[25] Salomon waited until Beckett and Chesterton's plans reached an advanced stage and then passed the information to Lord Robert Vansittart, who, in a speech to the House of Lords on 12 March, gave a wide-ranging account of recent fascist activities and paid particular attention to these talks.[26] The harsh light of day is a fatal thing for furtive fascist plans, and in the wake of the speech both Chesterton and Beckett's organisations shed members and the talks were swiftly abandoned. Backed by the Duke of Bedford's wealth, Beckett was able to ride out this setback and the BPP stayed afloat, but for Chesterton this was the death knell. With his nascent organisation now entirely without funds and peopled only by a handful of rabid anti-Semites, he decided to pack it in and emigrated to Africa.

The provenance of Vansittart's intelligence was of course unknown to the ex-servicemen who saw the JDC as nothing more than a talking shop, typical of the old pre-war Jews. When it came to dealing with fascism, the ex-servicemen were getting tired of jaw-jaw; they wanted war-war.

A Monstrous Exaggeration

There was one organisation that was only too happy to war-war with the fascists; they'd been at each other's throats for years. When the BPP had held their meeting at Holborn Hall, it was members of the CPGB who had broken into the hall and forced it to close. Leading the charge that day was Douglas Hyde, the *Daily Worker*'s anti-fascism correspondent, who at a public meeting a few hours earlier had called upon his audience to join him in raiding the meeting. Over the next few years Hyde exposed numerous fascist activities and his 'All Outs' often left fascist plans in tatters. This was never more the case than in March 1946 when Hyde's job was made that much easier for him by one fascist's hubris and idiocy.

A builder in his late fifties, John Charles Preen had before the war been a small-time BUF member and briefly its organiser in North Kensington. His one moment of minor fame in fascist circles came when he and three other BUF members were caught breaking into the home of an ardently left-wing Air Ministry official. Preen's defence was that he had done so under instructions from MI5, and there is evidence to suggest he was telling the truth; nevertheless, from then on, he became known in fascist circles as 'Burglar Preen'.[27] Preen was interned from June 1940 to the start of 1942, with a month-long hiatus following an escape in April '41. In 1942 Preen returned to London and resumed work as a builder, mostly working on war-damaged buildings, and became the subject of a War Damage fraud investigation.[28] Upon his return to fascist politics, Preen denied that he and 'Burglar Preen' were one and the same, and he served libel writs on anyone who claimed otherwise.[29]

Like Hamm, Preen saw the gap left by Mosley's retirement as a perfect opportunity to establish himself as a leading post-war fascist. In October he conceived The Britons Vigilantes Action League, which aimed to provide 'food, clothing and shelter for British people in need'.[30] In his literature Preen was unashamedly pro-British: 'It is the British people who have made Britain what it is, and it is the British people who should have first claim on what Britain provides whether it is goods, jobs or houses.'[31]

Although he claimed that being pro-British did not make his organisation 'anti-foreign, nor, indeed anti-anything', he was keen to make sure one particular group of people knew why they were so disliked. In his 'Open Letter to the Jewish People', Preen affected a collegial and friendly manner to explain to the Jews certain issues which perpetuated anti-Semitism:

> Why is there relatively little food shortage in the districts mainly occupied by Jews? Why is there such a disproportionate percentage of Jewish names among the persons convicted of Black Market offences? Why are Jews so prominent in the money markets of this country, and the big International Finance Houses?[32]

Of course all these anti-Semitic libels were entirely fallacious. However, in his attempt to appear reasonable Preen offered some top tips to the Jews on how they might diminish anti-Semitism, including 'Put Britain first', 'Take your proper place in the queue', and 'Don't put money first'.

For a fascist like Hamm even the vaguely conciliatory tone of this letter was excessively moderate. The purpose of their political activities, Hamm stated, was not to temporise with the Jews but to turf them out of England. Preen had in fact approached Hamm and suggested working alongside him, but

Hamm felt that with Mosley's previous promise of assistance and support there was no reason to tie himself to Preen. Furthermore, he doubted Preen's boast of aristocratic support and a membership of 100,000,[33] 'a monstrous exaggeration' according to a Special Branch report. This was on brand for Preen, a notorious liar.[34]

Far from having aristocratic support, the wealthiest backer Preen had been able to attract was a Mrs M. Lumley, a well-to-do upper-middle-class lady. However, this was support enough for Preen to indulge his monumental hubris and hire the Royal Albert Hall for the launch of the Vigilantes Action League. The news took his rivals aback, and led to a swirl of rumours of a secret, highly illustrious backer. This was quite normal; with Mosley retired at Ramsbury and keeping his cards close to his chest, every new fascist organisation was rumoured to have his backing. Even so, Preen's launch event sent the fascist rumour mill into overdrive.

Perhaps Preen's decision to book the Albert Hall was just hubris, but perhaps there was some tactical thinking behind it. If the Vigilantes Action League launch could be a success on a par with the great BUF meetings in that venue, then Preen would leapfrog his rivals and receive the support from Mosley he claimed to have. Of course, when Mosley packed the Albert Hall he already had a movement of tens of thousands; Preen most likely had tens. Ticket sales were so paltry that Preen made a catastrophically stupid mistake, and put up posters all over London.

'18B SPEAKS! ALBERT HALL. WEDNESDAY MARCH 13. 7PM 2000 FREE SEATS', declared the poster reproduced in the *Daily Worker* on the day of the meeting. 'ALL OUT Against Fascists TONIGHT', demanded Douglas Hyde's adjacent article, calling on 'the working people of the capital to demonstrate this evening against what threatens to become the ugliest piece of Fascist provocation since Mosley's black shirted hey-day'.[35] Beckman, Flamberg and several other ex-servicemen decided to heed Hyde's call.[36]

Held in conjunction with an organisation called the British Housewives League, Preen's meeting attracted a mere 200 people, which in the vast Albert Hall looked pathetic. They nevertheless included a good number of well-to-do fascist women – ladies who could be even more rabidly anti-Semitic than the soapbox speakers. Preen had also ensured that there were plenty of fascist stewards in the hall in case any disruptors should show up, and the police also had a presence. Hamm was in attendance, too. He sat surrounded by heavies near an exit, assuming an inevitable raid would force him to beat a hasty retreat.[37]

Preen and Lumley walked out onto the stage, and Preen began to speak. The heckling began immediately; the few dozen young communist men and women who had managed to get past the stewards and into the hall began a running commentary on the event, the empty seats, and Preen's speech. After a few minutes, Lumley came forward and begged for silence, claiming that she was doing what she was doing simply to fight for the homeless. When, in answer to a question, she declared that it was she who had paid for the meeting, she was laughed off the stage. Meanwhile, the Communist Party leaders in the hall were actually trying to get their comrades to keep quiet, as it was Hamm, who was on the programme to speak, that they really wanted to target.

Shortly afterwards the doors at the back flew open and a rush of young communists came charging into the room, made for the stage, and started tussling with the stewards. Chaos descended; Hamm took this as his cue to scurry away. All over the auditorium, scraps and altercations were breaking out. A *Jewish Chronicle* reporter described the chaos:

> The very many anti-Semites in the hall were screaming foul anti-Jewish slogans. One aged harridan in a fur coat was waving a stick in the air and shouting, 'Hang all the Jews!' A young man got up and said, 'You are a Fascist, madam.'
>
> A pro-Fascist was knocked down by a Jewish soldier when he (the pro-Fascist) abused him and told him to 'go back to Palestine.'

As I dodged around the arena, where almost everybody had gathered, I heard nothing but anti-Jewish remarks. 'Look at them,' said one young girl, pointing wildly, 'the dirty Yids, they all need a wash!' Another person was crying hysterically, 'They are all Russians!'[38]

Meanwhile, the communists had mounted a successful invasion of the stage where many of them had pretended to listen to what Preen was screaming. He was not up there for long, though, as he and Lumley beat a hasty retreat leaving the stage to the communists who held their own meeting, voted to ban fascism and sang the 'Internationale'. While the fascists congregated at a side of the hall and tried to work out what to do, police reinforcements arrived and, to a rousing chorus by the communists of 'When Irish Eyes Are Smiling', cleared the stage. Preen and Lumley reappeared once more, but the moment Preen tried to speak, a roar of heckling quickly drowned him out. It was at this point that Mr Cruickshank, the Communist Party leader in the room, announced to the comrades that if they dispersed, the police would close the meeting.

Later referred to by the fascists as the cheapest meeting ever held by the Communist Party, the Albert Hall debacle precipitated the closure of the Vigilantes Action League and Preen temporarily disappeared from view.[39] The following day, Chuter Ede shared with the House of Commons an account of the day's events and declared that even if it had not been interrupted by communists, Preen's meeting 'would have been a complete exposure of the futility of the Vigilantes' Action League'. For Ede, the Albert Hall farce demonstrated that post-war fascism was nothing to be feared and certainly not something that needed legislating against. Really, Ede suggested, all that was required was 'to leave these people to the sense of humour of the British people'.[40] It was true that in 1946 British fascism had reverted to being the domain of cranks, weirdos and infighting would-be dictators, but as the Labour MP Tom Driberg reminded Ede, despite their failings the fascists must be taken seriously. Unlike Preen, they were not all ineffective jokes.

The following day Mosley circulated an open letter to his supporters throughout the country, addressed to Alf Flockhart, in which he announced two upcoming publications: one a collection of old essays and speeches, the other an entirely new work. As for their distribution, Mosley wrote that while they would be sold through the normal channels, they would also 'certainly be supplied to any book clubs which desire to purchase them'.[41] Within days Mosley's supporters were writing to let him know they had got the hint. F. R. Cork of South Norwood told Mosley: 'The idea of area book clubs could be exploited to the full with particular reference to problems in the future . . . I am immediately making contact with many old friends and circulating the context of your letter to them.' Meanwhile, N. B. Rawlinson of Hampstead wrote, 'It will be my endeavour in the near future to commence a British book club, here in Hampstead.'[42] Over the ensuing months, fifty-seven Mosleyite book clubs were founded around the country. Primarily they served as a way of maintaining and growing Mosley's middle-class following, and would, Mosley hoped, provide a backbone of respectability to his next political organisation.

As for the foot soldiers of that next organisation, Mosley left their recruitment to Hamm, who was steadily growing the League. In part this was due to Hamm's decision to switch the focus of his activities from west London to east London, and particularly Bethnal Green, where he often found crowds far more receptive to his message. On 20 April, Hamm held his largest indoor private meeting to date with 100 people in attendance. During the meeting, Bill Carrit, a local councillor, castigated those present, shouting, 'This organisation is an insult to British servicemen. Men have fought and died struggling against Fascism and those who spread these filthy anti-Semitic lies!' Carrit was swiftly ejected from the hall by the stewards.[43]

The meeting was a high point for Hamm in a year in which he struggled so much he began giving serious thought to moving to South Africa and abandoning the British fascist cause for good. But when Carrit's interruption got into the papers, the owners of the venues Hamm tried to book became wise to the true nature of his organisation and denied him the use of their spaces. Meanwhile, Hamm noticed his street meetings were beginning to attract more and more organised heckling. However, these challenges paled in comparison to the problems that were emerging from within the League itself.

When Hamm and Burgess took over the League, they did so on the understanding that they would run it together. However, over time Hamm became the far more dominant figure and Burgess felt that the younger man was treating it like his own private fiefdom. Burgess was not alone in feeling that Hamm had started running the League like a dictator, and an ineffective one at that, as the League had encountered financial difficulties. Like all good dictators Hamm was rabidly determined to maintain his dominance and sidelined all challengers, especially Victor Burgess, whom he removed from the League's roster of speakers.

For Burgess this was the final straw, and he had a very useful ally: Hamm's lodger, a fascist called David Keith Barrow, alias David Hearn. Despite the fact he shared rooms with Hamm, Barrow agreed with Burgess that life in the League had grown intolerable under Hamm's leadership. There was of course only one solution: to split off and form their own movement. Barrow's decision was a major blow for Hamm, not only because he lost a lodger but because most of the young toughs who Hamm relied on to steward his meetings were loyal to Barrow, so when he left they followed. With the loss of Barrow's men, Hamm suddenly became very vulnerable on the platform.

Fortunately for Hamm, he was approached a month later by an ex-BUF man called Bertram 'Duke' Pile, who offered to send some old BUF stewards who were 'specially trained in the art of being tough' to Hamm's meetings. Hamm accepted, although he told Pile that his men should carry no weapons, as he currently had the sympathy of the police, which he wished to maintain. Secretly Hamm also suspected Pile of being a police informant, so thought it wise to be doubly cautious. Pile's men, who were, he said, East Enders with a score to settle against the Jews, appeared to adhere to Hamm's request. Not long after they met, Hamm began to notice organised hustling at his meetings, and believing this to be Pile's men at work, revoked his original suspicions of Pile, who would go on to become a key member of the League. Pile, who the police described as being 'of average mentality',[44] was a typical working-class fascist and had none of Hamm's intellectual pretensions. Pile, who proved to be a loyal ally to Hamm, in all probability joined the younger man in the belief that Hamm enjoyed Mosley's full support. He thought that backing Hamm would win him Mosley's approval. Over the ensuing months many other ambitious fascists came to the same conclusion and became Hamm's loyal lieutenants, allowing him to consolidate his position as the League's indisputable leader.[45]

Meanwhile, Burgess and Barrow had launched their own organisation, the Union for British Freedom (UBF). With Hamm's activities now solely focused on east London, the UBF stayed in west London and the two organisations kept out of each other's way. Consequently, there were now two Mosleyite organisations operating in London, but even this new development triggered no meaningful response from the Jewish community's official defence structure – the Jewish ex-servicemen were getting ever more frustrated.

'What, the five of you?'

On 24 May 1946 a letter signed by Morris Beckman and Gerry Flamberg appeared in *The Jewish Chronicle*.

On Sunday afternoon the British League of Ex-servicemen and Women held a meeting on Hampstead Heath. The speakers preached anti-Semitism and Fascism pure and simple . . . Amongst the audience Jewish people listened and suffered silently. They heard themselves threatened and slandered and read the anti-Semitic pamphlets handed to them – without so much as uttering one word of protest. Until my friend G. Flamberg, M.M. and myself, quite by chance, came across this meeting. By countering the speaker's arguments all along the line we swayed the crowd completely against him. I noticed the faces of Jewish members of the audience light up with relief.

This letter, which is the one and only primary source referring to the Whitestone Pond attack, typifies Beckman's overblown style. The Jews of Hampstead seem reminiscent of the subjugated Jews of Europe, and Flamberg and Beckman's appearance is almost messianic. The complete absence of violence from the encounter, however, is perhaps more understandable; after all, a public confession to a physical attack on a political meeting would have been unwise. Beckman concluded with a call to his fellow ex-servicemen. 'There must be no half measures and cowardly hiding of heads in the sand. It is up to all Jewish ex-servicemen to help fight this menace. All who are keen to join us in this fight are invited to write . . .'[46]

Clearly the letter served its purpose, as the following week Beckman wrote to the paper again and mentioned 'receiving many letters from those keen to join'. Beckman continued with an account of a second encounter with Hamm, this time at a League meeting in the East End, where 'with the very able support of some Jewish ex-servicemen, who happened to be in the audience, we closed that meeting in an orderly fashion within 15 minutes of its commencement.' Again, a pinch of salt might be required, as it seems highly unlikely that if a few ex-servicemen had managed to close down a League meeting within fifteen minutes they had done so 'in an orderly fashion'. The ex-servicemen in the crowd that day would have also been interested to learn that Hamm himself took the *Jewish Chronicle*, probably mentioning it in conjunction with Beckman's letter and the attack at Whitestone Pond. With this knowledge Beckman addressed himself directly to Hamm:

> Now, knowing full well that Hamm himself reads The Jewish Chronicle and will read this letter, we hereby tell him that we will not rest until his anti-Jewish activities are nullified.

Another person who had noticed Beckman's letter of the previous week was the JDC's Sidney Salomon. He also wrote to the paper and while he agreed that Beckman's letter made a legitimate point, he assured readers that 'observation is kept on all meetings of an anti-Semitic nature', although not the ones that were 'arranged at very short notice'. He concluded, 'I hope Mr. Beckman and his gallant friend, Mr. Flamberg, will agree as to the necessity for fighting anti-Semitism and Fascism on a united front.' In principle, Beckman and Flamberg had no problem with this wish: 'We are only too willing to work in conjunction with the Jewish Defence Committee. But, we stress, we demand action now! Nothing else will suffice.'[47] In practice the two sides were growing further apart. The small group of ex-servicemen – having seen success through more violent methods at Whitestone Pond and having witnessed how effectively the communists had shut down Preen's meeting – were moving ever further away from the JDC, which refused to budge from its preferred tactics.[48]

It was not just the young ex-servicemen that the JDC's intransigence was alienating. Discontent was also brewing in the higher echelons of AJEX. One of the Association's most respected and influential members was Major Samuel Weiser, a former member of Field Marshal Montgomery's staff. Along with Lionel Rose, Weiser was one of the driving forces behind the proposed anti-fascist Speakers Programme and consequently, as the months wore on and the JDC still had not signed off on it, Weiser grew annoyed. Unafraid to vent his frustrations, he discovered that he had an ally in a tall, wiry, bespectacled film producer. The son of a senior figure at RKO Pictures,

Geoffrey Bernerd was a well-to-do former army captain and war photographer from west London. Bernerd had participated in the raid on Dieppe in 1942 where he was shot in the leg and invalided out of the army. As a result, the 'tall, dark and handsome' Geoffrey Bernerd frequently carried a cane,[49] which along with his trademark trench coat and his cigarettes smoked from a pack of twenty – a sign of real wealth – made him a striking figure.[50] Bernerd was also a strident anti-fascist who was deeply unhappy with the passivity of AJEX's tactics, and so when Weiser floated the idea of starting their own organisation and breaking away from the 'official defence structure', Bernerd was all in.

Although they were all members of AJEX, it was quite by chance that the two groups of ex-servicemen came together. One Sunday afternoon Bernerd, his wife Trudie and their one-year-old son Elliot were taking a stroll through west London when they encountered a fascist meeting. They stopped at the edge of the crowd and listened for a few moments. When a large, heavy-set Jewish man with a flat nose began heckling, Bernerd was sure to signal his approval. At the edge of the crowd the two AJEX members started chatting, but Flamberg was immediately distracted by baby Elliot. Without asking for permission, he scooped the baby out of his pram and threw him right up into the air. Trudie's heart skipped a beat as she watched her first-born hover in mid-air before falling back into Flamberg's strong arms. The former boxer held the baby affectionately and handed him back to his very relieved mother. Baby-tossing out the way, Flamberg and Bernerd went on chatting and realised they shared the same frustrations.

Not long after Bernerd and Weiser met Flamberg, Beckman and their growing band of ex-servicemen, they floated the idea of turning the ragtag band into a real anti-fascist organisation. It was an idea that was met with excitement, and throughout the summer of 1946 the growing group of ex-servicemen began meeting in each other's living rooms where they discussed anti-fascist tactics and the plans for their new organisation.[51] Planning did not preclude action and the ex-servicemen continued turning up to fascist meetings, mostly just to heckle the speakers; a few scraps might have broken out with stewards, but they tended to avoided physical attacks. Heckling, however, could be surprisingly effective, and on a couple of occasions their persistent yelling forced Hamm to close his meetings. At each meeting there would often be one or two new faces, as more Jewish ex-servicemen heard about what was going on and got involved; sometimes people were even recruited at the meetings themselves.

Philip Evansky was a tall, hulking butcher's boy who, due to a childhood injury, was deaf in one ear, an impairment that kept him out of the services. During a Sunday morning walk with his brother he had seen the League's pitch at Hereford Street, Bethnal Green. Having grown up in the East End during the BUF days he immediately recognised the gathering and, fearing for his brother's safety, quickly walked on. The next Sunday he returned alone and stood against a wall watching the fascists set up their platform. It was there that he was approached by five unmistakably Jewish boys, one of whom was Flamberg, who demanded to know when Evansky's mates were coming. It took Evansky a few moments to realise that they thought he was a fascist. This was understandable; he certainly did not look Jewish. Evansky insisted that he was a Jew, but as had happened on numerous occasions, he was not believed. Evansky produced his identity card, with his obviously Jewish name, but someone pointed out this could be a fake. Exasperated, Evansky wondered how else, short of pulling down his pants, he was meant to prove his faith, when an unmistakably Jewish friend of his walked past. This friend confirmed Evansky's identity, informing Flamberg he knew him from a Jewish Boys Club. Flamberg relaxed and told the two boys about their plans to go after the fascists. 'What, the five of you?' exclaimed Evansky indignantly. 'Six, if I joined?' 'Seven,' chimed in his friend. Still, they accepted Flamberg's invitation to a meeting at Maccabi House. There were around twenty others there. They had no name, they had no idea whether they wanted to be out in public or remain underground, but they knew what they wanted to do, and their numbers were growing.

At the start of July, they were presented with the best possible opportunity to find and reach out to likeminded ex-servicemen. This came as a direct result of events in Palestine, where the British Mandate forces were struggling to contain the boiling tensions between the Arab population and the Yishuv (the Jewish community in pre-Israel Palestine). What made matters even more difficult for the British was that the Jewish paramilitaries, who felt that the British overwhelmingly favoured the Arabs, had begun to target the British. On 17 June 1946, one of these paramilitary groups, the Irgun, kidnapped six British soldiers. Twelve days later the British responded by arresting 2,700 members of the Yishuv, including many of its leaders.

Throughout the global Jewish community Operation Agatha, as it was called, led to a wave of outrage. The Anglo-Jewish community was particularly incensed. Even the Board of Deputies felt compelled to act. On 7 July, 80,000 Jewish people met in the East End for a march to Trafalgar Square to protest the arrests. Seeking to ensure attention from the British press, the organisers placed the community's leaders, including Board chairman Professor Selig Brodetsky, beside the most decorated Jewish ex-servicemen in the front row. Gerry Flamberg with his Military Medal was one of these ex-servicemen, and a photograph of the march shows him at the front standing a full head taller than everyone else. However, another gentleman in the first row held a decoration that dwarfed even Flamberg's.

Tommy Gould was a submariner who had served as a petty officer aboard the HMS Thrasher. In February 1942, the boat successfully torpedoed an Axis supply ship off the coast of Crete in enemy waters, but was then itself attacked with a three-hour barrage of depth charges and aerial bombing. The Thrasher survived, but soon it was discovered that two unexploded bombs were lodged within it; Gould and Lieutenant Peter Roberts volunteered to remove them. The first bomb was stuck in the submarine's casing, a light metal structure on the deck, and so was easily removed; the second, however, had got through the casing and was lying on the pressure hull. They determined that the only way to safely clear the bomb was for Gould to lie on his back, gripping the bomb firmly to his chest, while Roberts dragged him under his arms as he himself crawled through the tiny space. With only a small torch for a light source, the two men took forty minutes to move the bomb the necessary twenty feet – every time it moved it made an ominous twang. For the feat of removing the bombs and saving the craft while in enemy waters, both men received the Victoria Cross.

Gould was one of only three Jewish recipients of the Victoria Cross in the Second World War, and his decoration made him a hot commodity. He might have agreed with Flamberg that more direct action against the fascists was required – he would become the most high-profile of the 43 Group's founding members – but he was not willing to reject AJEX's less confrontational methods out of hand. So, when he was approached to join Lionel Rose and Major Weiser's Speakers Programme, which after several months had finally been approved by the JDC, he accepted. Flamberg, Bernerd and Beckman also joined.

On 8 September, AJEX set up their first platform at Speakers' Corner in Hyde Park. In front of a large crowd, Weiser opened the meeting and set out the core argument advanced by both AJEX, and later, the 43 Group:

> Every man irrespective of his religion, irrespective of his views shall be free, that is what we fought for. I do not stand here to argue for the privilege of the Jew, it is for your privilege that I fight. This is your fight equally as it is mine, and I shall hope to see on this platform not only Jews, but also non-Jews, Catholics, Protestants, or whatever he may be.

It was a performance that impressed Mr M. J. Roston of the JDC, although he had less praise for Morris Beckman: 'very unimpressive. The matter was quite good and given an impression of sincerity. His delivery though was atrocious.'[52] On the whole, Roston was pleased with the event and noted that the crowd 'seemed slightly puzzled and visibly impressed'. He concluded: 'While I am of the opinion that it would be highly inadvisable for any open-air Defence to be carried out elsewhere I was impressed by yesterday's platform in the Park.'[53] Clearly this view held sway in the JDC, and when Weiser submitted a proposal for a meeting in Bethnal Green it was swiftly rejected. This was exactly the sort of innate conservatism that had brought the ex-servicemen to the inescapable conclusion that the fight against fascism could never be successfully directed from within the official defence structure. It was time to break away.

One New Raincoat

During the summer of 1946, Flamberg and friends steered clear of any anti-fascist activities that would draw too much attention and contented themselves with just heckling public meetings. Come autumn, a decision was made to adapt their modus operandi and they decided to go after the fascists' private meetings as well. One of their targets, they revealed in a 1948 feature on the Group in the *News Review*, was a meeting of the BPP held at St Ermine's Hotel, which they attacked as it drew to a close.

> Only assessable damage was a ripped raincoat belonging to one of the Group. In a whip-round the sum per head of 3s. 6d. and one clothing coupon was raised. Net result: one new raincoat and the formal birth of a new and militant anti-Fascist organisation.[54]

Not long after, they struck again. Raven Thompson had been giving a series of lectures on the theme of Jewish black-marketeering and profiteers. When the ex-servicemen discovered one was scheduled to take place in Holborn Hall in Kingsway, they called the police with a hoax threat to blow the place up if the meeting was not cancelled. That failed, so they moved to Plan B and smashed up the meeting and destroyed Raven Thompson's magic lantern projector. However, it was as they lay in wait in the room next door that they had an unnerving yet fateful encounter with the law. Clearly on high alert following the bomb threat, two policemen walked in and were surprised to see a dozen or so young men hanging around without apparent purpose and demanded to know who they were. Standing nearest the door were Len Sherman and Jonny Wimborne, a smaller man with a thin moustache who was still technically serving in the Merchant Navy. 'We're a football club,' said Sherman. 'What's the name of the club?' asked the police. Sherman and Wimborne both spotted the number on the door at the same time. 'We're the 43 football club!' they said together. And that, insisted Len Sherman decades later, was how the 43 Group got its name. 'Anything else that you've heard forget it, because I named the group, it was an accident, it wasn't intentional, I never thought about it, it came exactly as I described to you, and that is historic.'[55]

It is not, however, the official account of how the Group got its name. In all its literature the Group stated that it was named for the 43 people in the room at its first official meeting. This is also Morris Beckman's version of events, describing how thirty-eight men and five women came together in an upstairs room at Maccabi House and decided to form an organisation which would defeat fascism by any means necessary. At that meeting, which lasted for several hours, two co-chairmen, Gerry Flamberg and Geoffrey Bernerd, were elected and the Group's aims and objectives agreed upon. These were subsequently laid out in a Group pamphlet:

1. To advocate the immediate passing of legislation to make Fascist and Anti-Semitic Organisations illegal.
2. To combat actively all Fascist and Anti-Semitic Organisations by:

      (a) Opposing their activities;

      (b) Publicly exposing them

3. To awaken and unite all sections of the public against the menace of Fascism.

4. To develop an organisation capable of communal defence.

5. To work and cooperate with all the other bodies combating Fascism and Anti-Semitism.

Other matters that were discussed included the Group's politics and who could be a member. It was agreed by all that the Group would have no political opinions or beliefs on any matter other than the question of fascism, and the only criteria for membership was a belief in anti-fascism. Even though it was going to identify as an organisation formed by Jewish ex-servicemen, there was no obligation to be either Jewish or an ex-serviceman.[56] This would have greatly reassured both Philip Evansky, the only non-veteran in the room, and Joe Zilliacus, a non-Jewish ex-Royal Marine and friend of Flamberg's; he was also the son of Labour MP Konni Zilliacus. After several hours of discussions Alec Black, a former territorial officer in the Essex Regiment and a captain in the Eighth Army,[57] summed up everything that had been agreed upon and said if anyone was uncomfortable with the declared objectives, they were free to leave.

When no one did, a brief cheer went up, and then the question of the organisation's name was raised. After several suggestions which aped the grandiose titles the fascists gave to their organisations, someone pointed out that they had been talking for hours and they'd rather like to get home: 'There are 43 of us here, so let's call ourselves the 43 Group.' The name was seconded and then unanimously adopted with another cheer.[58]

By September 1946, the 43 Group had formally come into existence, but that did not mean it was ready to come out into the open, and for the next couple of months its members continued to be active in AJEX. Bernerd was still determined to set up an AJEX platform in Bethnal Green, and when the JDC learnt that he did so with Weiser's support they demanded the Major 'take all necessary steps at once to call off this intention'. Weiser ignored the instructions, and he and Bernerd went ahead with their plans. The platform was, however, enough of a success that when Weiser met with the JDC a few days later he got them to sanction two further Sunday meetings in the area.[59]

The first was on 13 October, when Weiser and Bernerd stole Hamm's usual Bethnal Green pitch on Hereford Street. Hamm was forced to move a few streets away and Weiser attracted an audience that listened with some interest. He did the same the following week, but this time his audience of a couple of hundred was mostly apathetic. Meanwhile, on an alternative pitch Hamm had attracted a large and more sympathetic crowd, but he also faced determined opposition from 43 Group members who began heckling and jostling and creating a generally unpleasant atmosphere. Fearing a breach of the peace, the police stepped in and closed the meeting.

On 27 October, AJEX held another meeting in Hyde Park, with Bernerd and Weiser being joined on the platform for the first time by Flamberg, who offered a strong warning about the potential dangers of British fascism:

> They will not stop at the extermination of the Jewish race in this country. Such will be their lust for power that they will not be satisfied until every decent, freedom-loving Englishman is exterminated as well and Britain will become a nation of automatons like the 'Master Race', which has just been the cause of the destruction of half of Europe.

Unfortunately for Flamberg, his public speaking inexperience meant that when it came to answering questions from the audience he allowed himself to get drawn into an argument, and had to be rescued by Weiser who was suffering from a sore throat.[60] That was the last time on an AJEX platform for either of the 43 Group's co-chairmen, but they were not yet done with the

Association. In November AJEX held its executive elections, and Bernerd and Flamberg along with six other 43 Group members stood on a platform advocating an 'ACTIVE policy to combat the growing menace'.[62]

They could not have been surprised that this electoral bid ended in failure. After all, Flamberg, Bernerd, Sherman, Beckman, and Blacke had all signed a letter to the *Jewish Chronicle* in which they confessed to being, along with Major Weiser, behind AJEX's unsanctioned Bethnal Green platforms. Not that they were admitting to having started their own organisation; the 43 Group was never mentioned. But they were unequivocal about their mission, and willing to proclaim it from the rooftops:

> The battle against Fascism, much to our disillusionment and disgust must go on. But we shall fight it, and win! Again we appeal to all Jewish ex-servicemen and women to join us and help us *actively* in this fight. If we all put our shoulders to the wheel and muck in, Fascism can never survive. We must kill it, and kill it now! *Now, and not later.*[63]

3

The 43 Group

The winter of 1946–47 was to be one of the twentieth century's bitterest. Not only was it one of the coldest ever recorded in England – in January, temperatures fell to minus 21°C, and in February conditions were so bad that no sunlight was recorded at Kew Observatory for twenty days – the country was also completely unprepared. When it was discovered that the coal stockpiles had frozen, making them impossible to transport, factories were forced to close and in certain parts of the country people were banned from heating their homes, for three hours from 9 a.m. and two hours from 2 p.m. Even with these restrictions, blackouts were frequent, with staff at Buckingham Palace and Parliament often being forced to work by candlelight. Meanwhile, rationing got worse and worse, and unemployment skyrocketed from 400,000 at the start of January to 1.75 million in February. For the 43 Group this horrendous winter was the backdrop for its transformation – from a band of rogue ex-servicemen, haphazardly operating from the shadows, to a fully functioning, multifaceted anti-fascist organisation proudly stepping out into the light.

Of course, one advantage of staying in the shadows was the element of surprise. If the fascists had no idea of the nature of the organisation that had been formed to destroy them, they would have no idea what, quite literally, had hit them. On 10 November, two days after the Group's letter appeared in the *Jewish Chronicle*, a visibly cut-up and bruised Jeffrey Hamm mounted a platform in Bethnal Green.

'Yesterday a gang of Jewish terrorists—'

'Sit down you twerp!' someone shouted from the Jewish section.

'Fascist!' '18B!' and the like, yelled others unceasingly.

Hamm soldiered on and tried to make himself heard above the heckles as he told his small audience about the events of the previous night. 'Yesterday afternoon a gang of Jewish terrorists in a car, and some of them are here this morning, went around London breaking into private premises and attacking people.'

The events of that night, which, for fairly obvious reasons, we have only the fascists' accounts of, began at Victor Burgess's home in Westbourne Grove.[1] On the evening of Saturday, 9 November, Burgess was holding a meeting of the UBF when between 9 and 10 p.m. the doorbell rang; David Barrow went downstairs and answered the door. Two assailants sprang out of the night and launched themselves onto Barrow, who went sprawling to the floor with a shout. The UBF members leapt to their feet and charged down the stairs, coming face-to-face with half a dozen assailants. A melee broke out. The fascists had the numbers and home advantage, and beat the attackers out of the house. However, one of the retreating men, a twenty-four-year-old ex–Royal Navy man called Mark Fisher, was grabbed by Burgess and pulled back indoors. Fortunately for Fisher, if the fascists had any mind to give him a beating their window for doing so was small, as shortly afterwards a police officer arrived and Fisher was handed over. At the subsequent trial, where Fisher was fined 30 shillings for each of two charges of assault, Burgess claimed that Fisher had kicked him, and Barrow said Fisher had bitten him on the back of the hand. Fisher for his part told the court that Burgess had threatened and hit him with a spanner which had been thrown at Fisher from upstairs during the brawl.[2]

An hour after the raid on Burgess's home, William Francis McGrath, an Irishman who lived in Notting Hill, heard a loud knock on his front door. Standing outside were two gentlemen he did not recognise.[3] 'Is Dave or Jeff here?' one of them asked. Taking them to be members of the political organisation of his fellow tenant, he pointed towards the upstairs flat saying, 'You better go up and see.' Thanking him they walked into the dimly lit hallway and made their way up. 'These Jewish terrorists came up the stairs and knocked on the door of my flat,' Hamm told his Bethnal Green audience. 'When I saw the repulsive alien faces I closed the door. They smashed the lock and then assaulted me with knuckledusters.'

Gerry Flamberg the boxer and Len Sherman the martial arts expert had no need of knuckledusters and in a short and brutal fight they easily took down both Hamm, who had grabbed a fire poker, and his lodger, an ex-BUF man called Owen Holliwell.

The commotion brought into Hamm's living room, first his heavily pregnant wife who fainted at the sight of her husband being beaten up by Flamberg, and then McGrath, who went for Len Sherman. Sherman punched him in the stomach, sending him reeling to the ground. Flamberg and Sherman then scarpered, but not before someone had seen and noted down the licence plate of their car. At both Notting Hill and Westbourne Grove, a car full of reserves was also spotted.

Shortly after the attack, a UBF man named Woods arrived at Hamm's house to warn him that he should expect some unwelcome visitors, but he had arrived too late. Or rather, he had arrived right on time: after all, no one at the UBF would have been particularly bothered if Hamm got a good thrashing. That night Hamm and McGrath went to the police station, and in Bethnal Green the next day Hamm assured his audience that steps were already being taken, 'My wife, who is expecting a baby in the near future, fainted when she saw these terrorists.[4] I am applying for a summons tomorrow. The first step is being taken to stop these Jewish terrorists.' In the event, only Flamberg was subsequently arrested and charged.

Over at the JDC, news of Flamberg's assault was received

with exasperation but also some sympathy. Hearing of multiple witnesses, including one who took down the car licence plate, Louis Hydleman, the chairman, assumed this was an open and shut case but told Flamberg's lawyer, Mr Mishcon, he would be willing to provide mitigating evidence, including anti-Semitic materials published by Hamm. This offer of help was quickly rescinded when he discovered that Flamberg's defence strategy was to deny he was anywhere near Hamm on the night in question. 'Let Flamberg and his friends stew in their own juice,' Hydleman wrote to Sidney Salomon. 'We must repudiate them, as well as considering our whole attitude towards the Jewish Ex-servicemen's Association.'[5]

Clearly Hydleman had some unvoiced wish that when Flamberg v Hamm came in front of Mr E. L. Guest at West London Magistrates Court on 16 January 1946, the young Jew might be slapped with small custodial sentence; it would be an excellent deterrent for those who might follow his stupid example. The trouble was the case was far less open and shut than it first appeared. The car that had been spotted was a rental, and only Hamm could positively identify Flamberg. Neither Sally Hamm nor McGrath had got a good look at the assailants, and Holliwell, the BUF man, had disappeared. Without another corroborating witness the best Hamm could do was convince the magistrate that Flamberg knew where he lived. Flamberg confessed that he had been to meetings of Hamm's where literature was distributed, literature where Hamm's address was clearly printed.

By contrast, Flamberg's lawyer, Victor Mishcon, presented the court with a watertight alibi. His client had spent the evening at the Bray House, a private members' club in Piccadilly and to prove this was the case he called as first witness Captain Leighton-Morris, the club's secretary, who produced the signing-in book to show that Flamberg had arrived at 8:30 p.m. and left at 11:30 p.m. The second witness was the club's chairman, Joseph Webber. Webber told the court how towards the evening Flamberg and his friends had asked Webber if he would take them to the Blue Lagoon nightclub in Carnaby Street. Was it not strange, asked Hamm in cross-examination, that Webber had such a distinct memory of this conversation? Not in the least, retorted Webber: did he not remember the recent murder of a young woman which had been in all the papers? That had occurred the following day right outside the Blue Lagoon, and with a coincidence like that it was no wonder Flamberg's request lodged in the memory.[6] Hamm obviously had no idea that the club was a front for prostitution, as he asked no further questions. With no more evidence to be heard Mr Guest declared he was far from convinced by Hamm's case, which he dismissed; costs were awarded against the plaintiff.

But what if both the prosecution's and defence's versions of events were true? Early in the evening on 9 November, Len Sherman brought Gerry Flamberg and several other Group members to the Bray House Club, where Leighton-Morris greeted them and asked them to sign the guest book. The gentlemen, all of whom were wearing dinner suits, came in, had a drink and mingled for a bit. Then, one by one, they surreptitiously made their way towards the back door of the club where a couple of cars were waiting. As they sped off towards west London, the men changed out of their dinner suits into attire more appropriate for social calls. Following quick stops at Westbourne Grove and Arundel Gardens, they drove straight back to the Bray Club, and re-entered via the back entrance once again looking resplendent in their dinner suits. Other than when Flamberg signed the guest book on arrival at 8:30 p.m., it was only after 11 p.m. that Webber and Leighton-Morris recalled actually seeing him in the club.

Then again, Hamm claimed it was around 11 p.m. when he was attacked. So, either he, understandably, was mistaken as to the time of the attack or Gerry Flamberg never attacked him. Len Sherman certainly did, though; decades later he proudly boasted of his involvement, although Len's version has some crucially different details.

According to Len it all began with a phone call from the 'police' telling Hamm that they had information that he was going to be attacked and would be sending around officers to protect him. Hamm already had a couple of League men guarding his flat, but when the two 'police officers' arrived declaring that they were there to give added protection, they were immediately let in. They went up to Hamm's flat and knocked on the door. Hamm answered and was confronted with the sight of 'two big brutes'. Hamm started screaming for help, but before he knew it, he was getting, as Len put it, 'a very very nasty . . . *welcome*'. As Len's friend beat Hamm, Len raided his cabinets, and stuffed his pockets full of League documents that he subsequently handed over to Special Branch. Damage done, they charged down the stairs where they came face to face with one of Hamm's actual bodyguards. 'Hurry up you fools, can't you hear he's being attacked!' Len shouted. The moment's confusion this caused was enough to allow them to barge past and rush out the house, jump in the car and make their escape to the Bray House.[7]

Gasbag Gaster at the Halt Café

Late in the evening on 12 December 1946 the phone rang at the Reuters news agency. The caller refused to give their name. There were only two details they were willing to provide, the name of their organisation – the 'National Guard' – and their intention: to burn down the Clapton Synagogue. By the time the police arrived the synagogue had obviously been broken into, but superficially little damage had been done. The police went further in and found by the Ark, the special cabinet in which the sacred Torah scrolls are kept, the scrolls lying on the ground smouldering away in a stench of paraffin. Two weeks later, on 29 December, upon entering Dollis Hill Synagogue its custodians discovered all twelve of the synagogue's Torah scrolls had been thrown on the floor and burned. This time the vandals had left a message, scrawled on the wall: 'You Whip – we burn. 2nd N.G.'[8]

The 43 Group probably had no idea who was behind these two attacks, but they reckoned they knew who had inspired them. At a Bethnal Green meeting of the British League in September, Duke Pile raged about the actions of Jewish terrorists in Palestine, and told his audience that the Jews' next targets would be closer to home. 'I demand that every Jewish organisation be searched for arms!' a police shorthand reporter recorded Pile as saying. But, according to 43 Group founding member Alec Blacke, he went much further than that and yelled, 'Burn the synagogues! Kill the Jews!' The audience, said Blacke in the case brought against Pile in December, took up the call of 'Kill the Jews! Kill the Jews!' The case, which was thrown out, got attention in several newspapers.[9] So, whether Pile had actually shouted 'Burn the synagogues' or not, Blacke's suit had brought his words to public attention, perhaps unintentionally catalysing the vandalism. It's a possibility, but the man the secret services reckoned was behind the attacks had nothing to do with Pile, and certainly did not need anyone to encourage him in his anti-Semitism.[10]

A former public schoolboy who had been discharged from the army on medical grounds, John Marston Gaster was a young man who was no stranger to anti-Semitic organisations.[11] He had been one of the few members of Chesterton's National Front who had supported his vision of creating a deeply anti-Semitic organisation, and when that folded, following its foiled attempted to merge with the BPP, Gaster joined the British League. This was short-lived, as although Hamm quickly made him director of public relations, he was forced to purge him shortly afterwards owing to Gaster's embarrassing penchant for public displays of Nazism.[12] On Christmas Day 1946, Gaster, along with kindred spirits J. Minney and J. Atkins, officially launched the North West (Racial Defence) Task Group in Burnt Oak, north London,[13] an area which the *Edgware Local* described in its 18 December issue as being 'Alive with Fascists'.[14]

Particularly active in the area was Victor Burgess, whose

Corporate Utilities Print Shop had become the go-to printer for London's various fascist organisations, including the League. All this was laid out by Major Weiser, who was still with AJEX, at the December meeting of the Edgware and Stanmore Forum held at the Edgworth British Restaurant. Weiser concluded his remarks by declaring his amazement that some of the other speakers claimed to be 'unaware of any Fascist activities in Edgware, when the district [was] alive with Fascist propaganda'.[15] The following week, Burgess addressed a private meeting at the same venue and declared that he had a right to print pamphlets for whoever he bloody well pleased. Knowing he was among friends, he went one step further and announced the commencement of 'a war on Jews in an effort to free this country from their grip'. He announced that the campaign would start in Edgware by 'turning out the aliens and giving the houses back to the British ex-servicemen'. He advocated that 'for every British soldier assaulted by the Jews' in Palestine, 'one hundred British Jews should be publicly flogged.'[16]

While the offices of the *Edgware Local* were on high alert for potential fascist activity, the same could probably not be said for the patrons of the Halt Café on the Edgware Road, a popular destination of both lorry drivers and disaffected youngsters, looking to while away the hours between random bouts of crime. For John Marston Gaster it was the perfect place to find recruits for his new movement, and by the start of January 1947 he had built up quite the following of young people, many of whom referred to Gaster, who was not that much older than them, as 'the Professor'. A concerned local resident witnessing what was occurring at the Halt Café wrote to Barbara Ayrton-Gould, a Jewish MP who represented the Labour constituency of North Hendon. The resident informed her that he had of late been noticing the young people, most around the age of fifteen, who frequented the café leaving with all sorts of fascist and anti-Semitic propaganda. One particularly disturbing incident was when he saw two young girls, 'who do not know one iota, walking around with the backs of the hands inscribed in indelible pencil with these words TASK GROUP: WARN THE JEWS'.[17]

These impressionable youngsters were an excellent way for Gaster to disseminate toxic material into the north London community, including Arnold Leese's *Gothic Ripples*[18] and Gaster's own pamphlets, one of which was headed, 'WIR KOMMEN WIEDER' (We Come Again). Printed by Burgess and in part reprinted by the *Edgware Local*, the pamphlet made a number of claims:

SECONDLY: THE JEW IS AN INFERIOR BEING – if a Jew walks on the same pavement, knock him into the gutter where he belongs.

THIRDLY: THE JEW WILL CONTAMINATE YOU – if a Jew is on the same bus or train with you, throw him off.

FOURTHLY: THE JEW OWNS TOO MUCH – boycott their shops; if you work in a shop yourself, don't serve a Jew.'[19]

When Ayrton-Gould reported these concerns, a Special Branch officer looked into Gaster and the Task Group and noted how many of the young men who joined it already had criminal records for offences including shop break-ins, car theft and vandalism. They concluded that while Gaster had politicised these youths, he had not turned them into criminals, and it was in fact the Halt Café's reputation for attracting these youths that drew him to it. It was Gaster's ability to turn these young people to his own ends, however, that enabled him to cause what the *Local* described as 'an anti-Jewish reign of terror'. There was nothing unusual about the youthfulness of Gaster's followers, as teens who had been old enough to fight in the war made up a large percentage of the League and other street-based fascist organisations.

Towards the end of January, a young Jewish woman called

Peggy Bloom was walking her dogs one Sunday evening in Edgware when she encountered three youths who were loitering about and shooting an airgun at random front doors. When they saw Bloom, they aimed their gun at her. 'Go back to Palestine or I'll shoot you,' said one of the youths and immediately fired, the airgun pellet searing the back of her neck. She turned and fled, was shot once more in the back, but managed to make it home and subsequently recovered.[20] While there is no strong evidence that the youths were connected to the Task Group, the attack occurred during a time when the Task Group members were making lives very difficult for north London's Jewish community. Young people began harassing Jews, distributing anti-Semitic literature, breaking into and vandalising shops, and scrawling anti-Semitic graffiti on Jewish buildings in Edgware and its environs. This spree went as far south as Golders Green, where one Jewish shop had scrawled upon it 'Remember the Flogging'.

At the 43 Group's new headquarters at 54 Bayswater Road the phone rang. The caller was a disaffected and disgusted former Task Group member who had some information. Sunday, 2 a.m., members of his erstwhile organisation planned to daub anti-Semitic graffiti on every shop on Edgware's Station Road. On the night in question two cars full of trusted Group members lay in wait at one end of Station Road, with their lights off and smoking strictly prohibited. A white van pulled up and came to a stop around twenty feet away. Six men emerged and, after unsuccessfully checking their surroundings, they removed paint pots and brushes from the van. At that point the Group members charged towards the would-be vandals, petrifying them. The 43ers lined them up against the wall, grabbed their paint pots and dumped the contents over the fascists' heads.[21]

This was the only real victory the 43 Group scored against the Task Group. While the 43 Group had been alert to the threat of the Task Group since it became active, there was very little they could do. However, it was in response to Gaster's gang that the 43 Group developed some critical aspects of its operation, including its surveillance capabilities and its decision to subdivide into local sections, which would focus on monitoring and dealing with fascist activity in their own areas.

More significantly, it was the actions of the Task Group that led to the 43 stepping out of the shadows and into the light for the first time. On 27 March, the day after the *Edgware Local*'s headline declared, '"43 Group" is Jewish Answer to Fascists', the Group held a public 'Answer to Fascism' meeting at the Edgworth Restaurant. The meeting, according to the *Local,* was attended 'by a large and enthusiastic – predominantly youthful – audience' as well as 'a number of Conservatives, Communists, some Fascists and a number of plain clothes police officers.' Several of the Group's founding members addressed the meeting, including Alec Blacke who informed the audience: 'When the Fascists step outside the law, as they will, they will find a strong determined group of young men and women who will stop at nothing to thwart them. Our answer is Death to Fascism.'[22]

Among the fascists that day was Gaster himself, who clearly was getting frustrated with all the negative attention he was receiving. A few days after the meeting he stormed into the offices of the *Edgware Local* and demanded they print his denial that he was the author of the 'Wir Kommen Weider' pamphlet. The editor agreed on the condition that Gaster, who he described as 'piercing-eyed, close-cropped and pallid', answer some questions about his organisation. Gaster acquiesced and sent his responses in a letter in which he declared 'the Nazi ideology is ours'. As to the aims of the Task Group, Gaster stated: 'Democracy aims to rule the world. Task-Group aims to expose the true character of Democracy. This character is Jewish.' It was after this encounter that the *Local* began referring to him as 'Gasbag Gaster'.

The publicity surrounding the Task Group soon did it for

Gaster. He had already been banned from the Halt Café and by the end of April he had suspended his organisation. It was quite the reverse for the 43 Group, which utilised the publicity generated by the Task Group to announce itself and its anti-fascist mission.

43 Idiots

In February '47, one month before the 43 Group first featured in the *Edgware Local*, the Group finally came out into the open on the letters pages of the *JC*.[23] This was catalysed by a letter to the paper from Major Weiser, who had split from the Group following a clear divergence in priorities. Weiser believed nothing could take priority over the recruitment of young Jews to go and fight and live in Palestine, whereas the Group believed all their energies should focus on Britain. Weiser had also left AJEX and decided to set up his own organisation, the Jewish Legion, the creation of which was announced in his letter in the *JC*. The Group's response appeared directly below his and was signed by Beckman, Flamberg, Bernerd and Blacke.

> In the past our names have been associated with that of Major Weiser, as part of the 'rebel group' in the Association of Jewish Ex-servicemen. However, in view of Major Weiser's secession from the Association we wish to dissociate ourselves completely from his new group.
>
> We ourselves are members of The 43 Group which has been actively fighting organised anti-Semitism for some time. The Group was formed as we realised through bitter experience that the official defence bodies are still using the same methods that were so unsuccessful in the past, methods that are completely antiquated to-day when faced with a menace far greater and more subtle . . .[24]

Presumably one of the reasons the Group had waited so long to step out into the open was its founders' knowledge that doing so might attract the attention of the JDC, which would do everything in its power to shut it down.

A few days later Louis Hydleman, now the chairman of the JDC, wrote to a community leader expressing his annoyance at the '43 idiots'.[25] Hydleman, who proved himself to be one of the Group's bitterest and most intractable enemies, wanted to publicly denounce the Group at once; however, the rest of the JDC decided that the best course of action was to reach out and make clear to the Group that its 'members would be welcomed and given full scope for Defence work within the Board's defence organisation'. Shortly afterwards the Group responded, declaring that while they were 'prepared to co-operate completely' they would do so 'only on the basis of remaining a separate organisation'. Hydleman responded that the Group could continue to exist, but only as a social club. This suggestion, which implied the JDC saw the 43 Group as nothing more than a gang of stupid kids – a perception which it never really moved away from – infuriated the Group and communication between the two bodies completely broke down.

One month after the Group's first letter to the *JC*, the paper published Hydleman's response, in which he described his meeting with 'these self-appointed saviours', who 'were not ready to acknowledge or even listen to facts which disprove the case they appear to have built for themselves'.

The following week's paper carried a response from Bernerd alone, who put the case for the Group's existence to the entire readership, declaring that the fascists' new campaign needed to be met 'with courage and imagination, with a clearly defined active policy'.

> The battle against the Fascists will never be won on a platform in Hyde Park or by committees that 'sit and watch' . . . Every member of the '43' Group is a volunteer who works with the knowledge of what the lack of positive action cost our brethren in Europe.[26]

The following week Hydleman was spitting with rage, focusing his ire on the 'behaviour of certain '43' members:

> Their hysterical conduct is leaving a most undesired impression upon impartial listeners; shouting and excitable antics only prove helpful to the speakers by attracting much larger audiences than could otherwise be induced to listen to them.[27]

Despite the bad blood, the Group saw the value in maintaining a relationship with the JDC, and Bernerd suggested that the two organisations exchange representatives. When this suggestion was completely ignored, the Group applied for representation on the Board itself, but this too was subsequently denied,[28] despite one of the Board's constituent committees speaking in its favour.

The Trades Advisory Committee (TAC) had been set up by the Board to help combat anti-Semitism in trade and commerce, and it was mostly comprised of prominent businessmen. One of these gentlemen was Maurice Essex, a successful businessman as well as an active communist. Essex sat on both the TAC and the JDC and so when talks with the Group collapsed, he volunteered to try and mend bridges. Hydleman insisted that he alone should represent the committee, but Essex reached out to the 43 Group anyway, and discovered a group of young men with whom he strongly empathised.[29] Essex became one of the Group's most active supporters, advisers and donors, and introduced the Group's leaders to other prominent Jewish businessmen who were only too happy to reach into their pockets.[30] He also spoke highly of the Group to the TAC which wrote a letter in support of the Group to the Board. Another TAC member and left-leaning businessman, Jack Parry, used his position as a deputy on the Board to add his support.[31] Clearly these activist businessmen who cared deeply for their community and who despised fascism were delighted to see young Jews taking the fight to the fascists, even if they were not always comfortable with the Group's methods. For Hydleman, the TAC was one of the worst possible bodies to support the Group, as not only were its members prominent community members but could also, if they so chose, have bankrolled the Group for as long as they wanted.

Not that the Group was solely reliant on the TAC members for financial support. In early 1947 the Group rolled out a fundraising programme, including socials and dances. They also placed appeals for funds in the *JC*, and sent their members around Jewish areas to knock on doors and ask for donations. Group member Gerry Abrahams recalled that sometimes the door was answered by someone who was more than willing to donate a few shillings, whereas on other occasions the Group member would get an earful from someone who clearly disapproved of the Group's methods.[32] Many of it's wealthier supporters were East End businessmen, factory owners, traders, shopkeepers and bookmakers who remembered the horrors of the 1930s and were delighted the Group was doing something about the fascists. These individuals had no compunction about publicly supporting the Group, so that its prominent backers included the entertainer Bud Flanagan, boxing promoter Jack Solomons, and several famous Jewish boxers such as Ted 'Kid' Lewis.

It was not just the East Enders who supported the Group; the Group also had plenty of support from more middle-class businessmen who held prominent positions within the Jewish community at large. However, many of these individuals assumed that public support of the Group might jeopardise their position in the community, which is why some of the Group's most trusted senior members were on occasion summoned in the dead of night to the homes of the community's wealthy to pick up large cheques or wads of cash.

It became an impressively effective operation and in July 1947 in a meeting with representatives from the Board, the Group's executive declared they had over 500 members and an operating budget for the coming year of £30,000 (over a million pounds in today's money).[33]

A Few Hundred Idiots

There was, for the most part, a clear division of labour between the 43 Group's two co-chairmen, as each man played to his own strengths. Gerry Flamberg – strong, charismatic, fearless and a powerful presence – became the Group's figurehead and its unquestioned leader in the field. But it was the more operationally minded Geoffrey Bernerd who was at the forefront of moulding the Group into a dynamic and highly effective multi-faceted organisation. Despite wildly different temperaments and priorities, which at times led to ferocious rows, the two men made an excellent team. Over time, however, Bernerd became the far more influential presence, especially once he became the Group's only paid full-time employee. However, in the beginning the two men were equally influential, and one of the Group's major strengths was that it embodied the contrasting temperaments of its two leaders.

Bernerd and Flamberg did not run the Group alone, and from the outset they worked alongside a Provisional Committee comprised of some of the most active founding members.[34] One of their first tasks was to find a suitable headquarters for the Group, which in its early weeks operated out of Maccabi. This situation fast became impractical and when some rooms at 54 Bayswater Road, just opposite Hyde Park and next to the headquarters of the Football Association, became available the Group snapped them up. These were rather dowdy rooms on the ground floor of a large house, but with space for a few offices, a meeting room and a reception area for the secretarial pool, were apparently more than suitable. It would take almost a year before the Group realised the major security concerns the location created.

Shortly after moving into its new headquarters, the Provisional Committee was replaced with an elected National

Executive upon which sat the Group's executive officers, chairmen, deputy-chairman, secretary, and treasurer, as well as the heads of the social and fundraising sub-committees, the Group's area branches, and its head of intelligence, and field commander. Accounts differ as to the first head of intelligence, but the most likely candidate appears to be Jonny Wimborne, even though he was still technically serving in the Merchant Navy at the time. There is no debate though as to the identity of the Group's field commander, for occupying that role was one of its most memorable figures. Reg Morris was a six-foot-three, half-Jewish, devilishly handsome ex-guardsman, who once worked as a stand-in for movie star Stewart Granger. Like Flamberg and Sherman, Reg Morris was among the Group's toughest fighters and most popular members.

The Group's charismatic leadership was a big boon as it worked quickly to grow its membership. News of the fledgling organisation spread fast among London's Jewish ex-servicemen, and some wanted to join up the moment they learnt of it. Martin Block heard about the Group at a dance, and shortly afterwards went to Bayswater Road to sign up. Others needed a bit more convincing.[35] Gerry Abrahams got wind of the organisation from his friend Monty Solomons, but it was only when Solomons introduced him to Flamberg that he was persuaded to sign up.[36] Within a few months the Group had expanded to about 300 members.

One of the Group's favoured recruitment tactics was to go to Jewish dances on a Saturday night, get up on the stage and requisition the microphone. 'It may be all right for you to be here tonight,' the Group member would harangue the slightly miffed revellers, 'but tomorrow is Sunday morning and you should be out on the streets. There's still a war on, the fascists are still out!' The idea was to pick up a few young men who were trying to look big in front of their dates. It was not a completely unsuccessful tactic, but plenty of the guys recruited this way dropped out once they had experienced the rough and tumble of street meetings.[37]

The Group used more traditional methods as well, and held recruitment meetings in various venues around London, including several at Maccabi House. At these events, Group representatives talked about the fascist resurgence and explained the organisation's aims and objectives, asking, pointedly, why if they had been sent to Europe to fight fascism they should be in any way hesitant about doing it at home. The Group's spokesmen also made clear that there were no membership fees or subscriptions from active members.[38]

Also expected to chip in with the recruitment work were the Group's 'sections'. Early on, the Group decided that a decentralised structure with semi-autonomous local branches would more effectively allow Group members to monitor and deal with fascist activities in their areas. All the sections were London-based (regional branches were established later), and for a substantial period all were north of the Thames. Even when a South London section was formed, in response to a local increase in fascist activity, it was far smaller than the other sections, which usually reflected the size of the area's Jewish population. At its peak the Group had six sections – Central, North, North-West, West, East and South – and the vast majority of the Group members were attached to one of these.[39] Group members were by no means limited to their area though, and its most active members operated all over the city.

Each section was tasked with recruiting and organising new members, monitoring local fascists, distributing Group literature, harassing fascist paper sellers, and attending fascist meetings to observe, heckle, disturb and disrupt. Essentially, each section functioned as a smaller version of the larger group with a Section Head, who sat on the Executive, Field Commander and Head of Intelligence; the larger sections further subdivided into cells, each with their own leader. This further subdivision was essential for the Group's effective operations: it allowed the Group to mobilise quickly; it created a structure through which information could be quickly disseminated;

and in battle, smaller cells could function as far more effective fighting units.

The North London section, which covered areas including Clapton, Stoke Newington, Stamford Hill, and Dalston, was led by Stanley Marks, one of the original 43 and a former corporal in the Royal Engineers. Marks was a ferocious fighter, but one would have never guessed that from his slight frame, bohemian airs and deeply creative sensibilities. His friend and fellow Group member Ivor Benjamin recalled that he was a brilliant artist.[40] Marks's number two in the section was Gerry Abrahams, a former morse code operator for Air Sea Rescue. Abrahams, who was the North London field commander, later reckoned that at no time did the section have more than forty active members, with the personnel frequently changing. As far as Abrahams remembered the vast majority of the section's members were young Jewish men, although there were a number of women, who mainly did surveillance work. The section never had its own headquarters, and section meetings were usually held in the home of one of its members.[41]

As he lived around Tottenham Court Road, Martin Block joined the Group's Central London section. 'I suppose I had only been there for about a month or something when the guy who was the area commander [for Central London] – we liked to use the military terms because everyone was military at that time – had to leave and they wanted a new commander, and the only one foolish enough to take the job was me.'[42]

Block was a musical instrument repairer with a workshop in Kingly Street, an area thriving with Jewish activity and industry, which quickly became the Central section's de facto headquarters. There its members would hang out, discuss plans, and use Block's tools to fashion knuckledusters and other weapons. The fascists did not tend to hold that many meetings in central London, but fascist newspaper sellers, who often appeared in popular locations, gave Block's boys plenty to do. There was also a North-West London section, which covered Stanmore, Edgware, Hampstead, Golders Green and Finchley. This section, run by Ken Zimmerman (another of the original 43), was primarily responsible for dealing with the Task Group. Meanwhile, the West London section covering areas including Kilburn, Paddington and Notting Hill mostly found themselves tangling with Burgess and the UBF.

The East End section was by far the most notorious. Within its zone of operations were Mile End, Shoreditch, Bethnal Green, Hackney and Dalston, making it responsible for the area where Hamm's League was most active.[43] Violent clashes with the League was a major factor in the section's reputation, but so too were its own members, who having grown up in the poverty of the East End were willing to countenance exceptional levels of violence. The section was run by Harry Bidney, a wiry man of five-foot-four, who, unusually for the time, was fairly open about his homosexuality. A former warrant officer who had served in Burma, Bidney was one of the Group's most active members and one of the most effective intelligence operatives. An active chap, Bidney, who was never seen without a Woodbine cigarette in his mouth, perpetually had several 'interesting' businesses and projects on the go; selling nylons purchased from American soldiers at the back of a pub was his best remembered. 'He was a real weasel,' remembered Martin Block, 'but a fast thinker and an organiser.'[44]

Bidney's number two was Jackie Myerovitch, who, aged just twenty in 1947, was five years Bidney's junior but at well over six feet tall dwarfed his leader. Jackie's father had left home when he was two, leaving his mother to raise the children.[45] They lived in what Jackie's friend Jules Konopinski described as 'the poorest hovel in the East End, the Stepney Green Dwellings where there was a toilet on the landing and you had a butler sink between four flats'. Myerovitch enlisted with the Royal Engineers but a year later was released on compassionate grounds, so that he could look after his invalid mother. 'His mother was a little lady,' recollected Konopinski. 'But when she spoke he jumped.' As the war came to an end Jackie learnt that the majority of his cousins in Poland had been murdered and his aunt had been blinded in a concentration camp.[46] The combination of a tough childhood and recent trauma provoked a lot of anger in the young Myerovitch, who, as well as joining the 43 Group, turned to boxing to channel his rage. In his first fight, he won when a spectator from the Group told him his opponent had said: 'I'll bloody kill that Jew!' He was trounced in the second fight, and decided to call it quits.[47] With the gloves off, he was the most ferocious fighter, and his street-brawling skills were second to none.

Myerovitch and his gang were a major factor behind the East End section's notoriety, but so too was the Group's decentralised structure. Members of other sections heard plenty of stories about the East End section, but they might not have ever actually met them. People tended not to mix much outside of their own section, and even at Group dos, both the social and violent kinds, friends tended to stick together. Similarly, the sections echoed the city's class divisions. 'The East End [section] was very working-class,' Martin Block recalled. 'There were a lot of very posh guys in my section that we saw once or twice when somebody told them to be there. They were very loyal and were prepared to do anything but they weren't general hard-grafters, like the guys in the East End section.'[48]

Another consequence of the Group's decentralised structure was that nobody really knew who was a member and who was not. There were no subscriptions, and while a membership list had been briefly maintained, it had been destroyed to prevent it falling into the wrong hands. While anyone who applied to join at headquarters was subjected to an interview, these were not hugely rigorous. Jonny Goodman joined in 1948: 'There was a table like that, draped with an Israeli flag, and there were three guys sitting there, and I was interviewed and interrogated about how I would or wouldn't do this that and the other, and then they said, fine, OK, you're in. So I joined.'

For a member who joined the Group via one of the sections there might not have even been that level of scrutiny. The vast majority of members simply joined through becoming active in a section. Here the process was so ad hoc that anyone who had turned up a few times and proven themselves to be reliable was seen as a section member, and thus a 43 Group member. In truth, no quality was valued more than reliability. This being a voluntary organisation, nobody could be compelled to be anywhere or do anything, and no one could be punished for not turning up. However, the Group was run by former soldiers who valued military discipline, and who aimed to prosecute their campaign with military precision. This meant it was vitally important that members showed up when they said they would. There was nothing worse a member could do than leave his fellow members a man short. Over the years of research for this book, I compiled a list of Group members that I always showed to veterans I interviewed, and a comment they often made as they looked down the list was 'He was always there' – a true compliment to a fellow member who never left his friends in the lurch. For those committed members it was clear they took their duties very seriously, and were prepared to devote as much time as they could to the organisation.

Just as people were willing to volunteer their time, they were also willing to donate their skills and services. Geoff Bernerd's brother-in-law Maurice Melzack, for example, had recently qualified as a solicitor and did much of the Group's legal work. A number of members were taxi drivers and were only too happy to drive others around on various jobs. If someone had a particular skill or craft and were willing to put it to the Group's service, before long the increasingly ingenious Group was likely to find a use for it. As for payment, the Group decided that while advice could be accepted free of charge, any professional work undertaken, especially by tradesmen, had to be reimbursed in full. The Group was also happy to benefit from favours offered by supporters and community. For example, Joe Bloom owned a boxing gym in Cambridge Circus that would later be patronised by the likes of Sonny Liston, Rocky Marciano, and Sugar Ray Robinson. Bloom gave the Group members free use of his facilities where they could practise hand-to-hand combat, self-defence and martial arts, with Len Sherman leading the training.[49]

That this disparate, decentralised, multifaceted and sometimes completely chaotic organisation functioned at all is something of a wonder. This was almost entirely down not only to Geoff Bernerd and the Executive, but also to the Group's secretaries. Entirely consisting of female members, the secretarial pool quickly became the Group's central nervous system. It was the secretaries who were responsible for coordinating all Group activities, from fundraising events to major meetings and attacks, and collecting and disseminating information as quickly as possible. The Group tried to give the vast majority of the office and administrative work to its female members, as it wanted to ensure they could make a vital and meaningful contribution. Outside of the office the Group's female membership was employed in lots of different ways, including in surveillance work and as spies, newspaper sellers, fundraisers and so on, but office work was seen as the most useful way the truly committed could contribute.

However, a number of the women at HQ did not see why the boys should have all the fascist-beating fun. Mildred Levy was an early recruit. Having previously worked as a secretary at the War Office, she was immediately given a job in the secretarial pool.[50] A statuesque woman who stood six feet tall, Levy had a passionate hatred for fascists. 'I just felt when it was all happening that I had to fight,' she told a BBC journalist. 'I was a Jewish girl and I had to fight the fascists.'[51] With such strength of feeling she was hardly going to be satisfied with office work, and Mildred became a regular attendee at the fascists' bigger street meetings. She liked to throw herself right into the middle of the fighting, normally going for other women, as did most women who fought, and on one occasion came away with a good handful of fascist hair.[52] This sort of behaviour was frowned upon by the head secretary, Geoff Bernerd's wife, who felt that the fights were no place for her girls, and so her more pugnacious secretaries became adept at concealing their extracurricular forays and any resulting bruises.

Keeping Trudie in the dark was an impressive feat, as she was one of the most in-the-know members of the Group – as well as running the secretarial pool she sat on the executive. Geoff Bernerd also felt the need to keep members in line, but only the ones who felt like chatting about the Group's one taboo subject.

No Politics!

The 43 Group was from the outset determined to be an organisation defined entirely by its anti-fascism, and thereby one that welcomed any and all individuals who shared its anti-fascist philosophy. Of course an organisation comprised of frequently argumentative and opinionated young Jews, with multifarious political opinions, could turn into something of a tinderbox. Geoffrey Bernerd thought it safer to have a strict 'No Politics!' rule, banning all political conversations that did not directly pertain to anti-fascism. This, he hoped, might allow the Group's more conservative and liberal members to peacefully co-exist with the left-leaning majority.

The situation in Palestine could also be a source of major arguments, as even though the majority supported a Jewish state in the region others were strongly against the idea. Whether Bernerd was successful in his attempts to stifle irrelevant political talk is up for debate – as one Group member told me, trying to stop hundreds of young Jews discussing politics was a fool's errand, but that was not the policy's significance. By banning fractious political discourse, the Group made clear to all its members and new recruits that no one was ever going to be made to feel uncomfortable or alienated because of their beliefs; so long as you were against fascism you were at home.

The organisation saw this policy as a vital part of its identity, and in its paper's first issue the Group's nonpartisan nature was heavily stressed. 'Non-political in its own policy,' the *On Guard* correspondent wrote, the Group 'contains in the ranks members of all parties and where you may find Communist and Tory working together in complete accord.'[53] Similarly the Group was very keen to make clear that it was an independent organisation, 'THE GROUP IS NOT AFFILIATED TO ANY POLITICAL MOVEMENT,' declared one of its pamphlets. This was a point it made time and again as the police, fascists and journalists frequently saw them as indistinguishable from communists. This conflation of anti-fascists and communists was a holdover from the 1930s, when active opposition to fascism was seen as the purview of the communists. Thus even after the end of a war in which the entire country had come together to defeat fascism in Europe, there was still the perception, especially in the police force and the press, that anyone who fought fascism was by default a communist.

While the 43 Group was definitely not a communist organisation, it did have far closer ties to the Communist Party than it let on. During its existence, the 43 Group assisted the CPGB on a number of occasions when fascists threatened to attack their speakers, and the two organisations frequently cooperated. Among the Group members a decent number also had strong communist sympathies and a communist cell was operational within the 43 Group. This cell was headed by Lenny Rolnick, a tailor by trade, who after learning of the Group and approving of its methods decided to join. Rolnick was a member of the CPGB and a close friend of its leader, Harry Pollitt, whom he informed of his decision. 'Pollit gave me a choice,' Rolnick told historian Dave Renton. 'If you want to continue, try to organise a cell within the group.' Rolnick agreed, and then officially tore up his membership card, as

Pollitt was worried CPGB involvement might lead to the Group getting a bad name.[54] Once he became a Group member, Rolnick got to work recruiting people into his cell. Rolnick's primary aim was for his cell to provide a lead within the Group and in doing so hopefully get it to embrace socialist politics.[55] Believing had unspoken communist sympathies, Rolnick approached the chairman. He told him that 'although I felt that the direct action the 43 Group was taking was correct for the time being, I did not believe that in the long run it was going to solve the Fascist problem', and that embracing left-wing politics was necessary. Bernerd's response was not to kick Rolnick out but instead to invite him to serve on the Executive Committee, an offer Rolnick was delighted to accept, becoming an active and key member of the Group.[56] There have been suggestions that Bernerd's willingness to allow a CPGB cell to thrive within the 43 Group indicated Rolnick was correct in believing Bernerd to be a secret communist; this, however, is doubtful as Bernerd was somewhat bourgeois and came from an affluent background.[57] More likely is that Bernerd was just being canny, determining it was far better to have Rolnick close by where he could keep an eye on him.

Some historians have examined these facts to determine whether or not the Group was in fact a communist entity, but I fear they have rather missed the point. In the 1930s, when fascism first emerged, it was the communists who quickly became their main political rivals. Consequently, the fight against fascism was seen as part of the conflict between radical political opponents. Even though by 1945 Britain had been fighting Nazism for six years, those who took to the streets to oppose fascism were still characterised as communists. By declaring itself to be apolitical, the Group was making the case that the destructive nature of fascism was such that opposing it was a moral imperative and not one that should be left to a single political group. The Group wholeheartedly believed that if someone wanted a free, open and tolerant society in which all were welcome they should be actively participating in the fight against fascism, regardless of any other political affiliation. The Second World War had brought the entire country together to defeat fascism in Europe; why then should the country react any differently when it was home-grown?

4

Going East

In the spring of 1947, the fascists were ramping up their activities, fortunate to have an economic and political climate favourable to their goals.

On 2 March, the League set up a platform at Buckfast Street in Bethnal Green; this was a brave decision. The bitterly cold winter was still battering the country, and three days later there would be one of the worst blizzards in British history. To an audience of 300, which included 100 loudly heckling 43 Groupers who made his speech frequently inaudible, Hamm marvelled at how 'the Jewish Strachey and the part Jew Shinwell managed to organise a fuel and food shortage at one and the same time'.[1] This was a strange remark, as John Strachey was not even slightly Jewish and Manney Shinwell was entirely Jewish. However, aside from these weird inaccuracies, Hamm's speech showed just how easily he and his coterie of speakers could in 1947 turn current events and the nation's innate anti-Semitic prejudices to their advantage. As the minister of fuel, Shinwell had become the national scapegoat for the winter fuel crisis and had received death threats. Shinwell's failed leadership during the crisis would give the fascists fodder for their speeches for many months, as their audiences remembered the misery of that freezing winter, and it was not the only misery upon which they could draw.

Minister for Food John Strachey was not in the least bit Jewish,[2] and yet Hamm's attempts to make food shortages the Jews' fault rang true with his audiences. During the war years there was no greater blaggard than the black marketeer who, when everyone else was making do with rations, was using dirty tricks to consume more than his fair share. It was not long before the black marketeer became inextricably associated with Jews, and the Jewish black marketeer was such a prominent image that one almost appeared in a Ministry of Food propaganda video. It was the newspapers, ranging from the *Spectator* to the *Daily Mirror*, that were mostly responsible for this stereotype. In 1942 *The Grocer* reported on forty-three cases brought against black marketeers, only three of these involving Jewish perpetrators, and yet it was these three and only one or two others on which the papers reported.[3] In the post-war years rationing not only endured, it became more austere. Bread, which had never been rationed during the war, was put on the ration in mid-1946 after a period of prolonged rainfall, and in mid-1947 transport and dock strikes left meat rotting on the docks and virtually non-existent on the shelves.[4] 'Don't you know there's a war on,' became an even more common refrain during peacetime, as the victors remained perpetually hungry. Lamented one diarist for the social researchers Mass Observation, 'The peace is so grim it occupies all our time.'[5]

At a League meeting in Dalston in May, in front of an audience of 200 that again included a large 43 Group contingent, Duke Pile played on these miseries and calumnies.

I have not sabotaged the nation's food supply like various members of this audience. I am not a black marketeer. I am a danger to the British public – that is why I was in Brixton [prison]. It is about time some of the black marketeers were sent to Brixton for sabotaging the food supplies.

Later in his speech, Pile argued that the suffering of the British was down to their disenfranchisement. They needed, he said, 'to enter the struggle for political power in order to better the British people as a whole'.[6]

While some fascist speakers at League meetings attempted to be vaguely euphemistic in their anti-Semitic attacks, others were far more cavalier. One of the League's speakers was a young man of Indian descent called Otto Abeysakera who had been a sergeant-major in the King's Royal Rifle Corps.[7] Abeysakera's minority heritage did not make him any less anti-Semitic, and at a League meeting in Hackney in April he made full use of it:

> The Jew because he is born in England says 'I am as British as you are'; I say no. I am a coloured man born in England but that doesn't mean I am English. Blood is the law of nature. Blood determines race. Jewish laws of race and nationality should be abolished in this country . . . I know the cheap little Jew for what he is. He will appear very charming and say 'have a drink' but behind you, will hate you far more than the Germans.[8]

It's hard to believe that anyone in the immediate post-war years with the knowledge of Belsen and the Holocaust could have stomached these views, but as the Hampstead Anti-Alien petition showed, anti-Semitism remained rife. Certainly there had been some decline from the early war years, when a Mass Observation study found that around 55 per cent of the population harboured private prejudicial views towards the Jews, but how material this was is up for debate.[9] It should be remembered that the war was never framed as a repudiation of the Nazis' anti-Semitic policies, so one could easily support the war effort and remain a Jew-hater. As knowledge of the Nazis' crimes began to permeate British consciousness, there were some individuals, particularly those of a more reflective bent, who, understanding where such hate could lead, did not hesitate to abandon their anti-Semitism. However, as the historian A. J. P. Taylor observed, many in Britain were actually rather 'annoyed at having to repudiate the anti-Semitism which they had secretly cherished'.[10] In the post-war years many began to express both deep sympathy for the Jews of Europe and personal hostility towards their British coreligionists.[11]

In the wake of the discovery of the Nazi crimes, there was a small wave of philosemitism, but this was short-lived. But a 1947 Mass Observation report found that 'people are no longer moved by the thought of Jewish suffering in concentration camps.'[12] Anti-Semitism remained particularly bad in East London. A Bethnal Green psychological study carried out between 1947 and 1949 found that 26 per cent of respondents could be identified as 'extreme anti-Semites', believing Jews to be 'traitors', 'warmongers' and worse.[13]

To justify their attitude many of the respondents could easily have pointed to events in Palestine, where the British forces were struggling to deal with the Jewish and Arabic antagonists in the territory. The Jewish paramilitaries, in particular the Irgun and the Lehi (Stern Gang), were making life as difficult for the British as possible, attacking troops and senior figures. The assassination of Lord Moyne, a government minister, in November 1944, and the blowing-up of the King David Hotel in July 1946 showed how far they were willing to go to. Such acts caused outrage in Britain. In 1947, as a United Nations commission tried to decide on the territory's future, tensions escalated further still, and the British found themselves mired in a conflict with Jewish paramilitaries.

Unsurprisingly the British public did not readily recognise the division between the actions of the Jews of Palestine and those of the Anglo-Jewish community, whose leaders were continually and vociferously condemning their coreligionists' crimes. 'I don't accept as sincere the comments of Jews these last few days. In their hearts I believe all Jews are glad to hit us British,' wrote a socialist Sheffield housewife in her Mass Observation diary.[14] It was a view that resonated with much of the population. In the wake of the King David explosion, Stanley Evans, a Labour MP, observed how ordinary people were beginning to talk with frequency and great disgust about the conflict in Palestine, and that a seed of hostility against the Jewish community in Britain was being sown.[15] And it was not just the ordinary people. In October 1948, the *JC* reported: 'A survey undertaken privately for a national newspaper on opinions within the Labour Party has revealed that there has been a significant increase of anti-Jewish feeling in sections of the Party in the last few years.'[16]

However, it is vital to note that widespread anti-Semitic feeling did not produce pro-fascist sympathies. Of a conversation with her husband's friend, the same diarist wrote, 'He says he agrees with the Mosleyites that the Jews run this country though he has no time for Fascism of course.' A Mass Observation poll taken in the summer of 1946 found that 58 per cent of respondents believed that fascism should be banned.[17] In the 1940s the British public did not see anti-Semitism and fascism as inextricably linked, and so had no problem hating fascists and Jews in equal measure.

Still, for the League speakers the situation in Palestine was manna from heaven, and gave them a topic upon which they and the majority of the British public were in some agreement. At Dalston in March, Duke Pile, who claimed to be the League's 'expert on Palestine',[18] told his audience that he had a son serving in Palestine and that he was 'the only man in Britain today who has properly condemned the murder of our troops in Palestine'.

> During the past year we find that not one sentence has been carried out in Palestine. Hundreds of our lads have been maimed and killed by these murderers. Why have they not been carried out? I will tell you. The reason is because the government of today is rotten and controlled by the Shylock moneylenders of New York and the world.[19]

At a Dalston meeting in May, John James Spicer, whose 'cheerful, honest face' led the journalist Rebecca West, who was writing a piece on the fascists, to designate him as 'much the pleasantest of fascist speakers', declared that 'British troops were being murdered in cold blood' and that the League should 'attack the Jews for their activities in Palestine'. But was this, he asked his audience, anti-Semitic? 'Is it anti-Semitism to denounce the murderers of your flesh and blood in Palestine?'[20] To a fair-minded audience member willing to consider the arguments, Spicer might have had a point. The speaker who followed him onto the platform though, a man named Ronald Hargreaves, utilised no such potentially moderate argument:

> Communism is Jewish – Jewish in outlook, Jewish in objective, and Jewish in the methods which it uses. What I mean is that Communism stinks and that people who follow Communism are stinkers. There has never been at any time . . . anything done by the communists . . . that could be considered honourable. Shooting people in the back, raping women and doing all the filthy and low-down tricks that Western civilisation left behind in the dark ages.[21]

Many of these speakers had received some training from Hamm, training he sometimes carried out at fortnightly or monthly meetings at the Green Gate pub in Bethnal Green. This became Hamm's de facto East London headquarters. The landlord was sympathetic to his politics (for a time at least, Hamm was subsequently denied the use of the pub) and allowed Hamm to store his small platforms, literature and other equipment there and use it as a base of operations.[22] One of the first tasks Hamm gave his followers in the spring of 1947 was the distribution throughout the area of a leaflet entitled *Open Letter to the British People of Bethnal Green*.

ARE YOU SATISFIED WITH THE PRESENT SYSTEM?
Or are you looking for the ALTERNATIVE?
COME AND HEAR THE BRITISH LEAGUE OF EX-SERVICEMEN & WOMEN AT HEREFORD STREET, at 11.30 EVERY SUNDAY MORNING.[23]

In the spring of 1947, Hamm began to focus most of his efforts on East London. But he was keen for the League to cover more ground, and so he decided to decentralise and create local branches.[24] Soon, a regular schedule of meetings was established, beginning on Thursday evenings with a gathering at Gore Road in Bethnal Green. On Friday evenings the League held events at Brondesbury Villas in West London; Rushcroft Road in Brixton; and Victoria Park Square in Bethnal Green. Saturdays were a rest day for the League, as it was on their Lord's day that they really went to work.

Sundays began with a morning meeting at Hereford Street in Bethnal Green, after which Hamm and his 'boys', as he called his stewards and foot soldiers, repaired to the Green Gate for lunch. In the afternoon the League headed south to Clapham Common, before returning northwards to Dalston and Tottenham, where simultaneous meetings were held. The popularity of these events varied. Towards the beginning of the summer the less-successful pitches could just about cobble together audiences of fifty to sixty, whereas the better attended ones could attract a couple of hundred every week.[25] These numbers might have been a good deal smaller were it not for the 43 Group whose keenest members were forever running for buses or piling in ten to a car as they rushed from meeting to meeting.

One of the main attributes of the League's regular speakers was that they were unfazed by the shouting and could make themselves heard over it. Plenty tried their hand at speaking and came up short. Not that the regular speakers necessarily had many other oratorical skills. Abeysakera and Hargreaves were both prone to ramble. 'Hargreaves continued in that strain for some time,' wrote one clearly bored Special Branch shorthand writer at a Bethnal Green meeting, and this after he had already taken down a sizeable chunk of Hargreaves's political musings.[26] Meanwhile Alexander Raven Thompson, who began turning up as a 'guest speaker', in part to indicate that the League was a bona fide Mosleyite organisation, shared with his working-class

Bethnal Green audience some thoughts on issues that would clearly matter to them, including the government's policy for nut cultivation in East Africa.[27] 'I consider that this is but one of many industries which could be commenced on a large scale in that part of the Empire,' opined the fascists' chief intellectual.[28] On the other hand, working-class League speakers like Pile and Pipkin were effective rabble-rousers who knew how to stir up their audience.

It was Hamm, however, who was clearly the superior orator, with his style of beginning softly and working himself up into strident declamations that often featured some colourful turns of phrase, some of which landed him in hot water. Even the 43 Group members begrudgingly admitted that Hamm had talent, although one might debate whether is apparent on the page. 'Come out you little rats of the Communist Party,' he told a meeting at Hereford Street.

> Come out of your sewers and rat holes. Come in a bit closer my friend. There are two groups of people here today with two ideas. Our idea is this – to conduct peaceful and orderly meetings because we know we have an unanswerable case. There is a small group of alien traitors who have come here with the decided intention to cause a breach of the peace and we have had enough of it.[29]

It was 1 June 1947 when Hamm delivered that speech and he would have been wise to mind the wasp nest he was poking, for while the buzzing of the swarm had often made his words inaudible, it had so far withheld its sting. That was about to change.

A Large Welsh Male Voice Choir

At first the Group avoided deliberate violence at street meetings, knowing the small crowds left them all too visible to the police, who would not hesitate to arrest them. Instead Group members turned up to League meetings to heckle and barrack the speaker. Tony Charkham, who ran a menswear shop on Shaftesbury Avenue, had a real talent for this line of work. Gerry Abrahams recalled that Charkham's deep booming voice led to him becoming the de facto leader of the Group's barrackers – once he got going 'no one could hear anything else'.[30] On plenty of occasions Special Branch's shorthand reporters were forced to write 'hecklers made speaker inaudible', and several of the League's greener speakers gave up after one or two attempts. The 43 Group were by no means alone in their heckling and were frequently joined by their communist allies as well other Jewish and anti-fascist passers-by.

One tactic particular to the Group was its use of ridicule and insults, deployed to gall, provoke and rile the fascists. These were aimed at both the speakers and their supporters in the crowd, as Group members tried to get them to lose their cool and go on the attack, and hopefully get arrested. 'We used to call their girlfriends hermaphrodites,' Len Sherman told his family many decades later.[31] Scuffles and fights would follow, monitored by the police, whose presence at meetings was starting to grow. At first the Group tried to use the police's presence to their advantage, informing the most senior officer present that the speaker was a fascist and a former 18B detainee. This was usually met with a curt response that this was Britain and the speakers were Englishmen who had a right to freedom of speech. Even when the Group's tactics became more violent, its members would still make formal requests that the meetings be closed – requests that were always refused.

By May, Flamberg, Bernerd and the Executive had come to the conclusion that heckling achieved nothing and almost never led to a meeting's closure. The League was still finding sympathetic ears throughout London, and its audiences were slowly growing. The Group wanted to raise public awareness of the nascent fascist movement in Britain, but they were struggling to get even the local papers to pay attention. Something had to change.

At Bloom's Gym in Soho, Gerry Flamberg and Reg Morris brought together some of the Group's toughest members, all ex-servicemen. These were the men Morris Beckman referred to as the commandos, although this designation has been heavily disputed. Whatever term best describes this cadre, its mission was to come up with tactics that would force the police to close down the fascist meetings. Aiding them in this was the 1936 Public Order Act, which gave the police the power to close any public meeting likely to occasion a breach of the peace. What could be a clearer indicator of such an eventuality than the speaker being knocked from his platform? But this was easier said than done. The cordon of League stewards in front of the platforms was beginning to grow, along with the crowds. An even bigger issue was that someone had told Hamm that if he cited the Public Order Act to the senior police officer and requested protection for his meeting, it had to be provided.[32] At Bloom's gym, the Group began developing a manoeuvre which would allow them to clear all these obstacles, and at the start of summer they were ready to take it onto the streets.

On Sunday, 1 June 1947, the League held two evening meetings – one at a new pitch in Tottenham and the other at Ridley Road in Dalston. At 6:45 p.m. Spicer mounted the Ridley Road platform, introduced himself as the meeting's chairman and then brought in Hargreaves who addressed the 100-strong audience. 'We notice that today in this country there are people who are not British, who are determined to see that disunity, corruption, and degradation are the order of the day.' Fifteen minutes later, Jeffrey Hamm introduced himself from his new platform on Tottenham High Road:

'British people of Tottenham. This evening for the first time we raise the platform of our organisation in Tottenham for the first of what will be regular meetings. We are the British League of Ex-servicemen and Women.'

For forty-five minutes Hamm laid out his ideas, with little interruption, to a receptive audience. Then the local branch of the Communist Party showed up and erected their platform thirty feet away. At first the officers of Y Division were not particularly concerned; after all, this was a popular spot for political meetings and it was common for as many as five to be held in the vicinity at once. However, what the Division had probably not had to deal with for many years was two violently antagonistic organisations holding meetings in such close proximity. Before long the two crowds had started to merge, and disorder erupted; at 8:15 p.m. there was a 'definite effort by the Communist Party to break up the [League's] meeting and breaches of the peace began to occur among the persons assembled'.

Fighting broke out, the police intervened and four arrests were made: Thomas Starling, a fascist, and David Tiller, Stanley Marks and Harold Bidney, 43 Group members who the police took to be communists. Hamm was instructed to close the meeting. He obeyed, but then marched over to the Communist Party meeting with 100 of his followers in tow and confronted the speaker, George Reuben Cross. An altercation ensued and the two meetings turned into one violent rabble. The police demanded Cross close the event, and when he refused, he was promptly arrested, as was Hamm.[33]

Meanwhile at Ridley Road, Spicer and Hargreaves had been sharing the platform with little bother from the audience, beside the usual amounts of heckling. Then, at around 7:30 p.m., someone shouted from the crowd, 'Going back to the Isle of Man for your holidays?' 'I'm not going to listen to that fascist scum!' yelled another. 'They should have hanged you with Joyce!' 'Gairmany calling!'[34] 'Down with the bloody fascists!' The heckles grew and grew. Hargreaves could barely make himself heard. Morris Beckman was in the crowd: 'Down with the fascists! Down with the fascists!

The cries had simplified to the one slogan, gaining a mesmeric effect. I was chanting with the others and it was almost like singing with a large Welsh male voice choir.'[35]

For fifteen minutes the chorus persisted; meanwhile, a dozen of the Group's 'commandos' gathered at the far edge of the 200-strong crowd. Casually they got into formation, a wedge shape with the largest men towards the front. Now they hoped that all the practice at Bloom's Gym was about to pay off.

Surreptitiously they began to form a compact unit, arms were wrapped around bodies, and at 7:45 p.m. a new shout went up, 'Break the fucking meeting up!' The men in the 'Flying Wedge' began to move into the crowd, quickly picking up speed as they easily barged people out of the way. Within moments they had reached the cordon of stewards and crashed through them, then slammed into the platform causing Hargreaves to go flying. The wedge then broke apart, and the assailants turned on the stewards. Morris Beckman was in the crowd when the wedges smashed through:

> I glimpsed the wedge on our side drive through the fascist stewards. Fists were flying and I heard shouts that were a mix of fear and rage. The people in front of us were pushing back with alarm, panicking to get away from the fighting around the platform. Police in uniform were tearing into the melee trying to separate the combatants. Women were screaming and the chanting of 'Down with the fascists!' went on and on.[36]

With Hargreaves off his platform, the police were forced to step in, close the meeting and try to restore peace. There were eight arrests, seven Group members and one fascist.[37] Although the Group's lawyer subsequently argued that the imbalance in the arrests demonstrated innate police bias, it was exactly what the Group wanted. Among the arrested seven were Gerry Flamberg, David Golding and Alec Carson, one a paratrooper and two RAF pilots; Flamberg had been awarded the Military Medal and Golding the Distinguished Flying Cross.[38] Such was the nature of their distinction that the duty officer initially refused to book them, but Golding and Flamberg insisted, demanding their day in court.[39]

In post-war Britain, where military distinction was highly

celebrated, the Group knew that the arrests of its decorated members would generate the publicity and newspaper coverage it desired. The Group was forever seeking to emphasise that it was an ex-servicemen's organisation, whose members had distinguished themselves on active duty, while the fascists had all been detained under 18B. In focusing on the service records of its members, the Group was also challenging the fascists' claim that during the war the Jews only sought to profit from the conflict and did all they could to avoid the front lines. In actual fact, 15 per cent of the Anglo-Jewish population served, as opposed to 10 per cent of the population as a whole.[40] The military careers of its members were a vital part of the Group's PR operation, and its decision to play these up paid immediate dividends.

On the following Wednesday, sixteen-year-old Harry Kaufman's eye was caught by a headline on the front page of the *Hackney Gazette*: 'Disturbance at Ridley Road Meeting, Eight Sunday Night Arrests'. Curious, Kaufman read the article and discovered that Jewish ex-servicemen had been arrested fighting fascists. Living in Walthamstow, which had not yet been blessed with a League platform of its own, he had no idea about the fascists' activities and neither did his parents. The following Sunday, Kaufman went down to Ridley Road to see for himself what was happening. Standing at the edge of a crowd three times the size of the previous week's, Kaufman got chatting to Harry Bidney. Despite Kaufman's evident youth and diminutive stature – he was barely five-foot-three – Bidney recruited him into the East End section.[41] Kaufman, who for quite a while was the Group's youngest member, was probably not the only one who joined in the wake of that first attack.

The Group had an even bigger publicity boost after the trial, which was held on 23 June 1947, in front of Mr Daniel Hopkin, at the North London Magistrates' Court. Four days earlier, Stanley Marks, Harold Bidney and David Tiller had all escaped punishment for their role in the chaos at Tottenham, and their fellow Group members probably hoped for similar good fortune.[42] Like the three at Tottenham, the defendants were charged under Section 5 of the 1936 Public Order Act: 'Using threatening behaviour with intent to provoke a breach of the peace'. Of course, there was no doubt that they had breached the peace, and Hopkin was forced to bind them over for a year even though he was clearly sympathetic to their cause:

> If people come into this district, which is essentially a Jewish district, to talk anti-Semitism in this kind of way, to stir up racial hatred, to incite and abuse people here and provoke them, they must take what is coming to them. I should support the police if they took any action to keep such talk down . . . I am sorry that the platform were not brought in by the police as well as the eight defendants.[43]

Hopkin's remarks were printed in the *Manchester Guardian*, *Daily Worker* and *Hackney Gazette*, and this clearly had an effect. For the next six weeks the disorder around the League meetings continued, but there were no arrests.

This changed on 13 July at the Ridley Road meeting, when a plain-clothes officer grabbed a Jewish gentleman called Murray Silver, who was heckling the speaker, and shouted, 'You'll ask a bloody question at question time!' Silver protested and got loose, but the officer grabbed his arm again and twisting it dragged him to a waiting Black Maria.[44] Furious at this injustice, Silver struggled and hit the officer and immediately had several officers on him. When David Goldstein, a father of two in his forties who had been invalided out of the army in 1943, saw what was going on he protested. In response, four police officers leapt on top of him. He received several blows to the face and was knocked him to the ground before being dragged to the nearest police car. The police later claimed Goldstein had provoked them by kicking their superintendent in the balls.

At the station Goldstein and Silver waited for hours in separate cells, until one after the other they were brought into the charge room, where they encountered the man Goldstein had reportedly attacked, head of 'G' Division, Superintendent Charles Satterthwaite. 'Fucking Jew bastard!' Satterthwaite shouted at Silver as he repeatedly beat him, while two of his officers held Silver against the wall. With Goldstein, Satterthwaite went for his face, which, according to Silver, was left 'covered in a mass of blood'.[45] The following morning both men were released on bail but came face-to-face with Satterthwaite in court a month later, when the superintendent denied assaulting the prisoner. He was believed, Silver and Goldstein were not and were both found guilty and given custodial sentences. Goldstein was sentenced to three months' imprisonment; Silver got twenty-eight days.[46]

For the Group, Charles Satterthwaite would become as big a villain as Mosley or Hamm. He was, according to the journalist Rebecca West, called Porky 'by practically any crowd he is summoned to quell, and it is impossible not to see why; but the compared animal is no common porker but a pedigree boar'. West's portrait is vivid. 'He was an isosceles triangle balanced on its apex, its sides sloping sharply from his immensely broad shoulders to his small feet. In his eyes was loathing for these people whichever side they were on.'[47] This final judgement was one the Group would have taken issue with, convinced as they were that Satterthwaite was, as Lennie Rolnick put it, a 'first class anti-Semite who would have done well at Belsen'.[48] Beckman recollected Satterthwaite striding around Ridley Road pointing at 43 Group members with his truncheon, yelling, 'Grab him. Arrest him,' and giving a good whack to any Group member who came within swinging distance. Naturally the Group was not prepared to take this lying down. When Satterthwaite walked past Jules Konopinski in a courtroom, Konopinski fell to the ground shouting about how he had just been hit; Satterthwaite got in serious trouble with the magistrate. Len Sherman preferred a more direct approach. At one meeting Sherman snuck around the back of Satterthwaite, tapped him on the shoulder and, as the policeman turned around, smashed him in the face. According to Beckman, Sherman hit him so hard he was knocked to the ground with a broken nose.[49] Sherman's cohort would have approved of this without dissent; declared Gerry Abrahams, 'He was the biggest bastard of all.'[50]

An Unbiased Watch

'You are quite sure that it is an unbiased watch you keep at these meetings?' the defence lawyer at Silver and Goldstein's trial asked Satterthwaite.

'As police officers it is always an unbiased watch,' responded the superintendent.[51] The facts struggle to bear this statement out. In a survey of forty-nine cases where arrests were made at fascist meetings, historian Dave Renton found that anti-fascists were three times as likely to get arrested as pro-fascists.[52] The question is why.

Widespread anti-Semitism in the Metropolitan Police force is the simplest answer. Satterthwaite was by no means the only officer who made regular reference to the faith of the anti-fascist disruptors he was arresting. Two young Group members from the East End, a hairdresser's assistant called Vidal Sassoon and his close friend, a gentle giant of a boy called Mo Levy, had a particularly nasty run-in with the law, which Sassoon described in his autobiography.

> One evening in Kilburn, we chased the fascists into a pub and were ourselves chased by the police. They arrested three of us. It took a long time to get to the police station which was only a few streets away. Two policemen held one of my comrades, Mo Levy, while a sergeant pounded him, beating him everywhere but the face, at the same time calling us 'dirty Jew bastards', 'fucking Yids who Hitler missed' and 'sons of foreign whores'.[53]

There is no question that events in Palestine encouraged the innate anti-Semitism in the force. That disturbing tendency was exacerbated in 1948, when former members of the British Palestine Police Force were transferred to East London.[54]

Knowing they were dealing with an institutionally anti-Semitic organisation, the 43 Group's leadership were keen not to provoke the police. In fact, they went out of their way to be cooperative.[55] As mentioned, before the Group launched an attack on a platform someone would approach the most senior officer and ask him to close down the meeting. Away from the street battles, the Group was eager to assist with investigations and even sent intelligence to Special Branch. None of these approaches made much of a difference. But to put this down to anti-Semitism alone in the Metropolitan Police is misguided; other biases were almost certainly in play.

For one, the police were never convinced that the Group was apolitical and not secretly communist. Consequently, like their communist allies, the anti-fascist ex-servicemen were seen as radical agitators desperate to overturn the status quo. The conflation of the 43 Group and the communists is actually quite understandable. In 1942, 10 per cent of the CPGB's 5,000 members were Jewish, and most of that 10 per cent lived in East London.[56] In the confusion of a street battle, a police officer could be forgiven for confusing one type of anti-fascist with another.

As well as being anti-Semitic and anti-communist, the police also harboured pro-fascist elements. In October 1946, Mr Orman, a concerned local, wrote an open letter to Chuter Ede:

> I suppose it is perfectly in order for a lousy swine like Jeffrey Hamm to get up on a street corner in the East End of London and shout, 'Down with the Jews. Burn the synagogues. Kill the Aliens,' and he gets away with it, but if a person tries to pull him up, what happens? The so-called keepers of law and order, the police, go up to this person and tell him he'd better move away before he gets hurt . . . These guardians of the law and order from Commercial Street Police Station openly boast about being members of Jeffrey Hamm's fascist party.[57]

At one of his very first meetings in Bethnal Green, a year earlier, a police officer approached Hamm and asked if his movement was anti-Jewish. Once this was confirmed, the officer reassured him there would be no problems from the police around those parts.[58]

It was in west London, however, that the most alarming example of the close relationship between the police and fascists came to light. In July 1947, Victor Burgess started to hold outdoor meetings of the Union for British Freedom. The events lacked the scale and violence of the League's meetings further east, but that meant the Group could get closer to the platform, ensuring that Burgess would receive their feedback loud and clear. When faced with one particularly vociferous heckler at a meeting that August, Burgess had turned to a police constable and demanded the heckler's name and address. In the audience that day was socialist MP D. N. Pritt, an ardent anti-fascist and occasional barrister for the 43 Group. Pritt watched in horror as the policeman did as requested and subsequently handed the details over to Burgess. Pritt asked the officer, 'who was perfectly friendly', why he had done this and received the explanation that 'as the police find it difficult in practice to decide whether any particular interruption constitutes an offence or not, they have made it *settled practice* to take the names and addresses of all persons indicated by the chairman'.[59]

Horrified, Pritt wrote an article for the *New Statesman*, which led to an investigation from the Police Commissioner's Office. A circular was sent to all inspectors asking if such things occurred in their divisions, and it was revealed that such things were not rare. The inspector of F Division confirmed that names had indeed been passed on to Burgess.[60] Responding in the same magazine, Home Secretary Chuter Ede informed Pritt that this practice was permitted under Section 6 of the Public Order Act, so that promoters of meetings might bring cases against an interrupter; he clearly did not share Pritt's fears that the fascists might take the law into their own hands and make a house call instead.[61] With this knowledge, Group members, especially those who still lived with their families, were often understandably reticent when it came to identifying themselves to an officer, putting them at risk of a further charge of obstruction.[62]

Ede's reference to the Public Order Act is important. That legislation did a great deal to shape the police response. The 1936 Act had effectively banned private militias and declared that only the police could steward public meetings. Consequently the fascists had to depend on the police for protection, and so they went out of their way to demonstrate their respect for the boys in blue. This continued after the war. Fascists speakers always treated the police with great friendliness and always followed their instructions. The other consequence of the Public Order Act was that it put the police, who were sent to protect the fascists, right in the firing line of the 43 Group and their anti-fascist comrades. 'Given these circumstances,' writes historian Nigel Copsey, 'is it not unsurprising that the police arrested more anti-fascists than fascists?'[63] Another anti-fascist historian, Graham Macklin, suggested that while there was 'little evidence of sustained, active collusion between the police and the fascists', this did not mean they did not have 'a set of shared attitudes, assumptions and prejudices'.[64]

Of course, not all police officers sympathised with the fascists. Martin Block recalled being shepherded on a march, and a policeman whispering, 'Give 'em one from me, mate!' On the whole, said Block, the policemen who had war-ribbons on their uniform would be friendlier to the Group.[65]

When Morris Beckman was collared by a young copper, he spotted the North Atlantic Star among the constable's ribbons, a medal awarded to those who had served in the Battle of the Atlantic. Beckman was veteran of that same long-running campaign. He shared this with the officer, mentioned a ship the policeman knew. 'Go on!' was the reply. 'You better beat it fast before the Marias get here.'[66]

Interviewed decades later, Charles Haslow, a former officer of G Division, claimed that the police were not driven by politics or prejudice, they were just really annoyed. 'All we wanted as police officers, to be truthful, was a quiet night . . . Life was hard enough to do what you were supposed to be doing . . . And to have this added business of this political upheaval . . . You don't really have a great deal of affection for them, putting it mildly.[67]

It's a point with which one can empathise, and as the summer wore on, more and more police officers were being drafted in to deal with conflict. On 1 June, there was one inspector, one sergeant and fourteen constables present at the Ridley Road League meeting. One week later, G Division had fifty constables in the area. By mid-August, over a dozen inspectors and sergeants and up to 300 constables were being deployed, many having been called in from surrounding divisions. Ironically, recalled Jules Konopinski, the violence 'never really all got started until the police formed the cordon; the police seemed to be the catalyst. The reason was when they linked up they were pushing you back, and the people were pushing forward, it was like a pressure cooker.'[68]

The police would have seen things rather differently. They were not causing the violence; they were preventing it from turning into all-out gang warfare.

A Tank on Two Wheels

The 43 Group was aware that its critics portrayed it as a gang and was determined not to be seen in that light. 'We are against gang warfare,' said Gerry Flamberg to a journalist writing what would become the most high-profile article about them.[69] Certainly the Group was determined that when its members went out onto the street they would follow certain rules. Violence of any kind against a police officer was prohibited. On being collared by an officer, the instruction was simply to go limp, become a deadweight, do not make his life any easier but do not actively resist. It was also essential that no man ever be left behind. Caution when leaving the battlefield was regularly stressed, and Group members were always reminded not to return home if they were being followed. Similarly, anyone heading out to disrupt meetings was instructed to leave any personal papers in an envelope at Group HQ. Alexander Hartog was often sent out on these missions, and he boasted of how effective the Group's 'fighting contingent' could be:

> One Sunday we set up a record. We turned over thirteen meetings all in the space of about three hours. We didn't argue. We didn't ask questions. We just moved into a thing, turned over the platform, gave a few Blackshirts a beating and kicked them up the arse.[70]

The tactics were flexible. When police cordons formed in front of the platforms, the Group often might risk arrest by seeding chaos and disorder in the crowd. On other occasions, it might be decided to avoid the negative publicity this might create, and members would do no more than heckle and barrack. But recklessness could be a real advantage, at times, as Jules Konopinski explained: 'When there were ten of them and only three of us we never ran, we used to go for them. They couldn't understand that these Jews were coming for them. That's what Flamberg always said, when he ran forward to take out a machine-gun nest, they always stopped firing because they couldn't work out who this lunatic was who was trying to take them out on his own.'

For the big dos, tactics and plans were conceived by Gerry Flamberg and Reg Morris, but for smaller affairs the section heads were in charge. Sometimes the whole section would be briefed. The East End section often met up in factories or warehouses owned by members' families, but when smaller cells met up they often selected cafés or restaurants not far from the meetings they intended to disrupt. A favoured spot was the Lyons Tea Houses where, Morris Beckman recalled, very large men would hunch over their coffee and cake, often failing to hide their feelings of nausea and unease as they received their instructions. The noise of the popular restaurant easily drowned out the quiet chat of the ex-servicemen.

The veterans who made up the largest part of the 43 Group would not have liked being labelled members of a gang. But there was one subsection who had no such problem with the designation. 'You were part of a gang,' said Jules Konopinski, who used the word interchangeably with 'team' to describe the constituent parts of the wider sections, normally based on geographic location. Jules, however, was an anomaly: 'I lived in Clapton, all the others in my clique lived in the East End, in Stepney Green, real East End people, but I ran with them, not with the crowd from Stamford Hill.' In 1947 Jules, seventeen years old, had been the country for around seven years, long enough to become a fluent English speaker and a very active member of the Hackney Boys' Club, through which he first heard about the Group.[71]

The East End boys Jules ran with coalesced into a cell led by Jackie Myerovitch, Harry Bidney's number two in the East End section. Jules soon became one of its more notorious members. They were 'young tough villains' who could be 'bloody vicious', recalled Alec Carson. 'There were things that the East End boys did that head office didn't agree with and would sometimes turn a blind eye to.'[72] In contrast to others, Myerovitch's cell was by and large made up of men too young to have fought in the war. Aged around seventeen to nineteen, they had grown up in some of the poorest parts of the East End, where they had been fighting anti-Semitism for as long as they could remember. Feeling they had missed out on the war against the Nazis, they became some of the Group's most enthusiastic fighters. 'I might have been crazy,' Jules told me, 'but everything was planned. I was crazy for a reason.' Even so, the boy who came to be affectionately known as 'Mad Jules' was not the most violent member of his cell. Not by a long shot.

Among Jackie Myerovitch's East End lads was an apprentice hairdresser everyone knew as Viddy. Vidal Sassoon, destined for fame, was in 1947 a bright and friendly young man and a well-loved figure among his cohort. Other notable characters were

his close friend Mo Levy and Sid Tonga, one of the most popular of the members, a dim-witted, gentle giant of a man who
once required eight policemen to take him down. 'Big Sid' was
completely loyal to Jackie Myerovitch, once turning to his leader
in the middle of a melee to inquire about a fascist he had pinned
to the ground: 'Shall I break his arms or legs, Jackie?'[73]

Competing with Sid in the intelligence stakes were the
Goldberg twins. Born in 1926 to a desperately poor Jewish
family, with a violent father, Philip 'Philly' and Joe Goldberg
were unquestionably the Group's most ferocious members. At
about five-ten, the twins shared a wiry build with massively
knuckled hands and arms well developed from their work as
pressers in a clothing factory.[74] Identical twins, they could be
distinguished only because one of them sported a thin black
scar. 'Phil was OK, but Joe was a killer,' recalled Jules, who
once saw them tear a man's face apart with their fists. 'Oh God
help us, dangerous, dangerous!' recalled Murray Podro. 'I
wouldn't want to even be in a prison with those two.' Jonny
Goodman, on the other hand, was very curious about the
twins and took one of them out for lunch; it was like talking
to a brick wall. 'I asked are you ever scared, and he said,
"What's scared?"' Goodman reckoned all the twins knew was
that 'the fascists were giving us a hard time so we had to duff
them up.'

There was perhaps one member of the section who rivalled
the Goldbergs' violence, a woman called Julie Sloggen. 'She
wasn't so small, but she wasn't tall either,' recalled Philip Evans.
'She wasn't afraid of anybody, she used to go right into the
Blackshirts' meeting and start with them.' At first the Group's
boys tried to protect Sloggen, but quickly realised it was the
fascists who needed protecting from her. 'She'd just go straight
in, you wouldn't get in the way with her. But she was terrific,'
remembered Jonny Goodman. 'She was a fearless crackpot, a
tank on two wheels.'[75]

As well as often being more violent and more reckless, the
members of the East End section, especially the younger ones,

were more willing to experiment with weapons. At first most people only used their fists, but over time, and partly in response to the fascists arming themselves, more and more Group members began to carry weapons, although normally the kind of thing that might serve a peaceful purpose to provide a cover story should the police become involved. One ingenious weapon was a broadsheet newspaper that, when rolled up correctly, became a handy club, and of course a belt and buckle could double as a whip.[76] Those craftsmen and apprentices who used sharp or heavy objects could make a case for having the tools of their trade on their person, and Vidal Sassoon often went to war with a pair of pointed scissors clutched in his hand.

Then there were those apparently innocuous weapons found around the house. Jules Konopinski often carried a broken light bulb or two in his pockets, and sometimes employed a walking stick for the limp he affected. Gerry Abrahams owned an Alsatian he occasionally took to meetings and was not the only Group member in possession of a large dog. 'We never set the dogs on them,' Abrahams assured me. 'It was only if they came near us that the dogs would go for them. The dogs were just there for protection.'[77] Another unusual form of defence were cricket boxes, which some men took to wearing under their trousers. These became particularly useful after the police developed a tactic of linking arms and marching forward, raising their knees whenever they came close to an anti-fascist.[78]

The most popular weapon, possession of which was not particularly easy to explain, was the cosh. It could be made from a bit of lead or copper piping or a rubber tube or piece of wood, materials that might feasibly be lying around the house, although the presence of them at a political meeting couldn't fail to appear suspect. A cosh could at least be slipped up a sleeve, and if it couldn't readily be explained away it was at least easy to hide. It was the fascists who first began to use knuckledusters, and some Group members responded in kind. However, when some fascists were seen with razor blades, copying them was strongly discouraged. Phil Goldberg was vocal in wondering why on multiple occasions, and had to have it repeatedly explained what would happen if he was caught with one. The message clearly did not stick. At one meeting, when a fascist speaker declared, 'We will overthrow the Jewish scum,' Phil, calm as you like, walked up to him and slashed a razor down his arm.[79] Mostly the Group stayed away from razor blades, although some of the fascist meetings also attracted Jewish boys who were involved in the criminal underworld and were far more willing to use blades. One of them even gave Martin Block a lesson in razor slashing:

> He told me it's a load of rubbish, all that about cutting people across the face. That's only for the movies, he said. He said what you do is you come up behind them and you give them the snook across the touchus.[80]

In other words, a cut on the bum.

With the presence of actual gangsters at the fascist meetings adding to the wild violence of the East End cell, it's not hard to see why some less sympathetic critics saw it as no more than a gang of vicious hooligans. But that was a serious mistake. Behind the scenes, the Group was evolving into a sophisticated, multifaceted and highly effective organisation.

5

Not Just Hooligans

In the summer of 1947, the Group's profile was growing, attracting an influx of recruits. Most of these new members wanted to be out in the field, heckling and fighting, but there were plenty of others eager to make a contribution while avoiding the rough and tumble of direct action. The leadership was particularly good at talent-spotting and making the best use of a new recruit's skill set. As the range of abilities grew, the Group became far more than just a street fighting gang.

One job that always needed lots of volunteers was surveillance. A primary objective was to expose the fascists, a vital operation that got off the ground at a very early stage.[1] At first, the surveillance operation was rudimentary. One or two members would be sent to stand on a street corner or sit on a bench near the home of a known fascist, outside a fascist pub, or close to one of their offices and keep watch for hours on end, often in the pouring rain or blistering cold. Mostly the Group just wanted to know who was going in or out, but if, for example, a car licence plate could be taken so much the better. One of the few documents to survive is an extensive list of all the cars known to be associated with the fascists, and any known relevant information, including the owners, where the cars were spotted, and so on. Another list of known fascists collated in 1949 also still exists and reveals the extent of the surveillance operation.[2]

As the sections were responsible for keeping an eye on the fascists in their own area, most active members could expect to spend some time standing out on a street corner. It was a task often given to new members, whose reliability needed testing, and women, who the section heads preferred to keep away from the fighting; often a boy and a girl would be sent out together.[3]

Surveillance was something everyone could participate in, but only the blond-haired, blue-eyed or gentile were asked to contribute to the Group's other intelligence strand. When Doris Kaye, a Jewish veteran of the ATS, first came to Group HQ, the eagle-eyed Geoff Bernerd quickly brought her into his office.[4] When he discovered that Doris had an Irish-Catholic boyfriend called James Cotter who shared her hatred of the fascists, Bernerd asked if she would bring him by. Together with Jonny Wimborne, the head of intelligence, he pitched to Cotter and Kaye an undercover mission to infiltrate the enemy.[5] By this point, the Group had already successfully planted a few men and women into a number of fascist organisations, so the protocols had already been established. Wimborne, who became their handler, subjected them to a series of mock interrogations and prepared them for life undercover.

Eighteen months after he first went undercover, James Cotter told the story of his and Doris's time amid the fascists in *On Guard*, an early edition of which he had used as a handy prop to get himself admitted into the Modern Thought Book Club in Chelsea:

It had been agreed that I should pose as an anti-Communist, violently anti-Semitic ex-soldier, attracted to Fascism by events in Palestine.

The door was opened by a tall, heavily built blonde. Her brown eyes surveyed me curiously.

'Have you seen this article,' I began, waving 'On Guard' at her.

'Oh that rag!' she exclaimed . . .

'Well,' I started, 'if this Jewish rag dislikes what "Modern Thought" stands for – then I'm for "Modern Thought".' Then I treated her to a long anti-Jewish tirade which I concluded by asking if I could join the 'Book Club.'[6]

The blonde was Tizzy, the wife of Allan T. Smith, one of a number of former rank-and-file BUF members who saw starting a book club as way of propelling themselves into the big leagues. Smith had had the good fortune to attract Raven Thompson as a co-founder, and consequently Modern Thought became the largest book club, with sixty-eight members in September 1947.[7] Cotter waited in the living room for a couple of hours before both of the club's founders showed up, and it did not take long for him to win their trust. That evening he introduced them to Doris, who easily convinced them that she was a bona fide fascist and rabid anti-Semite. The couple became signed-up members of Modern Thought.

From inside the club, Cotter and Kaye were able to collect intelligence on the post-war fascist element most invested in by Mosley. Not only were the book clubs started on his orders and used as the main channel for the sales of his literature, Mosley saw them as a vital way of maintaining and growing his following among genteel middle-class folk, who would give his return an air of respectability. Consequently, in September 1946 Mosley went on a national tour of the book clubs in an effort to help boost their popularity. He spent far more time with book clubs than he ever did addressing organisations like the League.

At book club meetings, Mosley's writings were read and praised to the rafters; the issues of the day were discussed, and all blame placed firmly on Jewish heads. Book club members were instructed to identify potential new recruits and bring them along to meetings. On those occasions Mosley would not be mentioned, but Wagner would be played and German culture discussed, while a couple of subtle comments about Jews were aired. Depending on how the newcomer reacted, Mosley might be praised once or twice, and if these comments were received positively then the members might reveal their political affiliation.

A couple of these new recruits proved themselves to be over-eager. Unprompted, they started sharing their opinion of Jews and encouraging others to do likewise. Such behaviour tended to put the book club's leaders on high alert. One of these potential joiners was beaten up as he walked to his car; another was followed home and subsequently had all his front windows smashed. Both had been sent by the 43 Group. In the wake of these failures, the Group instructed its book club spies to simply observe and report.[8]

For Cotter and Kaye, observing soon required them to do much more than sit around and listen to Wagner. Book club members, it transpired, were expected to get their hands dirty. Having attended a few Modern Thought meetings, Cotter and Kaye joined other members of the club in an evening spent posting pamphlets through letterboxes. Not long after, Cotter was asked to come down to a League meeting at Ridley Road, where he was immediately sent to guard the platform; it was not long before he was regarded as a most trustworthy steward. Several other spies ended up as stewards or bodyguards and all received frequent beatings from 43 Group members unaware of their true affiliation. Apologies after a spy was extracted were common, but the beatings were understood to be very much an occupational hazard.[9]

There were three parts to the Group's intelligence operation: two might be thought predictable, the running of spies and surveillance; but the third was most unusual – Harry Bidney. It appears that the East End section head not only handled his own spies, but he also had an uncanny ability to extract information from the fascists himself, even though they knew exactly who he was. According to Jonny Goodman, 'He somehow managed to worm his way inside of the fascists, he got to the stage where he could go into a pub and end up having a drink with them . . . they knew him so well and he knew them so well . . . he could get into a situation where he might have got heavily cuffed up but he somehow didn't.'

A possible explanation is that Bidney was blackmailing them. Bidney was fairly open about his sexuality, but there were homosexual fascists who most certainly were not – Alf Flockhart in particular. Similarly, as someone who very much operated on the fringes of legality, Bidney could access intelligence not always available to the Group's intelligence heads. Murray Podro, who ran the Intelligence Section from 1948 onwards, remembered running his operation in tandem with Bidney's. Each had different sets of contacts and different and secretive ways of working. Podro was full of praise for Bidney, calling him 'very sharp' and a 'loveable rogue'; however, 'you couldn't say you trusted him, because the way he worked you couldn't trust him.' But there was no question whose side he was on: 'He was a true anti-fascist, he hated them like poison.' Together Bidney, Podro, Wimborne and the spies gathered a plethora of information and passed it to Geoff Bernerd and the executive, who occasionally decided to share what they'd learned with the wider world.

On Guard

July 1947 saw the first publication of the 43 Group's newspaper, *On Guard*. The paper was the brainchild of Geoffrey Bernerd, who had always thought the organisation needed a paper of its own, but lacked the know-how to set one up. Then one Sunday afternoon he had a stroke of good fortune when a young woman called Rita Goldstein came to his office for an interview. In passing, she mentioned her boyfriend, Tony Bensusan, a journalist at the *Jewish Chronicle*, and his younger brother Roy, who was a printer. Bernerd made Rita promise she would bring the brothers in and then, to show how much he was willing to trust her, he left her in charge of the office while he and the boys went out to a public meeting.[10]

The Bensusan brothers grew up in a cramped and noisy home in Stepney, the only boys in a brood of eight, much mollycoddled by their older sisters. Born in 1921, Roy served in the RAF, against which he bore a lifelong grudge after they denied him permission to return home from Egypt after his mother died. Eighteen months older, Tony had been prevented from joining up by a heart problem.[11] When Bernerd told the brothers his idea, they immediately agreed and quickly got to work. Roy spent many happy hours at his kitchen table, working on the typeface and layout for the paper that would become his pride and joy, while Tony and Bernerd began planning the content and editorial position.[12] Originally to be called *Combat*, the name was subsequently changed to *On Guard*, in part as a tribute to a paper of that name published by the Republicans in the Spanish Civil War.[13]

Not everyone in the executive was thrilled with the idea of having their own journal. Stanley Marks, who at one point led the intelligence section, believed no good could come of the Group having a paper, as it would be a source of information for the fascists.[14] Bernerd, however, was insistent, having wanted to start a paper from the beginning; but it may have been in response to Marks's objections that he, the Bensusans, and the rest of the editorial team decided that the paper's primary purpose was not to serve as a newsheet for the 43 Group, but to lay bare the actions of the fascists. In fact, the paper set out to appear as independent from the Group as possible. When someone from the Group was quoted, an impression was given that *On Guard* and the 43 Group were completely separate entities. 'In an interview with one of the executive members I was informed that the 43 Group has better things to do than haunt Hamm's meetings,' wrote an *On Guard* reporter in November, who probably worked opposite his 'informant'. He then joked about Hamm: 'He must be getting a 43 Group complex.' When the paper received a letter from a non-Jewish army captain about joining the Group, it responded neutrally that it understood membership to be 'open to men and women of every religion and political party who are sincere anti-fascists.'[15]

In publishing this letter, *On Guard* demonstrated how keen it was to advertise its and the Group's inclusivity. But *On Guard* went beyond this, embracing a truly internationalist outlook, with the first editorial giving global context to the fight against fascism:

> The United Nations won their fight against the Axis, against Germany, Italy and Japan. Was the war won so that today there should be colour hatred and lynching in America, persecution for political belief in Greece, so that the broken remnants of German concentration camps might be denied their promised home in Palestine, so that Fascism should come to be the accepted form of government in the Argentine and in Franco's Spain?[16]

This interest in foreign affairs persisted throughout the paper's existence. *On Guard* frequently carried stories of far-right activities in Europe, as well as reporting on fascism, racism and intolerance all around the world, with a particular focus on the United States and South Africa. African-American actors Hilda Simms and Paul Robeson both gave interviews to the paper, and Dr M. Joseph-Mitchell of the League of Coloured Peoples wrote an article on the prejudice and intolerance faced by African migrants to Britain.[17] The paper also had a regular 'One World' column, which focused on global prejudice, with its first instalment focusing on the colour bar in boxing:

> While a Negro may by skill and stamina prove to be the finest ring fighter in this country, he still cannot win the British title. This prejudice has been unfairly maintained to uphold the supremacy of the white man, in a profession which prides itself on a sense of fair play.[18]

On Guard was not a paper for one small community, but a publication with an internationalist outlook, convinced that the fight against fascism and intolerance was a global one which should be joined by all. The writing tended to employ a matter-of-fact tone, avoiding the strident polemic typical of a paper like the *Daily Worker*. Nevertheless, it was still very much a campaigning publication. It shared the Group's lofty ambition to see 'all Fascist and pro-Fascist activity made illegal, to ensure that those things that happened in Germany will never, can never, happen here'.[19]

Despite these goals, *On Guard* did not consider itself radical. It looked beyond activists to address 'every human being who believes in freedom and democracy'.[20] Among its most engaging writers were journalists such as Ralph Jeffries, the paper's special correspondent, who could be wonderfully evocative, as demonstrated in the very first leading article:

> In almost every town of any size in Britain to-day there is a Fascist group, quietly but busily preparing for launching of a big Mosley party, whose aim will be the establishment of a Fascist state.
>
> Most of Mosley's former lieutenants are back in action. The men who in pre-war days led black-shirted marchers to meetings which were demonstrations of an uncontrolled thuggery, and who organised the nocturnal Jew-baiting expeditions, are once again rallied around the 'Leader'.[21]

That first edition contained what would become regular features, such as 'Undercover', a satirical diary by someone referred to as 'J.M.'; 'One World' cartoons by Yak; reviews of fascist publications by 'Radar'; and 'Little Sir Echoes', a humorous spoof of a leading fascist. Later issues contained a column on pertinent parliamentary business by Labour MP Harold Davies. Also appearing in that first issue was Judith Michaels, who wrote the paper's regular column asking for donations to its Combat Fund. Michaels was one of *On Guard*'s most scathing and compelling writers. Her first column already set the tone:

> Are you a Protestant, a Catholic, a Mohammedan or a Jew? Do you believe in Democracy, the Atlantic Charter, freedom of speech, the United Nations, the rights of man? Do you belong to a trade union? Is your skin black or brown instead of white? Because if so the Fascist hates your guts.[22]

A few issues later Michaels launched into a vitriolic take-down of the far-right enemy:

> Fascists prove themselves again and again to be dishonourable and wretched scum. These creatures who discarded all notions of fair play, who gang up in numbers to attack a single, unarmed opponent with the weapons of the Apache and the hired assassin have no right to call themselves Englishmen, or for that matter to call themselves men at all. They are nothing but sub-human cretins who have lost all self-respect and humane instincts.[23]

The first issue also carried messages from famed well-wishers including the 'Red' dean of Canterbury, Hewlett Johnson, anti-fascist journalist Frederic Mullally, MPs Tom Driberg and D. N. Pritt, and actress Dame Sybil Thorndyke, who wrote: 'May I send this message of good luck and good wishes to your new publication. All things that stifle freedom must be fought.'

That explosive first issue described the founding of the 43 Group itself, in a piece entitled 'Ex-servicemen Form Anti-Fascist Group'. It stated that the lead its founders gave had 'been enthusiastically followed, their aims and ideals now have the active support of young, energetic men and women, wide-awake to the Fascist menace'.[24] This would not be the only time that the paper subtly or not so subtly promoted the 43 Group and its activities, although those activities rarely made the headlines.

The first issue, like every one that followed, was just four pages long and sold for three pence. It was printed initially by South Essex Recorders Ltd, in Ilford, Essex, but this arrangement did not last for long. The printers feared reprisals if they continued to work with the anti-fascists. This was not unrealistic, as several presses were smashed up during the conflict. However, it was almost always the 43 Group who were doing the damage.

Throughout its life, *On Guard* had a circulation of around 5,000 copies, although no sales figures were ever published. In the paper's third issue, Judith Michaels declared that 'there exists a demand for at least twice our permitted number of copies', but like all publications *On Guard* was limited by post-war paper rationing.[25] More than a few fascists numbered among its readers, and their leaders were known to read the paper. At one point it must have been felt that rather too many fascists were perusing *On Guard*, as in October 1948 the paper reported that fascist leaders had threatened to severely discipline anyone they saw reading it.[26] It was available in a number of newsagents, especially in those areas where fascist meetings were common, and not just in London. *On Guard* was sold in Manchester, Leeds, Newcastle and other cities where the 43 Group had a presence.[27] The main method of distribution was via street vendors, who could be seen on high streets, outside busy Tube stations, and in popular spots like Piccadilly Circus and, of course, Speakers' Corner. As with surveillance work, everyone in the Group was expected to muck in and hawk the paper, although again it was a task borne primarily by younger members and women. Of course, paper sellers were easy targets, and the Group often sent out a couple of shtarkers in case anyone threatened them. Jonny Goodman recalled one time when their protection was very welcome:

'I was selling *On Guard* once outside Piccadilly Tube Station and a couple of fascists came by, including an off-duty post-man, and they started to threaten me, and I had two minders standing out of sight. It was so dramatic, I just made a gesture, and these two guys appeared, and these two Fascists took one look at them and took off. We had to be protected if we were selling *On Guard* sometimes, because we attacked their paper sellers so we had to rationalise that they would attack ours.'[28]

It was true. The 43 Group very much set the precedent when it came to beating up paper sellers. Ivor Benjamin was one of the few members who owned a car, and on occasion he'd drive a couple of shtarkers to one of the fascists' favourite paper-selling spots. The shtarkers would jump out 'and bang, bang, bang then no more papers to sell'.[29] Fascists selling newspapers outside Tube stations sometimes found themselves caught in a pincer movement, as Group members jumped out of taxis in front of them while others emerged from the station behind. Little convincing was required to get them to drop their literature and scram when that happened.[30]

On Guard lent the Group a degree of legitimacy, enabling it to function publicly under the cover of a proper and respectable concern. It provided members with an excuse for being at fascist meetings, too. Previously, they had often struggled to explain their presence to magistrates and police officers. However, in the capacity of newspaper sellers, they not only had a perfectly legitimate reason to attend, but could receive police protection, because, like the fascists, they were merely exercising their freedom of speech.[31] Naturally, this was especially galling to fascist speakers, and Victor Burgess once got so angry at one of his meetings that he leapt off his platform and confronted a seller at the edge of the audience, yelling, 'So you call me a traitor!' before grabbing him by the lapel and punching him in the face. He was promptly arrested.[32]

On Guard became a useful form of provocation both at fascist meetings and elsewhere. Harry Kaufman was once sent with a large contingent of other sellers and shtarkers to hawk *On Guard* near a popular fascist watering hole in Bethnal Green. The fascists came out, eyed them up, and retreated. 'It was a bit of a waste of time really, but we just showed them that we were there, that was the point,' recalled Kaufman.[33]

The Group also sent vendors to spots favoured by fascist paper sellers. Although this sometimes resulted in jostling, name-calling, and the occasional fight, it was far more likely that the two sides would just ignore each other as they stood around and half-heartedly tried to sell their wares; sometimes they got so bored that they started chatting with each other. Life as an active member of the 43 Group could often mean very high levels of boredom and drudgery.

Quiet Work

As with all organisations, and especially those that take some inspiration from the military, there were generals and there were foot soldiers, and whereas the generals, including Gerry Flamberg and many of the founding 43, would turn up for the 'high days, holidays, and big dos', as Martin Block put it, they rarely did 'the general dog's work that we did'.[34] Jules Konopinski was typical of a committed foot soldier:

'We were individuals leading our lives, and doing what had to be done. Everyone had a job . . . I was training to be a handbag designer, doing an apprenticeship. I was with the group in my spare time . . . But a lot of us were prepared to go out in the daytime when available, and do things. Daytime activities were based on availability, the Group did not ask people to take time off their jobs.'[35]

Those who donated their time were usually given a stack of *On Guard*s and a location to sell them, or told to watch a particular fascist or household or instructed to canvass for donations. Then there were the regular meetings, of course, the small-scale affairs that each section was responsible for attending and opposing. For example, Martin Block and his Central section went every Saturday morning to the fascist meeting at Notting Hill Gate, where they would heckle, try to provoke the speaker, and sell *On Guard*. But over time this became like any other day at the office, full of ritualised behaviour and predictable outcomes. It was hardly thrilling, and most likely the only tangible results were a few copies of *On Guard* sold and some slightly weakened voices.

Even more of a drag was the constant need to be fundraising. As the fighting intensified more members ended up with hospital bills, legal fees, bail to be posted, and fines (which were always covered). Finding the means to finance these expenses was one of the jobs those based at HQ were particularly involved in, and they would reach out to donors, arrange fundraising socials, or send out direct mailers. An even more crucial task for the Group's secretaries was postcard writing. In the days before most people had telephones, this was the Group's preferred way of passing on the times and dates of upcoming meetings to its members. 'Not the most secure method of communication,' reminisced Jules Konopinski, 'but there was no other way. You had to hope that they turned up.'[36] The members that is, not the postcards. This, Jonny Goodman explained, was one of the major problems the Group had as a volunteer organisation.

'Because it wasn't a military organisation we couldn't command people to be anywhere at a special time. So often you're going off into the unknown as you didn't know how many were going to turn up. You could get there and there could be 300 Blackshirts and there might be fifteen of our blokes, which didn't augur well, so these were the kind of complicated things the Group was always fighting, trying to get the right number of people, to the right place, at the right time, because everyone was voluntary, you weren't under threat or anything.'[37]

One way the Group tried to stack the deck in their favour was through what Jules Konopinski called the 'quiet work', intercepting fascists on their way to meetings and convincing them not to attend. On occasion this involved beating them up, but more often than not a casual supporter could be dissuaded with a chat. 'If you say to people, look you are going to get a bloody nose or a punch in the face if you bother to go, then they won't go, and their numbers start to dwindle. You don't have to have fights with these people, you just made them scared about what would happen to them if they went.' This was a particularly effective tactic to use on those more middle-class fascist supporters who far preferred heavily stewarded indoor private meetings, which in 1947 were mostly being held by the British People's Party.

As the Duke of Bedford's organisation never held public street meetings and tended to have a more middle- and upper-class membership, it largely avoided the 43 Group. However, on the few occasions Beckett arranged a larger private meeting in a hall, the Group did whatever it could to disrupt proceedings. There were a number of different tactics to disrupt public meetings. As the fascists often booked venues under pseudonyms, when Group intelligence learnt of scheduled meetings, the venue would be contacted and told the true nature of the organisation who wanted to use it. Some cancelled immediately; others needed to be told that if they allowed the meeting to go ahead the meeting would be attacked and damage to property was a certainty. Some venues ignored these warnings, in which case the Group began leafleting the local area in the hope of turning out a large demonstration. Meanwhile Group spies were under instruction to get their hands on tickets which would be duplicated by master printers who supported the Group before being returned to their rightful owners. If tickets came with seat numbers, Group members got to the venue as early as possible so they could take those seats, and proceeded to start arguments when the seats' rightful owners turned up. A fracas would usually ensue and delay the meeting for quite some time.[38] There were other even more effective ways of disrupting meetings. Recalled Martin Block, 'If we could research a place and find there were fire buckets with water in it, great; put dry ice in the fire buckets and smoke would engulf the place. I remember doing that at the Duke of Bedford's meeting; everyone was trying to get in and then trying to get out. The meeting finished quite early. It looked fearsome the dry ice in cold water.'

Dry ice was not the only thing that Block could get his hands on. 'We had firebombs as well, that weren't kerosene or paraffin based, they were chemical powders that smouldered and smoked rather than burst into explosive flame.' As an ex-RAF engineer, he could also get his hands on sodium flares that were used for 'RAF runways when all the lights had failed, they gave off clouds of orangey yellow smoke, they wouldn't hurt anybody, they would just disrupt.'[39] In August 1947 it was these tools of disruption that the 43 Group needed in abundance, as they became one of the main protagonists in a series of battles that were reported on around the world; a struggle that was itself triggered in part by events over 3,000 miles away.

6

The Battle of Ridley Road

The situation in Palestine was escalating. On 4 May 1947, the Jewish paramilitary Irgun attacked the British prison in Acre, and freed twenty-eight paramilitary members. During the raid, three members of the Irgun were killed and five were arrested. Two of the five were minors and so could not face the death penalty. The other three were tried and sentenced to death. In an attempt to prevent the executions, on 11 July 1947 the Irgun kidnapped two sergeants, Clifford Martin and Mervyn Paice. The British, however, were not interested in any form of prisoner exchange and on 29 July they executed the three Irgun members; Martin and Paice were hanged on the same day. The following day the Irgun took the bodies to a eucalyptus grove near Netanya, put bags over their heads, hung them from trees and placed upon them a sign declaring that they had been found guilty of 'criminal anti-Hebrew activities'.

On Friday, 1 August the *Daily Express* published the photograph under the headline 'HANGED BRITONS – Pictures that will shock the world'.[1] It caused an immediate stir in Britain, and on that Friday afternoon the slaughtermen of Birkenhead, near Liverpool, declared their refusal to process meat for Jewish consumption until Jewish atrocities in Palestine ceased. That evening rioting began in Birkenhead and quickly spread to Liverpool. The brunt of the rioting focused on Jewish shops and property; a few Jewish people were also attacked. On Saturday there were sixty-eight reported incidents in Liverpool and on Sunday a further 101, the vast majority targeting Jewish shops and businesses. The rioting also started to catch on in other cities, and there were a number of incidents in Glasgow and Manchester. By Sunday, rioting and violence had broken out in Hull, Brighton and Leicester, with London, Birmingham, Bristol, Cardiff and Newcastle witnessing some sporadic incidents. In Manchester and Glasgow the disturbances continued through to the Bank Holiday, while in Liverpool it took a full week before all the unrest died down. While the rioters mostly attacked business properties, there were also attempts to attack and burn synagogues and cemeteries. Of the few people who were attacked, only a solicitor in Liverpool and a shopkeeper in Glasgow were badly hurt, although their injuries were not life-threatening.[2]

Even in those places where those was no rioting, the situation could be precarious. Henry Morris, a young AJEX member, made his first public speech at Buckfast Street in Bethnal Green, the weekend after the hangings.

> When I stood up to make my first speech it just kept going round and round: 'Why don't you go back to Palestine' and 'What about the sergeants?' And it ended up with my platform being smashed. A similar situation occurred at Durdham Downs in Bristol. One of our speakers, a lady, was addressing a meeting, when one of the men in the audience introduced himself as being the father of Sergeant Paice, who was one of the two soldiers. She sympathised with him, explained the situation and then closed the meeting out of respect.[3]

A further example of the strength of anti-Semitic feeling in the country was provided five days after the riots commenced in an editorial by James Caunt, the editor and proprietor of the *Morecambe and Heysham Visitor*, a small local paper based in north-west England with a circulation of around 18,000.

> There is the growing feel that Britain is in the grip of the Jews. There are more Jewish M.P.s than at any time in British

history, and, for the purpose of emphasis, we repeat that if any analysis could be made of the people convicted for black market offences the Jewish community in Britain would come out an easy first.

The Jews, indeed, are a plague on Britain . . . Violence may be the only way to bring them to the sense of their responsibility to the country in which they live.[4]

It was an editorial that brought Caunt much publicity and a criminal charge of stirring race violence. Before dismissing the jury, the judge, Mr Justice Birkett, told the jurors: 'It is in the highest degree essential . . . that nothing should be done in this court to destroy or weaken the liberty of the Press.' The jury adhered to the judge's wishes and found Caunt not guilty.

The riots and Caunt's editorial were manifestations of the considerable hostility that was felt towards the Jewish community, a product of long-held anti-Semitic views magnified by the worsening events in Palestine. The fascists might have stoked the riots, but they certainly had not instigated them, nor, the security services determined, had they had any part in organising or promoting them.[5] Nevertheless the atmosphere was a major boon, particularly for Hamm, whose meetings at Ridley Road were attracting larger and larger audiences.

Days and Nights on Ridley Road

By the middle of August the chaos surrounding the League's meetings at Ridley Road were beginning to draw thousands of people, including several prominent journalists. One of these was Rebecca West, the renowned novelist, who had recently returned to London from reporting on the Nuremberg Trials. First in a series of seven articles for the *Evening Standard* and then in two long feature articles for the *New Yorker* published in 1948, West reported on the violence. In her *New Yorker* piece, 'Heil Hamm', she shared with her American readers her impressions of when she first entered Ridley Road, on 24 August 1947.

> Across the square, as backdrop to the scene, was a public house, the Ridley Arms, its upper windows beacons fired by the reflections of the sunset that we could not see. On each side of it a road stretched away, at an angle, to the blue distance. The one on the left was a crescent consisting of tall houses built in villa style but of the cheapest materials and coarsest workmanship, which was the bad old way of housing the poor, but not so very poor, in mid-Victorian days. Each house would be inhabited by several families. It was not at all an unattractive street and had its trees and gardens and a pleasantly built church school. The road that branched off on the right side of the public house was a long, straight street lined on its left side with shops and houses and on its right with a row of one-storied shops, hardly more than market stalls. They were, it appeared, balanced on the edge of a railway cutting, for every now and then there shot up from behind them a puff of black smoke that chugged off in a line parallel with the street.[6]

It was a strong belief of the fascists that their most fertile recruiting grounds were those areas with large Jewish populations, which, they assumed, would always elicit hostility from their gentile neighbours. It was this logic that had led the BUF to the East End before the war. During that same period a steady stream of Jews who had accrued enough wealth were beginning to escape the area's cramped ghetto, with most moving slightly farther north towards Hackney, where a Jewish enclave had been present since the start of the century. During the Blitz the East End's proximity to London's docks meant it endured a horrific bombing campaign, and anybody who could afford to live elsewhere, whether they were Jew or gentile, got out.

For the majority of the Jewish community Hackney was the logical choice, and many families settled in areas such as

Stamford Hill, Stoke Newington and Dalston. In May 1943 the MP for Hackney estimated that around 60 per cent of his electorate was Jewish, and he feared a growing ill-feeling between Jews and Christians in his constituency. Certainly the *Hackney Gazette* did not help matters, accusing the Jews of cowardice in the Blitz, running a campaign against gaming clubs, and supporting discrimination against Jewish tenants. The *Gazette* was also more than happy to publish letters from those residents who were antagonistic to the Jewish population.[7] Such prejudices were beginning to abate by 1947, but the residual resentment towards Hackney's Jewish community was something that the fascists hoped to exploit.

The Jewish flavour of the area was most clearly sensed at the market on Ridley Road, called 'Yidley Road' by the fascists. Up to 200 stalls could line the long wide road on market days, catering to the needs of the local community. Traders shouting in Yiddish were as common as those shouting in cockney rhyming slang, with East Enders speaking Yiddish just as much as the Jewish traders used cockney.

Behind the market stalls was a long parade of shops, rarely more than one storey high and, like the market stalls, many of these were Jewish owned. One of these shops was M. Joseph's – a grocery store owned by my grandparents, which was famous in the area for its smoked salmon. My grandmother Pat often helped out in the shop and remembered how vibrant, lively and fun walking through the market could be. 'It was like Speakers' Corner without the politics,' she recalled. 'It was always the same traders, and most of the same shoppers, so people knew the trader's patter and would shout back their responses. They were heckling the traders.'[8] Next door to my family's grocery store was the fishmongers owned by the famous boxing promoter Jack Solomons, who was also a prominent 43 Group supporter.

It was the area's mixed population that brought Hamm and the League to Ridley Road, but it had been a popular spot for public meetings since 1913. In the post-war years Ridley Road once again became a hive of political activity, and the return of the League and the publicity surrounding the Group's first attack activated numerous political organisations in the area. The vast majority of these were communist organisations, with the CPGB being the largest, but there was also the Revolutionary Communist Party (RCP), the Young Communist League (YCL), and the Common Wealth Party (CWP).

The CPGB and YCL held meetings with organisations like the 43 Group, and the more violent communist organisations were more willing to go on the attack. Another vital part of the anti-fascist effort was community organising, and here the Hackney Trades Council (HTC), the area's main trade union coordinating body, played a large part. On Sunday, 15 June, the HTC organised a march to Ridley Road, consisting primarily of local trade union members but headed by the local branch of the British Legion, whose ex-servicemen's band led the procession.

Four days later the National Council for Civil Liberties (NCCL) held a meeting at Hackney Town Hall and launched a petition to the Home Secretary demanding action against the fascists. In addition both the HTC and NCCL held marches, meetings and conferences and other forms of community organising, all of which formed a rich part of the anti-fascist tapestry in Hackney during the summer of 1947.

On the day of the Trades Councils march to Dalston, Jeffrey Hamm's boys had a rather unpleasant surprise when they arrived at Ridley Road. The communists had stolen their pitch. In order to keep order in the area the police had a strict policy that only one meeting at a time could be in progress, so when the fascists arrived to discover that their spot had been taken they were forced to decamp to John Campbell Road, a residential street on the other side of Kingsland High Street. In the summer of 1947 arriving earlier than the fascists to steal the Ridley Road spot, or 'Jumping the Pitch' as it became known, was one of the favourite tactics of the League's anti-fascist rivals.

To regulate this competition the police upheld a set of unofficial conventions. It was 'first come, first served' and no pitch could be reserved. If another organisation had a meeting in progress they could not be turfed out. But a meeting had to be in progress; organisations were not allowed to hold pitches. Consequently, speeches were being given from the platforms many hours before the meetings were officially due to begin.

The week after the pitch was first jumped, Hamm's boys got to Ridley Road before any would-be pitch pilferers and continued to do so for the rest of June. However, come July and August the communists redoubled their efforts and were beating the fascists every other week. The scramble to bag Ridley Road first led to both sides turning up earlier and earlier on Sunday mornings, then Saturday nights, and then Saturday evenings – a full twenty-four hours before the meeting was actually supposed to begin.

The next challenge was that, as the police prohibited meetings while the market was open, it was impossible to claim the pitch before its closure for the weekend at 5 p.m. on Saturday. On a couple of occasions platforms were hidden beneath market stalls, with the disguise being thrown off and a meeting declared open the moment the market closed.[9]

The absurd upshot of this competition for the Ridley Road pitch was organisations having to hold twenty-four-hour-long meetings. Of course, as Hamm remembered, the speaker on the platform 'would obviously not speak continuously, but if challenged by a rival organisation he would go through the motions of addressing an invisible audience, even at two or three o'clock on a Saturday morning'. Be caught napping and the other side would try to steal the pitch. The League often sent Jock Holliwell to Ridley Road on Sunday mornings when they had been beaten to the pitch. Holliwell would turn up carrying a brown paper bag and if he spotted the communists snoozing or at an all-night coffee stall, he would drop the brick that he was hiding in the bag onto the ground, mount it, and announce in a loud voice: 'I declare open this British League meeting!'

To thwart such tactics, it was necessary for the League's opponents to have a substantial roster of speakers to hold the platform for hours on end, as well as a few heavies who could protect the speaker should the fascists try to steal the platform through more violent means. A policeman was normally on duty to ensure this did not happen; but even so, in the deserted marketplace in the small hours of the morning the speakers would surely have been glad of a bit of extra protection. Here the 43 Group, who were not holding meetings in 1947 and so could not steal the pitch themselves, were happy to lend a hand and would sometimes send a few shtarkers down to help guard a stolen pitch.

By the summer, Len Sherman reckoned, the Group had about 500 active members it could call down to Dalston every week.[10] In June and July when crowd sizes averaged around 6–800, turning out a third or a half of the active members was more than sufficient; as crowd sizes climbed into the thousands at the start of August, the Group needed all hands on deck.

As news of events at Ridley Road began to spread, many who were not members of one of the organisations active in the area started coming down. There were plenty of Jews who made their way to Ridley Road, but for various reasons never joined the 43 Group or AJEX. Alan Foreman was a youngster who often went to Ridley Road with his gang of friends, but was so unaware of the Group's activities that in later life he questioned whether or not it had actually existed.[11] This is hardly surprising, as at Ridley Road it was hard to differentiate between Group members and other young Jews who were happy to get their hands dirty. Certainly, there was little to differentiate the boys of the East End section from all the other East End Jewish youths keen for a go against the Mosleyites.

Similarly, not everyone who was supportive of Hamm's platform was a fascist. Plenty of the Hackney locals who cheered the League's speakers did so because they either agreed with their positions on the Jews, especially the ones in Palestine, or because they concurred with the fascists' claim that there existed a Jewish and communist element in Hackney that was denying Englishmen their fundamental rights of free speech. The League also attracted those who shared none of their politics but were drawn to Ridley Road to satiate their violent urges. One such individual was Arthur Harding, a notorious former East End criminal, who in the post-war years was trying to stay on the straight and narrow:

> I would never have belonged to the Mosley people. I mean it's daft to set about somebody for nothing. But I did give them a hand after the war, when they were holding their meetings in Dalston, at Ridley Road Market. Think the reason was this. I was a married man with a family growing up, and I didn't want to get mixed up with crooked people. But I wanted to get out of myself. There was that urge of excitement – I couldn't sit at home all the time and so I used to go down there.[12]

Harding was by no mean alone. Ridley Road provided a cathartic space where men of all ages could throw a punch and burn off some aggression, safe in the knowledge that the general chaos made it significantly less likely one might be collared by the police. The growing and increasingly violent crowds provided advantages and disadvantages to both sides. For the Group, getting anywhere near close enough to the League's platforms became next to impossible, but the crowd itself could be weaponised. Fireworks, bangers, and other pandemonium-causing incendiary devices were often deployed, and the ensuing chaos often forced the police to instruct the fascists to close the meetings.

Meanwhile, although the League's speakers had more protection, it was becoming harder for them to be heard above the tumult, heckling and constant shouting. Hamm's solution was to rent small loudspeaker vans, but these soon became no match for the roaring crowds. Even worse, the vans were constantly getting damaged, and rental companies where charging more and more. The fascists realised it was imperative to own their own vehicle Raven Thompson and Allan Smith spearheaded a national appeal to purchase an armoured loudspeaker lorry, but this took months to come to fruition. Until then Hamm would just have to make do.

Mr Mullally Pays a Visit

On 10 August 1947, a crowd of over 1,000 came to watch Hamm at Ridley Road; the first time, according to police estimates, it reached this milestone. The larger crowd, the overwhelming majority of which was supportive of Hamm, was a product of the febrile anti-Semitic atmosphere triggered by the hanging of the two sergeants in Palestine. Although the 43 Group was present they were completely nullified by the 90 per cent of the crowd who supported the League's position.

Frederic Mullally was not a member of the 90 per cent. A prominent anti-fascist journalist and the political editor of the *Sunday Pictorial*, Mullally kept a low profile as he closely observed the meeting in order to describe its full horror for the readers of his weekly column.

> Last Sunday evening at Ridley Road, Dalston, I had a sickening experience. For one hour, between 8 and 9 pm about a thousand working-class men and women cheered, wildly and hysterically, as one fascist speaker after another paid homage to Sir Oswald Mosley ('The greatest Englishman alive today').
>
> When Jeffrey Hamm . . . shouted to the crowd that he was 'preparing the ground' for the triumphant return of Mosley, a thousand dupes of fascist demagogy roared their imbecile approval. The few interruptions from anti-fascists on the fringe of the crowd were dealt with swiftly by the large body of uniformed police.[13]

Born to a working-class Irish Catholic family in 1918, Frederic Mullally had witnessed the BUF's famed 1934 Kensington Olympia meeting. It was an experience that both 'appalled and excited' him. Three years later, Mullally set sail for India, where he began his journalistic career. It was not long before he was made editor of Bombay's *Sunday Standard,* making him one of the youngest-ever editors of a national newspaper. Mullally returned to Britain in 1939 on a German ship, fully crewed by devoted Nazis who 'would play the Horst Wessel Lied and Deutschland Über Alles on the ship's radio regularly'; the radio operator kept trying to convert him to Nazism. It was this experience that alerted him to the seriously destructive dangers of Nazism and convinced him that war was imminent; he became a lifelong anti-fascist.[14]

Rejected the military on medical grounds thanks to a severe bout of tuberculosis as a child, Mullally worked in editorial roles at several newspapers before joining the *Sunday Pictorial* as its political editor. He was also given his own column, with his photograph next to his byline. Describing Mullally for her *New Yorker* readers, Rebecca West gushed:

> He is an intelligent and public-spirited person, but what mattered most at this moment was that he is a great beauty . . . His hair is jet-black, his skin is milk-white, he has an Elizabethan beard, and, like all great beauties, he knows the trick of wearing contemporary clothes so that they look like romantic period costume.[15]

A debonair bon-vivant and society man, Mullally was also incredibly astute, and in the months following VE Day got wind of the Mosleyite rumblings and their dreams of glorious return. Realising the alarm bell had to be sounded in 1946, he wrote and published *Fascism Inside England*, which included both an account of the pre-war BUF and of the fascists' more recent schemes. The historian Nigel Copsey credits Mullally and his book with challenging the prevailing perception in Britain during the war years that fascism was a foreign invention, alien to British society and values. Mullally argued that there was a sizeable minority of people who continued to be attracted to fascism's anti-communist and anti-Semitic principles. He was particularly fearful of a successor to the BUF attracting a middle-class clientele who were disillusioned with politics following the Conservative defeat in the 1945 election.

Mullally, says Copsey, was the first of many anti-fascist writers to argue that Britain did not possess intrinsic immunity to fascism, and that anti-fascists therefore had to be continually on their guard against it and not bury their heads 'deep in the sands of complacency'.[16] This was a sentiment that Mullally repeated a year later in a self-published pamphlet, 'Fascism Again in 1947'. 'The price of liberty is eternal vigilance. If you value liberty, play your part in stamping out its bitterest enemy. FIGHT THIS MENACE NOW!'[17] As for those who were actually engaged in the fight, Mullally was only too happy to offer his public support.

However, his trip to Ridley Road on 10 August prompted him to jump right into the heart of the fray. 'Okay, Hamm, let's see the stuff you and your audience are made of,' challenged Mullally at the end of his 17 August column. 'I'm coming down to Ridley Road again – tonight. I'm going to ask you for your microphone and your platform for just ten minutes. I know you can dish it out. Let's see if you can take it.'[18]

At 54 Bayswater Road, Geoff Bernerd's immediate response to the article was to call Mullally and offer him a bodyguard of the Group's toughest fighters. 'No bodyguard,' Mullally told Bernerd. 'I'm not walking in there with a bodyguard. I'm a member of the fourth estate and I don't need to walk around with a bodyguard. I'm going down by myself.'[19] 'You might be sorry,' Bernerd warned the journalist and began planning for the worst. Mullally had boxed in his youth and still fancied himself quite the pugilist; he reckoned he could take care of himself.

As the communists had jumped the Ridley Road platform that day, Mullally made his way to John Campbell Road. From a distance he could hear that the fascists were not the only ones who had turned out. As he approached the outskirts of the crowd he was immediately recognised and the staunch anti-fascists, who were in the majority towards the back of the crowd, began cheering: 'We want Mullally! We want Mullally!'

Then Mullally, with assistance, began to make his way through the crowd and towards the platform. He later insisted the protection came from the police. In the accounts of both the police and Hamm it was communists who surrounded Mullally and propelled him towards the League platform where Duke Pile was declaiming. The League supporters were encircling the platform, and as Mullally got closer the cries of 'We want Mullally!' became drowned out by a chorus of 'We want Mosley!' in response. Then the attacks started. Punches and kicks were aimed at him through the protective cordon. But still he pressed on. He was only a few feet away from the platform when the cordon was overwhelmed and the blows rained down on him. Decades later Mullally remembered:

> The fascists were breaking through that police line, one of them pulled me down to the ground, others struck across police shoulders at me and I had a rough time getting through. The police opened out into a circle and they left me right in the middle of the circle, I couldn't go to the platform, I couldn't retreat, I couldn't go right or left. The hubbub was enormous, it was bedlam . . . I was right in the middle of the fascists. I thought if this blue line breaks I've had it. That's when the 43 Group appeared, they punched through the police lines.[20]

Just a few feet away from the platform the Group's 'commandos' materialised and used their bodies to shield Mullally, who had been hurled to the ground. They insisted on him turning back, going forward was just too dangerous. Mullally agreed. They retreated back up the road, matching the fascists' aggression while keeping a tight ring of bodies around the journalist. Fortunately, more police officers appeared in the crowd, extricated them and escorted Mullally and his bodyguard towards Kingsland High Street, where the 43 Group and other anti-fascists were in the majority.

Now being followed by a far friendlier, 43 Group–dominated crowd, Mullally was taken across the high street to Sandringham Road, another side street. Here the Group set up an impromptu platform, Mullally mounted it and began addressing his audience. Meanwhile, Mullally's appearance had unleashed complete bedlam at John Campbell Road and Pile was instructed to close his meeting. The crowd then pushed towards Sandringham Road, but a police blockade on Kingsland High Street, which was attempting to keep the fascists and anti-fascists apart, made this almost impossible.

Over on Sandringham Road, Mullally was delivering the speech he'd planned to give on the League's platform, telling his young audience that the British League, which had no policies of its own, was trying to breed racial hatred by using the Jewish problem as a 'red herring'. A policeman stepped forward and told Mullally to close his meeting, fearing more disorder if it continued. Mullally obliged, ending his speech with a shout of 'Up with democracy and down with fascism!'

Next, Mullally and the Group went down the side streets to Ridley Road where the communist meeting was in progress. This was a far smaller gathering than usual, as most people, fascists and anti-fascists both, were still stuck in John Campbell Road. A car with a loudspeaker fixed on its roof served as the communists' platform and Mullally clambered up to address the small crowd. He had not been speaking long when he and his audience were distracted by a horrendous noise, the 'Horst Wessel Lied' growing louder and louder. A procession of fascists had escaped John Campbell Road through its unblocked exit and taking a circuitous route round Dalston arrived via a side street on Ridley Road. A police blockade was formed but not before some 200 fascists had broken through. A rush of Group members and communists met their attack.[21] Mullally's most indelible memory of the ensuing brawl was of a 'good old anti-fascist woman on top of the platform with a large bar in her hands smacking down anyone who came at her'.[22]

Mullally wanted to stay with the fight but a dozen or so Group members bundled him into a nearby pub. With the journalist safe, half returned to the action and half remained behind the bolted door. It was a decision Mullally later acknowledged might have saved his life, as the fascists soon broke through the police cordon and severely outnumbered their rivals, who could not be reinforced due to the police blockade of Ridley Road. It was a decided victory for the enemy, as they smashed up the communists' platform and carried off their banner in triumph.[23] It was well into night before the police were able to end the hostilities and clear the area, and only then did the Group feel comfortable shepherding Mullally out of the pub and back to the station.[24]

The police records for the meeting allege there were no injuries, a statement which stretches the bounds of credulity.[25] Perhaps no one was taken away in an ambulance, but the fights at Ridley Road often led to injuries ranging from cuts and bruises to concussions and broken bones. However, no deaths ever occurred, either there or in any other battle in this conflict. This might sound surprising, but the same was true of the fights against the BUF in the 1930s; fascist and anti-fascist violence in the first half of the twentieth century was never a deadly affair.

All the same, the prurient readers of London's newspapers lapped up the coverage of Mullally's Ridley Road appearance, and when his own column appeared in the *Sunday Pictorial* the following week many would have avidly hoped for all the gory details. They would have been disappointed. 'My brush with the East End fascists last Sunday has caused sufficient comment without my adding to it,' wrote Mullally, who wanted instead to discuss the politics of the matter.

As in the years of appeasement before the war it is considered not 'quaite naice' to be a militant anti-Fascist. It is taken for granted, by a surprisingly large cross-section of self-styled democrats, that anyone expressing strong anti-Fascist views must be either a Jew or a Communist.

As one who is neither, I can only regret that so many citizens of a nation which only a few years ago poured out its blood and wealth to halt the Fascist march towards world domination should have such short memories.

My thanks to the hundreds of staunch anti-Fascists who have written and telephoned during the week. And a special greeting to those who supported me last Sunday. You'll be hearing from me again.[26]

For a second Sunday morning in a row, Mullally picked up his ringing phone to hear the voice of Geoff Bernerd. The communists and 43 Group had jumped the Ridley Road pitch, Bernerd informed Mullally, and they wanted him to speak. Mullally agreed; even he had not expected to be returning so soon. This time at least he would have a 43 Group bodyguard; he was not foolish enough to turn down Bernerd's offer a second time. The two men arranged to meet at Dalston Junction, and then Bernerd was off the phone and over to the League's meeting at Hereford Street, from which the police, for reasons which remain unknown, escorted him away.[27] Bernerd was not an infrequent presence on the battlefield, although due to his gammy leg and the fascists' awareness of his role in the Group, he was also driven to and from the meetings and had a bodyguard whenever he was on the battle ground. Philip Evansky was assigned to this detail, and once got struck on the back of the head with a bottle while protecting Bernerd.[28]

Bernerd met Mullally at the station and the two men began to walk to Ridley Road, accompanied by a contingent of the Group's shtarkers, but nowhere near as many as Bernerd had promised. 'Well, Geoff. Where are all these guys who are going to save us if we get into trouble,' asked Mullally. 'Just look behind you,' replied Bernerd. Mullally turned and realised that standing in every doorway was a large man in khaki shorts. The

Group, he figured, had around 100 heavies stationed all along the route.[29]

The communists had also turned up in force following an enthusiastic response to the call for an all-out. Their Ridley Road platform was surrounded by a 2,000-strong supportive audience comprised of members from many different left-wing organisations. Mullally addressed the throng and told them how he had had to come to Ridley Road with an escort and how he was 'working for the day when every Fascist speaker will be escorted to jail'.[30]

Meanwhile at John Campbell Road the League's speakers were having a rougher time of it. Their audience of around 1,200 largely consisted of anti-fascists, with the police estimating that at least half the crowd was Jewish.[31] For the first twenty minutes there was relative order, but when a firework went off at 8:10 p.m. pandemonium broke out, and Superintendant Satterthwaite ordered the meeting closed. A police cordon once again stretched along Kingsland High Street, keeping the fascists in John Campbell Road away from the communists on Ridley Road. Of course, with so many anti-fascists still in John Campbell Road fights were breaking out right, left and centre on both sides of the High Street.

The disorder gave the police more than enough trouble, and so they once again failed to notice a large body of fascists disappearing down the other side of John Campbell Road. Again the fascists evaded the police blockade by meandering through side streets, and twenty minutes after their own meeting closed they came to Ridley Road. This time, however, Ridley Road was prepared and cordons of police and anti-fascists kept the adversaries thirty metres from the communist platform. From that distance they could only heckle, and, according to the *Daily Worker,* hurl stones; a barrage that was met in kind. When the communist meeting closed with the singing of the 'Internationale', the fascists tried to interrupt with cheers of 'We want Mosley!' The police did, however, manage to keep the two sides from violently clashing.[32]

Meanwhile, Rebecca West, who had spent the day touring the League's numerous meetings, had found herself trapped in a side road with a large number of fascist youth.

> There we were sealed. When we turned about and ran to the other end of the crescent, hoping to get out of there and follow a roundabout route and have a last smack at the Communist meeting, we discovered another cordon waiting for us. So up and down the street we walked in the gathering darkness, yammering and catcalling, not seriously discomfited, for nothing mattered to us very much.[33]

It might not have mattered to the youth with whom West was caught, but it meant a vast amount to Frederic Mullally. His editor Hugh Cudlipp, however, did not share his columnist's feelings and, having grown increasingly uncomfortable with Mullally's activism, he reined him in. Mullally argued that his coverage of resurgent fascism was necessary, but in the end he relented. He wrote a few more articles about the Mosleyites over the next few years but played no further role at the Battle of Ridley Road, which had barely even begun.

Pale Pink Palpitating Pansies

In his 1952 novel *With Hope, Farewell*, the Jewish novelist Alexander Baron, who had been an active anti-fascist in the BUF days, captured the weekly chaos that plagued Dalston in the summer of 1947:

> The mob was on the boil, with nerves fraying, tempers rising and the undercurrent of panic growing more powerful. The red, sweating faces of policemen, which could be seen here and there, betrayed – in place of their customary calm – a black, scared anger of this great beast of a crowd that had to be kept under control. The tall buildings that rose on both sides added to the impression of confinement, as if the people who rolled on in a

compressed mass, all unwilling, but all carrying each other forward, were beasts pouring between stockade walls into an abattoir.[34]

Naturally the carnage led to both sides claiming they had local support while their opponents were external disrupters. Rebecca West interviewed several residents to learn what they actually thought; one woman offered an insightful take on local reaction, and particularly that of the young people marching with the fascists.

> You see they all used to sleep down in the tube stations when the war was on, and they had a wonderful time then, with the concerts and all, and the company. . . . The boys and girls miss it all dreadfully, and the chasing around fills up the evenings for them. They'd forget it if anything else came along.[35]

'I don't blame these youngsters,' the woman continued, 'I blame the British League of Ex-Servicemen, and this man Hamm.'[36] The very youthful make-up of Hamm's followers was noted by plenty of other visitors to Ridley Road, one of whom, a Mr Ian Mikardo, wrote to *On Guard*: 'Most of the Fascists are under 25 years of age and many of them are under 20. One lad I saw had a knife in one hand a knuckle-duster in the other; when I asked him his age, he said he was 15.'[37]

Hamm surely welcomed his new young supporters, but he was also becoming a victim of his success, as the swelling crowds made it virtually impossible for him to hold his Dalston meetings. The League's 31 August meeting on John Campbell Road was closed after only fifteen minutes; with about 50 per cent of the 600-strong crowd being Jewish, this was hardly surprising. Once again a police cordon down Kingsland High Street kept the fascists to the west and the communists to the east, but once again the fascists reached Ridley Road via the backstreets. By now they were expected, and the police cordon mostly did its job. A few managed to get through and were

immediately met by some Group members who had been loitering at the edge of the crowd; in the ensuing punch-up, five were
arrested.

Meanwhile, over on Kingsland High Street a procession of
150 League members and a few prominent fascists, including
Victor Burgess, were marching and chanting 'We want Mosley!'
and 'Down with the Jews!' as they tried to drown out the
communist speakers at Ridley Road. At 8:30 p.m. the police
ordered the communist meeting closed, which was done with
the singing of the 'Internationale'; the fascists used the national
anthem for all their drowning-out needs. The communist exodus
out of Ridley Road tested the mettle of the police cordon; the
communists were forced east towards Hackney Downs, the
fascists west towards Islington.

The combatants had other ideas, and both sides circled back
to the high street. The police cordon down the middle of the
road held strong, however, and the two sides were limited to
chanting and throwing projectiles. Then, at 8:50 p.m., the police
were met with the alarming sight of Gerry Flamberg at the head
of twenty-five Group members marching down the west side –
mere inches away from their antagonists. Shouts and scuffles
ensued, before the police were able to separate the two sides.
Twenty-five minutes later a crowd had gathered around the
station with both sides, the 43 Group and the fascists, well
represented. The brawl was prolonged, and the police made
several arrests as they tried to mop it up.

One of those arrested was Philip Goldberg, who was with a
bunch of his fellow Group members when he shouted, 'There's
the fascist rats, let's get them!' He charged into the enemy, his
friends at his tail. Several policemen quickly collared him and
dragged him 150 yards down the road, before he finally agreed
to walk; two weeks later Magistrate Daniel Hopkin fined him
£7 for his antics.

Standing trial alongside Goldberg were two other Group
members arrested that day, Harry Cohen and Laurie Curtis.
Charged with 'threatening behaviour', Curtis had got into a

fight with a couple of fascists after they called him 'Jewish scum' and attacked him. However, at trial the arresting officer denied hearing the slur or seeing anyone attack Curtis, although he agreed he had numerous bruises. Cohen, an ex-RAF man, had been violently arrested by the police who subsequently discovered four Thunderflash fireworks on his person. Cohen told the court that he had merely found the fireworks on Ridley Road and had no plans to light them: neither lighter nor matches were found amongst his effects. He was believed and the possession of fireworks charge was dropped, although, like Curtis, he was found guilty of 'using threatening behaviour' and bound over to keep the peace. In total eight people were arrested on 31 August, five of whom were Group members.[38]

One week later there were over 2,000 people in Dalston, and rumours were rife that Mosley himself was going to speak. This, observed a Special Branch officer, was most likely put about by the League to boost their audience size.[39] Also working in the League's favour was a communist mass meeting in Hyde Park. With no competition in Dalston, the fascists were able to secure the Ridley Road pitch and keep their meeting open much longer than they had in previous weeks. The 43 Group were still there, of course, but the vast police presence meant they could do little by themselves and were limited to heckling and starting scuffles. The police could easily deal with this and had the situation mostly under control until around 7:35 p.m. – when a procession of 200 communists appeared on Dalston Lane seemingly out of nowhere, behind a banner that demanded 'Ban all Fascist Organisations!'[40]

Chaos ensued, and Satterthwaite shut down the League meeting. Then for the first time a full complement of mounted police were deployed to clear the crowds. Meanwhile the communists had set up a meeting on John Campbell Road, but this was interrupted by numerous fascists who got into the road and began chanting 'Sit down – sit down!' and 'We want Mosley!' Fights broke out and the police ordered the communists to close their meeting. This time the police were able to clear Dalston without any major brawls breaking out.

The following Sunday, 14 September, there were between 5–6,000 people at Ridley Road, but the police were prepared enough to deal with the masses, which by now also included hordes of sightseers. Two hundred fascist stewards and police officers guarded the platform. The Group had a contingent of a similar size, which the police were by now able to identify and separate from the rest. Good order was maintained throughout the meeting.

For the members of the Group, though, the day's most significant event had already occurred. Earlier in the afternoon, Harry Bidney, Bernard Shilling and Harry Stein were walking through Dalston, most likely on a reconnoitre. Walking up Kingsland High Street they passed a gang of fascists who were hanging out around a loudspeaker van, parked on the corner of Ridley Road. The fascists started jeering at the 43 Groupers who walked on without responding and turned into deserted Sandringham Road. Here, Bidney dropped back from his friends in order to fish out one of his perennial Woodbine cigarettes. He stopped to light it.

'You dirty Jew bastard!'

Metal and flesh slammed into the back of Bidney's head as a knuckleduster-clad fist smashed him to the ground. Bidney screamed. Shilling and Stein whipped around to see three thugs standing over their friend. They sprinted back and attacked his assailants, but from the outset the fascists had the better of things. The situation turned from bad to worse when a dozen more charged into Sandringham Road. But the commotion stirred the residents who came out of their homes to see what was up, and the fascists scrammed.

Bidney had had several teeth knocked out and his gums split,[41] but one of his assailants, a chap named Parker, might have come off worse. He had been recognised by Shilling and Stein and a few days later half a dozen of the Group's shtarkers gave him a severe beating outside his front door, sending a clear warning to the fascists about the consequences of fighting dirty. Clearly this visit had some effect, as Parker himself made a house call to Bidney to apologise. 'I hope I did not hurt you,' said Parker, according to *On Guard*. 'I am not really a Fascist. I am half Jewish. I will tell you all you want to know about Mosley. I am in charge of a defence squad in Hackney and received orders to beat you up.'[42] Why Parker thought this excuse made the attack OK is anyone's guess. A month after the assault he and his two accomplices were found guilty of assault and sent to prison for twenty-eight days.

The attack on Bidney was part of a growing pattern of violence rippling out from the clashes at the meetings. The *Daily Mail* wrote of gangs of thugs roaming the side streets off Kingsland Road looking for people to attack, and *On Guard* listed hecklers being followed and attacked and local protesters being intimidated.

The week after the attack on Bidney another, far more prominent, fascist was arrested. In an indirect manner this was also as a result of Group activity. The fascists' appeal to help buy their own loudspeaker van had inspired an unlikely benefactor, Jonny Wimborne, who had given the money to his undercover spy Cotter to enhance his standing in fascist circles.[43] Standing on top of the loudspeaker van's floodlit roof, surrounded by fascist flags,[44] Hamm tuned on the microphone to addressed an audience of thousands at Ridley Road on 21 September. The crowd included nine Labour MPs, who could hear Hamm clearly over the tumult telling of how he had recently received a court summons due to the use of particular phrases in previous speeches, phrases he then repeated for his Ridley Road fans.

We will fight to the death and never will you impose your Oriental, Mongolian, Asiatic creed of Communism on us!

The pale pink palpitating pansies with their long hair and painted toenails have been chanting 'We don't want Fascism', but I say 'We don't want Jewish Communism here!'

We will fight to exterminate your alien creed and build a new and greater Britain where no Communism will be tolerated! We don't want Jewish Communism here! We don't want Jewish Communism here!'[45]

The police immediately ordered the meeting closed and Hamm was arrested under the Public Order Act. Hamm subsequently went on trial in front of Magistrate Blake Odgers, who advised that should he wish to avoid prosecution in future he should limit his remarks to 'Jewish Communists' and not implicate all Jews. Hamm was bound over for twelve months at a cost of £25, but Odgers did not ban him from speaking at meetings, which he said would not be justified.[46] *On Guard* thought the Odgers verdict was correct, but only because the words Hamm had been summoned on were insignificant in comparison with 'the much stronger and more provocative propaganda Hamm has been pouring out over the last twelve months.'[47]

Towards the end of September, the CPGB decided it no longer wished to be associated with the disreputable violence surrounding the meeting at Ridley Road. It took the view that its participation in the conflict enabled the government to portray communists and fascists as two warring factions, both of which were a danger to the public. Consequently the CPGB decided to pivot to less controversial forms of anti-fascist organising, including petitions and advocacy work, and its members were instructed to no longer turn out at Ridley Road. In the vacuum left by the CPGB, other communist organisations – including the RCP and CWP, who held the Ridley Road pitch together on 5 October – were able to come to the fore.[48]

On 12 October the fascists, who had now taken to wearing Union Jacks in their buttonholes, so they knew who was on their side, got the jump on their rivals by arriving at Ridley Road nineteen hours before their meeting was due to start.[49] By this point the crowds had started to dwindle, but the belligerents were still out in full force with at least 400 League supporters and 100 Group members at Ridley Road. Violent

heckling quickly turned into more serious disturbances, and
the police had to separate the two sides in order to keep the
peace. Hamm's mounting of the loudspeaker van was greeted
with a firework going off in the crowd, and he had only uttered
a few words before Group members began to pelt him with
tomatoes, potatoes and light bulbs.[50] After a few minutes of
this the police informed Hamm that the meeting had to close.
For the crime of throwing tomatoes at the loudspeaker van,
Group members Norman and Gerald were found guilty of
'insulting behaviour' and fined £15 each.[51] In the next few
weeks the cold weather began to set in, even the faithful were
less keen on venturing outside, and the League soon stopped
erecting its platform.

The Battle of Ridley Road was the defining conflict of the
clash between the fascists and the 43 Group, and so there was
value in being seen as the victor of the conflict; a victory Hamm
tried to claim in a pamphlet published towards the end of the
year.

> Jeffrey Hamm and the British League have won their case. They
> have surmounted both organised hooliganism on the part of
> Communists and Jews and all legal attempts to ban them from
> the streets of East London on the pretext that they incite disor-
> der.[52]

Hamm's argument that the League had won because it was still
holding meetings was hardly compelling. Moreover, its anti-
fascist opponents were just as active at the end of the summer as
they had been at the start, and there was no indication that
either side had won the affections of the good people of Dalston.
It is therefore impossible to call a winner for the Battle of Ridley
Road, but Rebecca West believed she knew who was to blame:

> By a quite simple mechanism the Communists have heartlessly
> exploited the grievances of the Jews against the Fascists in order
> to create disorder under the Labour Government, to capture the

Jewish vote in forthcoming municipal and Parliamentary elections.[53]

For *On Guard*, which normally tried to keep as much distance in public from the communists as possible, this was a disgraceful charge and one that demanded a response.

> We feel it is our duty to deprecate Miss West's allegations that the Communists are heartlessly exploiting the Fascist provocation of the Jewish residents of Dalston.
>
> The Communists have been the only Party to erect a political anti-Fascist platform at the scene of Fascist meetings and many sincere young ex-servicemen have spoken from Communist platforms to denounce the Fascism they have encountered on returning to England.[54]

Chief among the numerous flaws in West's claim is that it fails to account for the role of the most belligerent anti-fascists, the 43 Group. The Group had no ulterior political ambitions, but it could be argued that all they were doing at Ridley Road was throwing fuel on the fire and giving publicity to the fascists. They were. But this was not necessarily a bad thing. First, in a period when the fascists desperately wanted to detoxify their image and appear to be a legitimate, sensible and civilised choice, the Battle of Ridley Road ensured that the fascists remained associated with street violence and chaos. Second, through the Battle of Ridley Road the Group was actively challenging the perception that theirs was a community that would take persecution and victimization on the chin.

Despite the Warsaw Ghetto uprising and the actions of plenty of Jewish soldiers during the war, there was still a prevailing stereotype in post-war Britain of the weak and cowardly Jew.[55] So when the fascists targeted the Jewish community, the last thing they really expected was for the Jews to fight back. As Morris Beckman explained to Dave Renton, 'the fascists were indoctrinated into believing that the Jews were soft targets . . .

They never believed that the Jews would out-violence them.'[56] At the Battle of Ridley Road, however, the perception of the conflict as one between communists and fascists meant this lesson was getting lost, and although the fascists were by this time well aware of the 43 Group, they had yet to fully comprehend the threat it posed.

7

Mosley Returns

When Mosley announced his retirement in 1945, he offered his lieutenants a prediction: the glow of victory would quickly fade, the people of Britain would grow tired of post-war austerity, and an inevitable financial crisis would bring the country to its knees. This, he told his minions, would give them the opportunity they needed; fascism would return, offering strong and clear leadership in troubling times, and people would flock to their clear-headed economic vision. Their rise to power was assured.

According to *On Guard*, Mosley believed that this financial crisis would come towards the end of the Labour government, which gave him plenty of time to organise, reunite the movement, and 'accustom the public to the idea of Fascism in post-war Britain'. However, when the currency crisis of 1947 began that summer, Mosley was convinced that an economic crash would ensue and his moment to seize power had arrived. Consequently, he sped up his plans and brought forward the date of his return.[1]

That the Labour government was able to successfully navigate the crisis and stave off a complete economic crash was not something Mosley had anticipated. This was typical. Mosley was clear-sighted enough to see the dangers, but his gargantuan hubris convinced him that only he could save the day.

One of the things Mosley wished his followers to do was to bring his name back into people's minds. Book clubs and organisations like the League and the UBF expressed an appreciation for Mosley and his politics, but denied any official connection and did not actively campaign for his return. However, by July 1947 any such pretence had flown out the window. Mosleyite speakers began actively calling for his return, and movement foot soldiers marched down streets shouting 'We want Mosley!'[2]

While the vast majority of the attention the fascists had been receiving was due to events at Ridley Road, there were many throughout the country who had been active in proselytising for Mosley, and even Hamm had not limited his radius to London. On 23 August he travelled up to Liverpool and opened his first meeting on a small platform in Islington Square. He was almost immediately bundled off by some young communists; the platform was smashed, and the pieces thrown at Hamm and his few supporters. The League's literature was next for the projectile treatment, and while the fascists were bombarded with their own materials an unsympathetic local audience hurled abuse. The lack of a police presence ensured this went on far longer than Hamm was used to. The League did not return to Liverpool.[3]

A more productive setting for League activity was Brighton, where it had gained a small foothold. Responsible for the League's presence in Brighton was one Leslie Jones, whose own organisation 'The Twentieth Century Socialist Group' was subsequently incorporated into the League.[4] Jones became the League's local officer and began holding his weekly meetings at the Level, a Brighton park and popular political meeting spot, under the League's banner. However, while Jones was able to create and maintain a small regional group he struggled to build up wider support among the local community. Nevertheless, the fascists remained confident that Brighton could be turned into a stronghold on the south coast.

Meanwhile, a fascist called John Webster had started holding weekly meetings in Bristol at Durdham Downs, an area of parkland popular with political speakers. Webster held his meetings under the aegis of the British Worker's Party for National Unity, affiliated with Victor Burgess's Union for British Freedom.

Webster was a wily operator. For his first meeting on 20 July 1947, he invited representatives of the local Communist Party to debate with him on the motion: 'That there is no case for discrimination against the Jewish race'.

The debate was held in front of an audience of 2,000, and when the motion was defeated, Webster must have felt like he had found fertile ground. The following week Webster spoke from his own platform before a far more hostile crowd, who pulled him from his platform. Also at Durdham Downs that day were AJEX, who held a successful counter-demonstration and subsequent weekly meetings at the same time as Webster's, and was usually able to attract mostly sympathetic audiences of as many as 2,000 people.[5]

Over in Derby a small and preposterously named organisation, The Order of the Sons of St. George, was in operation. This small group primarily worked like a book club, but one of its members began taking a platform out into the centre and holding public meetings. Tommy Moran was often regarded as the second most popular figure in British fascism after Mosley. An ex-coal miner and a Royal Navy boxing champion, he became a legendary figure amongst the fascists after newsreel of the Battle of Cable Street showed him flattening anti-fascists in a series of fist fights.[6] Moran's popularity among the fascists was clearly not shared with the people of Derby, and his solo efforts on the platform failed to result in any substantial following.

One of Mosley's regrets about his leadership of the BUF was that he had neglected to court support among the intelligentsia.[7] With such support Mosley believed he could properly articulate and sell his vision to the wider public, while at the same time his new organisation would be buoyed by gravitas and credibility. So, in an endeavour to ensure his new party would not have the same failing, alongside founding book clubs Mosley set about establishing 'Corporate Clubs' at Oxford and Cambridge.

The Oxford club was launched by a student called Desmond Stewart, after Mosley had visited Oxford to address a small number of ex-officer graduates where he encouraged them to seek out like-minded individuals among their university colleagues. Stewart ran the club out of his room at Trinity College. When his activities were discovered, a letter of protest signed by representatives of all the University's recognised political organisations appeared in the student magazine *Isis*, and the Club was forced to move to a private house.[8] Mosley was far more hands-on with the Corporate Clubs than he was with either the book clubs or larger organisations, and Stewart and his friends made frequent trips to Ramsbury where Mosley would expound his ideas and advise them on how to gain recruits and infiltrate the university.

Unfortunately for Mosley, the gravitas and credibility he hoped to gain from the Corporate Clubs were conspicuously lacking from the fascist cause, especially in west London. John Preen, the disciple who had failed so abysmally at the Albert Hall, had his sights set on this part of the capital, now mostly vacated by the League. In May 1947 Preen launched the Britons Action Party (BAP), and was joined by David Barrow who had abandoned Burgess and the UBF. Preen decided this time to announce his new organisation through standing in the elections for Paddington Borough Council. Standing against Preen for the Harrow Road Ward seat was a Jewish communist called Dan Cohen. During the campaign, not only were Cohen's meetings frequently disrupted, his car was overturned and he was physically assaulted. Even more disturbingly, Preen taught bands of children to chant 'Up with Preen, down with the Jews!' and had them march up and down the street during his meetings. After the campaign, in which Preen received 316 votes to Cohen's 211, both losing to the mainstream parties, he tried to sue Cohen for the libel of calling him a fascist, a case the magistrate dismissed as 'an idle piece of optimism'.[9]

Violence was less common at Victor Burgess's UBF meetings, which he began to hold regularly in July around west London; but they could still be very heated affairs. The 43 Group became a constant bugbear for Burgess and he often attacked them by name in his speeches. The Group did not however try to knock Burgess off his platform as often as they did Hamm. Instead they experimented with other tactics, and on 1 August 1947 held their own public meeting near Burgess's at Earl's Court. Both Flamberg and Bernerd spoke on the platform; but they must have decided they preferred their standard, more confrontational approach as the meeting was closed down and the majority of those in attendance headed over to heckle Burgess.[10]

For the most part the Group was content to heckle, jeer and goad Burgess, while selling copies of *On Guard*. Of course scuffles were not infrequent, and on one or two occasions attempts were made to knock Burgess off his platform, but the Group tended to be more cautious. At a September meeting in Notting Hill Gate, Burgess, showing his familiarity with the Group, made a comment about Joel and Sylvia Holder, a very committed young couple. In response Joel Holder charged at Burgess, shouting, 'I'm going to do him,' before his fellow Group members grabbed him and talked him down.[11] On another occasion a playwright called Benedict Ellis, who happened to be passing by, heard what Burgess was saying and was so incensed by his words he yelled 'These ***** Fascists!' and went straight for the platform, but was apprehended and arrested before he could reach it.[12]

The BAP continued to be active throughout the summer as well, but Preen had disappeared from sight and Barrow was mostly running the show. By this point he was a target of both the communists and the 43 Group, so it is impossible to say who it was who attacked him and three fellow BAP members outside Paddington Town Hall in September; however, just a few days earlier he had called out the 43 Group from his platform:[13]

I notice members of the 43 Group in my audience. I can tell you members of the 43 Group to take back to Mr Bernerd and the rest of them that by the time this year is out you will be a damn sight more sorry. Because we are going to chase the 43 Group from the streets of London . . . We will fly the Union Jack from all the street corners we want, and you won't see the Star of David flying again. This is our boast.[14]

It was a bullish tone, but one that accurately reflected the mood among the British fascists, for it had become an increasingly unguarded secret that Mosley was about to re-enter the fray.

The Alternative

When Trevor Grundy was a young boy, he was privileged to witness a most significant moment: Jeffrey Hamm informing his virulently fascist parents, with whom he had once lodged, that Oswald Mosley was about to return to public life.

My father returned with a bottle of whiskey and poured a substantial amount of the golden liquid into the three glasses. The adults stood up and raised their glasses, and I stood up pretending I had a glass in my right hand.

My father said, 'The Leader!' and we responded, 'The Leader!' I put my hand to my mouth and knocked it back.

It was a moment of great meaning and passion. I remember thinking that it must have been just like this when the disciples were together in the locked room, when crowns of fire settled on their heads and they went out and spoke in tongues to people who were amazed. But Jesus was dead and Mosley was still alive.[15]

Even without the ecstatic religiosity of a child's imagination, the fascists framed Mosley in a messianic light. When James Cotter first met Raven Thompson, the fascists' chief philosopher 'laid down a framework that seemed to prove Mosley alone had the answer to Britain's present difficulties'.[16] Raven Thompson had shared this truth at Book Clubs all over the country, and told of how Mosley was at that very moment writing a new tome in which he set out his glorious vision for the post-war world. That book, which Mosley began composing in the back of an old diary in February 1947, was *The Alternative*; its road to publication was plagued by obstacles.

Mosley's first new venture after the end of the war was the establishment of Mosley Publishing, based at his home in Ramsbury. Its first publication, in June 1946, was *My Answer*, a collection of essays including a scathing attack on 18B, and the seventh edition of 1938's *Tomorrow We Live*, the most comprehensive statement of his philosophy. This was put out through the Book Clubs, and was followed in November by the *Mosley Newsletter*, a monthly periodical that featured essays by Mosley and other fascist writers.

Publication of this literature had been fraught with difficulties. As printing and bookbinding were heavily unionised trades, it was near impossible for Mosley to find anyone willing to handle his output. On one occasion a master printer with fascist sympathies was found, but his men were resistant and had to be convinced by Mosley himself when he paid a visit to the printworks.[17] It did not take long for the print workers' union to find out, though, and it set about continually disrupting the production process. Mosley subsequently brought a case against the union for 'malicious interference with the business of his firm', but this was thrown out.

Seeking a more permanent solution for Mosley's problem, Raven Thompson and Victor Burgess began making enquiries into purchasing a printer. In March 1947 they learnt of one called the Merton Free Press that was for sale and sought Mosley's backing for the venture. This they received, on condition that they funded it themselves and went about the purchase with extreme caution, keeping it as secret as possible.

'Former Mosley Men Buying Printing Press' announced the *Daily Worker* on 28 March.[18] Mosley was furious. Burgess and Raven Thompson were left red-faced and forced to abandon their plans. This debacle, which the two men never lived down, was a product of the petty jealousies that forever dogged the fascist movement. In this case, worried that his influence with Mosley might diminish if Raven Thompson owned his own printers, it was Alf Flockhart who anonymously tipped off the *Worker*.[19]

A month later, Mosley's secretary was giving him a far more public headache. At a dance of the South Western Book Club, Flockhart said of Mosley's forthcoming *The Alternative*: 'As far as O.M. is concerned this is his last word . . . His political future depends on the reception this book has.' This caused quite the stir among Mosley's supporters, and Mosley was forced to deny that the sales of his forthcoming book were in any way connected to his political future.[20] It was hardly ideal timing for Mosley, who had come to realise that he was going to have to start writing *The Alternative* all over again, because it had a major problem: it was too nationalistic.

Here was the issue: fascism, wherever it emerged, had always had a fundamentally nationalistic quality that celebrated and argued for the dominance of the nation and the people from which it had sprung. However, Nazi expansionism had not only deliberately pushed out from national boundaries, but had also introduced an internationalist element – one that linked Aryans the world over, regardless of their nationality. For post-war fascist thinkers around the world, of whom Mosley was by far the most prominent, there was a need to adapt to this new internationalism. Mosley's answer was to expand the borders for his idealised fascist state 'from the nation to the continent' and unite those 'nearest to us in blood, tradition, mind and spirit'.[21] Mosley favoured creating an 'Idea of Kinship' among the people of Europe, who 'as a family of the same stock and kind . . . should have always been united in Ideal'. Into this European family Mosley also included 'kindred of our same kind in both Americas . . . Their spiritual life is also ultimately based on nearly three millennia of European History and Culture.'

By claiming history and culture as the unifying factor, over nation and language, Mosley and other post-war fascists sought to create a narrative of white Anglo-Saxon and European unity – a narrative that seemed to conveniently forget the perpetual disunity that had been the overriding character of Europe for the past two millennia. Instead, Mosley preferred to view Europe more monolithically, as a collective entity united against its enemies, with the apotheosis of those enemies arriving in the twentieth century as 'Asiatic' communism.

To fight this new threat Mosley proposed a united European state that he dubbed Europe-A-Nation,[22] for which he advocated the same corporatist and elitist principles he had proposed for Britain before the war. Also unchanged was Mosley's belief in the virtue of imperialism, and in *The Alternative* he argued that Britain and Europe's colonial assets should be expanded and exploited. If Europe was a Nation, then Africa should be her colony, its natural resources and riches sustaining the new European state.

Such ideas might have been appealing to race-obsessed fascists, but Mosley was not appealing to them alone; he also hoped non-fascists would read and be converted by his book. Mosley thus needed to articulate why Europe must come together to form Europe-A-Nation. To do that he had to explain why, without such an ambitious project, Europe would wither away and become an emaciated husk of its once glorious self.

For Mosley, with Europe a wasteland of rubble and ash in the wake of two world wars, radical action was needed if the continent was to sustain her global standing and resist being crushed between the United States and the Soviet Union. Only through the countries of Europe uniting and forming a bloc of their own would they be able to reassert their old dominance. Mosley saw economic collapse and subsequent privation as inevitable, and Europe's only hope was those few men who could save it from inevitable ruin at the hands of 'mob' and 'money', terms which Mosley used to describe the forces of speculative finance, decadent values, and communism. The Mosley faithful understood precisely which group of people was associated with these destructive causes.

Mosley, just like the more restrained fascist speakers, knew exactly how to keep reminding people that the Jews were always the enemy even without having to speak of them directly. Of course, writing about 'the Jewish question' in the post-war years was fraught with danger for anti-Semitic writers, who yearned for a Jew-free Europe but did not want to evoke the genocidal practices of the Nazis – at least not publicly. It was in this context that Mosley became a pioneer in the field of Holocaust revisionism, the practice of questioning and problematising the stated facts of the Nazi genocide.[23]

Mosley reminded his readers how in the 'last thirty years, the great countries . . . have accused each other of almost every crime in the calendar',[24] and then proceeded to list every crime of which the Allies had been accused. He then moved on to the Germans, who have 'been accused by a Court . . . at Nuremberg in terms too recent, familiar and voluminous to require, or permit, any repetition here';[25] Mosley then alluded to the scale of the killing. Is it legitimate, he asked,

> to enquire whether a man is any less a murderer if he has committed only half a dozen murders than if he has committed a thousand; once a crime has been committed the repetition appears more a matter of additional temptation, or opportunity, than a question of further immorality.[26]

Having dismissed the Nazis' crimes in such glib fashion, Mosley had to offer his own solution for the problem of Europe's Jews. In his 1938 polemic *Tomorrow We Live*, he had rejected the Jewish claim of a homeland in Palestine and suggested instead moving all Europe's Jews to Africa. By 1947 he had changed his tune slightly and, acknowledging the right of the Jews to live in Palestine, he suggested a partition of the region and Jerusalem under 'supra-national authority which will afford Christian, Arab and Jew impartial access to their Holy Sites'.[27] Although this proposal was virtually the same as the one the United Nations subsequently voted on, there was one substantive difference. Mosley recognised that even without enraging the local Arab population, Palestine could not play host to all Jewish people, and so he proposed Abyssinia (present-day Ethiopia) as a country in which the remainder of the Jewish population could be settled. Mosley supported a Jewish state only because he believed it had been proven quite impossible for Jews and Christians to live alongside each other without friction and disruption.

Mosley's anti-Semitism was catnip to the faithful, but the greater part of his book failed to live up to the hype. *The Alternative* was meant to lay out a roadmap to a glorious fascist future, but the central idea of Europe-A-Nation was a strange new concoction that failed to inspire Mosley's base. Although many fascists might have rooted for the Axis powers in the war, they were still patriots at heart; and while they might have felt strong fellowship for fellow whites around Europe, they still believed first and foremost in the greatness of Britain. Even devoted Mosley loyalists later conceded that 'Europe-A-Nation' never achieved 'quite the same zeal as the BU', and in 1950 Raven Thompson told Mosley it lacked a 'strong psychological appeal for the membership'.[28]

Not all fascists took against it – lifelong Mosley devotee Jeffrey Hamm was a fan – but on the whole Europe-A-Nation found its most enthusiastic readers on the continent. *The Alternative* became an influential work of pan-European fascism, with the German-language version outselling the English original.

Even if Europe-A-Nation did not inspire the fascist faithful, it was at least an idea that most could get their heads around. The same could not be said for Mosley's concept of the idealised fascist leader, which he called the 'Thought-Deed Man'.

He is the hope of the peoples and of the world. His form already emerges from this thought, in an idea which has derived from both theory and practice.[29]

The Thought-Deed Man was the type of fellow Mosley considered essential for the actualising and running of his European fascist utopia. Among the Thought-Deed Man's most important qualities was the will to achievement, which 'unites mind and will, and combines the executive and imaginative qualities'.[30] Fascist thought had always championed great men who they cast in the mould of Greek heroes, individuals who would not only lead with wisdom but who could shape the world to their will. The Thought-Deed Man was a philosopher, scientist and statesman combined, a man whose genius allowed him to see how the world should be, and then, through his prodigious will, make it so.

Mosley saw himself as just such a Thought-Deed man, as an individual who not only understood the world's problems, but also knew what must be done to put them right. What's more, he had both the ability and will to do so, even if it meant doing things that might seem cruel or unfair.[31] Still, he wasn't at liberty to say so aloud, hiding his self-aggrandisement in lofty drivel:

> This was the great vision of Goethe in the prophetic rapture of his Faust. The harmony of Greece – that sublime at oneness with self and nature, which needed no beyond the ecstasy of a genius for life-fulfilment – was married to the eternally aspiring and heaven-reaching Gothic of eternal dynamism, which can know no final fulfilment in the ever new becoming of ever higher forms.[32]

Satisfied with his work, Mosley put his lieutenants to work preparing the book for publication. Following a strike at the printers that had been contracted, Mosley employed a much smaller outfit he had previously worked with, but had to draft in some of his men, almost none of whom had printing experience, to help out.[33] A similar hands-on approach was necessary at the bookbinders, which the fascists had actually had to buy. Unsurprisingly the finished product, finally published on 1 October 1947, was a fairly shoddy affair, and Raven Books, the distribution company founded by Raven Thompson, had far fewer books than would be necessary to satisfy demand.

Still, Mosley was in good spirits, and the day after publication he told a meeting of the book clubs' secretaries that he considered *The Alternative* as the best book he had ever written. It was, he said, to be regarded as a text book, and although he did not expect everyone to understand it fully, the fundamental points could easily be extracted.[34] That said, he planned to give the work a couple of months to sink in and would then release a leaflet with a ten-point programme based on the book 'for the masses'.[35]

This was very much needed. For, whilst the presentation of the book might have disappointed, its actual content confused and alienated. 'It will leave some former friends as well as foes behind,'[36] wrote an early fascist reviewer. Very far behind, according *On Guard*'s J. M., who got it from his man on the inside that:

> Low foreheads are puckered and cauliflower ears are scratched perplexedly as Mosley's morons try in vain to digest their Leader's latest literary effort . . . As one of the Book Club leaders said as he sold a copy to an acquaintance of mine, 'You will not find it easy going, I'm afraid. In fact some of our members are making very heavy weather of it.'

The acquaintance in question was almost certainly James Cotter, who was quickly becoming one of the Group's most effective spies.

Under Cover

The day after one of the League's violent late August encounters with the Group at Ridley Road, Cotter and Kaye were at the weekly meeting of Modern Thought, where Allan Smith was addressing the club on the matter of Mosley's unwillingness to return to active politics.

> You cannot expect the 'Old Man' to stick his neck out again: he took one rabbit punch – he will only return again at the call of

the people! This is what we have to work for – to make the people Mosley-minded!

That, Cotter explained to the *On Guard* readership, 'was the broad outline of Fascist strategy at that time'. Mosley had to appear reluctant to come out of retirement and resume command, and would only do so 'at the request of separate individuals and organisations that were supposedly not already under his leadership'.[37] Cotter, however, was beginning to gain the trust of the fascist leadership who were confessing to him the truth of the matter. At a meeting in Hackney, Raven Thompson revealed to him that Mosley would be returning in November and gave him 'the low-down on why this particular time had been chosen', reminding Cotter of the previous winter's fuel crisis, the constant rationing and the situation in Palestine. 'Fascism thrives on such conditions, and, of course, Mosley saw a chance to get in at a time of difficulty and strain.'[38] Raven Thompson, not the only leading fascist to confide in Cotter, also told him of Mosley's imminent return, adding that this 'was considered "top secret" information and it was most gratifying that I should be trusted ... to such an extent by men in their position in the Fascist line-up.' It was Hamm, however, who gave the Irishman the most important detail:

> The actual date of his 'Leader's' come-back – November 15th. I felt pretty good, at last information that really mattered was coming my way. I knew the 43 Group would make good use of it; they did, too, and ... 'On Guard' carried one of its biggest scoops in its next issue.[39]

Under the headline 'MOSLEY DUE TO APPEAR IN NOVEMBER', the October issue of *On Guard* revealed detailed knowledge of the fascists' plans:

> From now, until Mosley reappears on the political scene, strict orders have been issued from his headquarters for the minimum

of hooliganism from, and notoriety for, his so-far unofficial supporters. After November – when Mosley has taken the salute of his once again united Blackshirts – the heavy artillery will open up, alarums and excursions, rowdyism and brutality will be the order of the day.[40]

The article must have raised suspicions that the Group had a mole among the fascists, but Cotter and Kaye were not suspected. Nevertheless, Kaye lived in constant dread of being found out, or being recognised by friends or family when she was out with the fascists. Cotter paid tribute to Kaye's steely personality and strong constitution as follows:

> That they never even began to suspect her of not being all she appeared was due in great measure to the iron control she kept over her feelings; never, even when most shocked and upset by the things she heard and witnessed, giving the slightest sign of being anything but one of the most virulent little anti-Semites in Mosley's ranks.[41]

The position of trust that Cotter had earned by late 1947 came at a very useful moment for the Group, as with winter approaching, the majority of the fascists' activities were moving behind closed doors. Moreover, with the coming of Mosley, seismic changes were occurring as the disciples prepared to merge all their organisations and Book Clubs into one large organisation, which Mosley would lead. This meant that fascists like Hamm, Burgess and Preen were no longer focusing on promoting their own organisations but on jostling for power to see who would be, as Cotter put it, 'the biggest boys around the Leader'.[42]

Preen, who had always been looked on derisively by the others, was again treated as a laughing stock when he brought a civil case against three Willesden councillors, but then failed to show up in court, and was fined £1,000 for legal costs. Meanwhile Hamm, who looked like he might be getting into trouble for his incendiary remarks at Ridley Road, had just been let off lightly by Blake Odgers. Not everyone was happy about this, however; Raven Thompson had rather hoped Hamm would go to prison and become a martyr for the cause.[43]

One fascist whose star was rising was Desmond Stewart of the Oxford Corporate Club, who on 23 October debated in favour of the motion 'This House Would Deplore the Introduction of Legislation to Curb Fascism' at the Oxford Union. His victory of 350 votes in favour to 178 against must have cheered Mosley, and outside the venue members of the Corporate Club, its ranks swollen by the arrival of some fascists up from London, sold copies of *The Alternative*.

Nonetheless the ambivalence surrounding Mosley's new tome had done little to dampen the sense of anticipation that surrounded his return. He had promised he would only come out of retirement when the time was right, so *ipso facto* when the fascists learnt their leader was coming back, they knew the optimum moment had been selected and their glory days were imminent. The 43 Group also saw Mosley's return as a critical turning point: if they could wreck the moment Mosley officially returned to public life, they could smother the fascists' dreams and render any movement stillborn.

Of course, the fascists were aware that Mosley's first public appearance in years would be a major target for their enemies, and they did everything they could to keep the details a secret. While the Group already knew the date of Mosley's return, they were clueless as to the location. The fascists were taking no risks. Only a select few of the most senior figures knew, and they were all, for once, tight-lipped; try as he might, Cotter could not discover the venue, nor find a way to steal or duplicate tickets.

Each member of a Book Club or neo-Fascist group was given an invitation to attend a 'Winter Sales Conference' at which Mosley was to speak. Each invitation was numbered and leaders of the various units were provided with a list of their members to whom tickets had been issued, together with the number of each ticket.[44]

As 15 November approached, the Group remained in the dark about the location, knowing only the sites of the various rendezvous points across the capital. Still confident that its spies would come through, they decided to mobilise the membership. Out went the postcards with the date of the 'Winter Sales Conference' and one other word, 'ARNOLD'. Decades later, this was the code word all the Group veterans remembered. ARNOLD, the sign for a major event. ARNOLD meant you were needed. Everyone was needed.

Needed for what, though? To sit around in the home of whoever had a phone, which more often than not meant sitting around in the house of some friend's parents. Scattered all over the city, groups of young men waited for the phones to ring with the location of where to go. Also on standby were all the Group's taxi drivers, requisitioned for the evening to help any members who needed to make a hasty getaway. Meanwhile, at 43 Group HQ, Bernerd, Wimborne and other leaders waited with a full complement of secretaries all staring at silent phones, hoping, praying, that James and Doris would come through. If things were tense for the waiting 43 Group, it was nothing in comparison to what Cotter and Kaye were going through.

Eighteen months later, Cotter shared in *On Guard* the events of that day and talked of the fascists' security arrangements, of the rendezvous points around the city, and of the prominent local fascist assigned to supervise them from his home, which served as temporary headquarters. Ticket-holders arrived at the rendezvous points and had their tickets checked by unit leaders, accompanied by a couple of heavies, who were constantly in contact with headquarters via public telephones. Cotter and Kaye had to navigate all this to get the whereabouts of the meeting to their 43 Group contact. It was decided that Cotter would head to Modern Thought slightly earlier than Kaye, in case there were any last-minute changes to the plans that had to be relayed to the Group. This was a prescient decision. When Cotter arrived at Smith's house at 2:30 p.m., Smith, who 'had a length of rubber tubing secured to his wrist', informed Cotter that all the rendezvous points had been changed following their publication in a newspaper. Fascist headquarters had been thrown into chaos and new locations had to be quickly found. This was a serious problem for Cotter, as the previously agreed point, the Chelsea Variety Palace, was where they were going to pass the location of the meeting onto their Group contact. Fortunately, with Doris still on the outside and scheduled to call, as long as Cotter could discreetly relay this information to her all should be well.

> In the midst of my panic the phone rang. Smith answered:
> 'Hello; who? Yes, he is here . . . hold on, Doris.'
> He handed me the receiver and said: 'Doris wants to speak to you; be careful what you say.'

With Smith listening closely, Cotter and Kaye began to play the parts of long-suffering boyfriend and clueless girlfriend who thought she had time for some last-minute shopping. Cotter explained the situation to Smith as if he had not been listening. 'She should not be penalised by being made to miss the Leader's meeting,' Smith said, and told Cotter to give her the new rendezvous point: South Kensington Underground Station.

With this information relayed to Doris, and from Doris hopefully on to her Group contact, Cotter was sent to the station as the bodyguard for J. C. Brampton, a former civil servant in his sixties who had been made rendezvous organiser. Brampton was, according to Cotter, a 'slight, short wisp of a man' who 'invariably carried a cane and wore a wide muffler,' and who 'seemed to possess a mania for joining as many of the Fascist organisations as possible'.[45] There was a reason for this: Brampton was the key spy for the Board of Deputies' Sidney Salomon,[46] meaning one spy was protecting another and neither had any idea of the other's true identity.

Brampton assigned Doris to the public telephone at the station, with instructions to answer it if it rang. Soon the Book

Club members began to arrive, and milled around the station waiting for instructions. Similar scenes were unfolding throughout the city including at the Angel, Islington where thirty or forty fascists were waiting for a local leader to turn up. When another gentleman joined them, they asked if he knew when X was coming. The man said he would make a call and find out. Five minutes later he was back. 'Well boys, I have made enquiries. X is not coming and the meeting is off. It's those Reds who published our plans in advance and messed the whole thing up.' Disappointed, they headed back to the station and made their way home, never suspecting that the man they took to be a fellow fascist was in fact a member of the 43 Group.[47]

Meanwhile, back at South Kensington station the members of Modern Thought had been joined by another group of fascists, many of whom Cotter and Kaye had never met. Among them was Hans Stauffer, ex-SS POW in London for denazification; he carried a personal invitation from Mosley. Accompanying Stauffer was League speaker Pipkin, who bumped into Cotter and Kaye at the top of the station's stairs.[48]

> Pipkin who had not seen Doris before, peered closely at her, then shot a question in German to Hans.
>
> '*Jüdin?*'
>
> There was dead silence all around . . .
>
> Stauffer stared curiously at Doris for what seemed like hours. Then he shook his head and smiled, '*Nein.*'

Pipkin was not satisfied, but things were beginning to move too quickly. Brampton called Smith at Modern Thought, who at last had the location.

> 'Memorial Hall, Farringdon Street.'
>
> I managed to scribble this address on a scrap of paper and passed it to Doris without being observed. Some minutes later we were shepherding the main body of the blackshirts to the booking office.

Going down to the platform a woman stopped Doris and asked her the way to Liverpool Street. She told her – and the woman went upstairs with the precious bit of paper stuck in the cuff of her coat.[49]

Memorial Hall

The phone rang. A rendezvous point was quickly selected, and the leaders charged out as the secretarial pool descended into a flurry of activity. Telephones began to ring all over London, and the gathered clusters of 43 Groupers leapt to their feet and bolted towards the nearest bus stop or Tube station. Few, however, would have known enough of the history of the BUF to spot the significance of the location. Memorial Hall was where Mosley had founded the BUF in 1932. It was ideal for momentous occasions, for it was an imposing beauty of a building constructed in the mid-nineteenth century in the Gothic Revival style; a grandiose setting perfect for Mosley's grandiose ambitions.

The fascists began arriving at the Hall around 4 p.m. in groups of six. Their tickets were checked first by a commissionaire outside the building and then again by a steward once inside.[50] There were also 'three fascist toughs patrolling outside,' wrote Cotter, 'with two other strong-arm boys on the steps and more in the lobby. At each turn of the stairs there were guards, some of them wearing black shirts, sweaters or ties' – with the return of Mosley, the old garb, hidden away for years, was making a comeback. Outside the venue, a deployment of ten policemen helped the fascists with security, and the rest of the area's force was waiting on standby at Snow Hill Police Station just around the corner.

By 5 p.m. the Hall was filled with 950 members of the faithful, belonging to active organisations such as the League, UBF, BAP, Corporate Clubs and the numerous Book Clubs. Also in the hall were all the ex-BUF people who had never joined one of the post-war organisations. The plan was for representatives of each of these groups to plead with Mosley to return to public life. But first, of course, the 'Leader' had to make his entrance. At 7 p.m. he emerged to a rapturous welcome, an entrance later described by Cotter in *On Guard*:

> When Mosley walked on to the platform the whole audience rose to its feet, gave the Hitler salute, and sieg heiled him for a full ten minutes.
> The hysteria died down and Mosley started to speak. Almost in the first few seconds he mentioned the 43 Group and boasted that they had not been able to find his meeting place.
> At that moment the familiar cry – 'Down with Fascism' – was heard from the street outside.[51]

The 43 Group had rendezvoused at the Express Building on Fleet Street, just around the corner, and Flamberg, Bernerd and Reg Morris devised a strategy as they waited for the rank and file to arrive. Monty Goldman, one of the Group's youngsters, was sent to scout out the venue and report back.[52] With Goldman's intel a plan was quickly made and 43ers set off in small groups, some walking straight down the main thoroughfare of Farringdon Street, others taking the side streets. Whatever the route, they had to ensure that they all appeared outside the Hall at roughly the same time, if they wanted to have any chance of busting in.

There is a discrepancy in the sources. Police records suggest that at the time of the Group's first attack there were only ten officers present, but most Group members recalled an entire cordon, which Flamberg, Lennie Rolnick wrote, approached with civility.

> He asked the police to cancel the Fascist meeting, which they refused to do. Gerry mustered all of us into a formation unit. He marched in front and led us forward with the purpose of breaking through the police and into the meeting, thus creating enough havoc to force the police to stop the meeting. The police

had drawn their truncheons. That was to our advantage, for they normally locked arms which made it difficult to penetrate their lines.[53]

By that point, Philip Evans recollected, fascists had started to appear at the massive ornate windows above. 'Some of us started shouting up at them and there were loads of police and we knew there were loads more around the back too. Eventually, again Gerry Flamberg said "GO GO GO" and those who were in the front ran toward the police cordon and suddenly things were flying out of the window: bricks, bottles, even broken chairs, they must have broken a couple of chairs and thrown them out the window at us.'[54]

An exodus of men and boys had deserted the hall to repel the invaders, while Mosley retreated to the wings along with his wife and mother and a number of other prominent ladies.

While some fascists took to pelting the Group from above, others sprinted down to the entrance hall planning to intercept any Group members who broke through the cordon. A few 43ers did and were met in the hall with an impressive staircase on which dozens of fascists were waiting. A few of the more foolhardy Group members ran up the stairs but were quickly grabbed and flung back down. No one was going to be throwing massive Reg Morris anywhere, however, and when he managed to get into the hall he broke all tackles and charged up to the massive bookcases that stood at the top of the stairs, heaved one off the wall, and sent it crashing onto the fascists below.[55] But Morris and the few others who had stormed the hall realised there were nowhere near enough of them to upset the meeting and they beat a hasty retreat out the building.

After a few minutes, the police reinforcements stationed around the corner had arrived, and they were able to force the Group back to the road's central reservation where the hundreds of Group members brought traffic to a standstill. With no chance of getting into the hall, the Group changed tactics; when

Flamberg seized a large projectile and hurled it at one of the windows, the others followed suit. Unfortunately, he was spotted and officers moved to arrest him.

This was dangerous: Flamberg had been bound over; if he was arrested there could be serious repercussions. The 43 Groupers jumped on the policeman who had hold of Flamberg and wrestled him out of the copper's clutches. Flamberg dived through the melee and escaped, and for some reason Len Sherman was arrested instead.[56] Like Flamberg, Philip Evansky was also currently bound over and so when he was grabbed by a police officer in the act of throwing a brick one of his comrades shouted, 'Come on we've got to get him out', deliberately avoiding using his name. Several boys jumped on the officer who had hold of Evansky, allowing him to escape. According to PC Wells, when he attempted to make an arrest he was picked up by ten or twelve men who proceeded to throw him between two stationary cars in the middle of the road.[57]

Farringdon Street was by now at a complete standstill, but the 43 Group's taxi drivers were waiting just up the road towards Ludgate Hill, and it was to them that Evansky, Flamberg and the other Group members who needed to make a quick getaway sprinted. The taxi drivers then whisked them back to HQ and safety.[58]

Within an hour the police had successfully dispersed the Group and order was restored. The fascists were not taking any chances, however, and all tickets were rechecked before the meeting recommenced. Mosley returned to the stage and spoke for an hour, lecturing his audience on many of the same economic and political themes with which he had thrilled them in *The Alternative*, in particular his idea of Europe-a-Nation.[59] After he concluded, Mosley asked for questions from the audience; this was the signal for the stage-managed moment where his supporters would plead with him to return to public life. Duke Pile, on behalf of the people of East London, was invited to 'ask his question' first. According to the *Mosley Newsletter*:

Amidst tumultuous applause, [Pile] opened the matter with an impassioned appeal for 'the greatest living Englishman' to resume his natural leadership, not only of the people of East London, but of England as a whole.

Other such 'questions' were asked in a similar vein with representatives of different areas, organisations and groups making their appeals. Mick Clarke spoke on behalf of 'the Old Guard, who had been waiting with deep feelings of frustration for this dramatic moment'. Hamm was one of the last to speak and he 'offered to merge the British League in a new movement under Mosley's leadership and to support the new movement in any capacity to which he was called'.[60]

As each fascist got up and offered their impassioned pleas to Mosley for his swift return, he nodded and looked pensive, as if this was all most unexpected and he would have to give serious consideration to these requests. Once Raven Thompson, the final speaker, had finished, Mosley returned to the microphone, thanked his supporters and, proving himself the master of the anti-climax, said he would need a few weeks to think about it. If, Mosley informed his congregation, a new party was to be formed, its name would most likely be the Union Movement (UM).

8

Behind Bars

The events at Memorial Hall kicked off a period when momentum was very much in the fascists' favour. Hamm's work at Ridley Road had put fascism on the ascendant and Mosley's return had bolstered his supporters' morale. Two weeks after his return appearance, Mosley addressed his first meeting in the East End since his internment, choosing for his location the Wilmot Street School in Bethnal Green. It was a most defendable location, benefitting not just from the high walls that surrounded the school but also the narrow street which led up to it, for this enabled the police to surround the school with two heavily manned cordons.

Such precautions were needed, as the anti-fascists turned up in their droves. The 43 Group and communists' numbers were swelled by members of the local population who were none too happy to see Mosley back in their midst. This coalition might not have been able to break through the police cordon, but they could provide a veritable gauntlet for any fascists entering or leaving the safe zone. Around 200 members of the fascist faithful did manage to make it through, most likely with a good deal of police assistance. Mosley himself arrived in his sports car, with bodyguards standing on the running boards to ensure that no one got anywhere near the Leader.[1]

As Mosley delivered his speech inside the hall he was forced to compete with the cacophony coming from outside. Taking a leaf out of the fascists' book, the 43 Group had turned up with a loudspeaker van of their own, with Captain David Rebak declaring on the megaphone: 'Mosley is doing today what Hitler did in 1933. We don't want a fascist Britain!' Rebak was subsequently arrested and bound over for 'using "a noisy instrument" for the purpose of calling persons together'.[2]

But this was merely the hors d'oeuvres, for while the police had just about managed to keep the two sides away from each other before the meeting, the afters proved a far more substantial challenge. As the fascists emerged from the school and left the safety of the cordon, the police struggled to keep the foes apart, and soon barbs and insults were giving way to scuffles and fights. For twenty minutes a full-on street battle raged, and officers from surrounding divisions were called in to help deal with the mayhem. Also deployed to the scene, rather bafflingly, were two fire engines, despite the complete absence of fire.[3]

Jackie Myerovitch was right in the middle of the fray when he head somewhere just behind him someone shout, 'You dirty Jew!' Myerovitch spun and saw a fascist couple walking away quickly. Myerovitch, full of the heat of battle, launched himself onto the man's back yelling, 'You fascist bastard!' and proceeded to pummel him. This was witnessed by PC Roberts who seized Myerovitch and tried to drag him off the fascist, at which point Myerovitch committed the cardinal sin: he struck Roberts on the forehead.

Myerovitch, realising what he had done, broke free of both Roberts and the fascist and legged it down the street, knowing that if he was caught he was for it. But another police officer had witnessed the transgression, and he and Roberts caught Myerovitch and tried to wrestle him to the ground. Myerovitch, realising he was done for anyway, kept fighting and gave Roberts a kick in the leg, before the two constables were joined by several others who helped to pin the big youth down for long enough to cuff him. They then picked Myerovitch up and carried him fifty yards to the nearby police station. Several Group members tried to intervene, including Lewis Lee, another twenty-year-old and a friend of Myerovitch's, who made several attempts to jump on the arresting officers' backs and was himself arrested and charged. Once the police got Myerovitch to the station, they carried him directly into the yard, where, while his colleagues continued to hold him, Roberts repeatedly punched Myerovitch in the face. Jackie was then charged and thrown into a cell. He was subsequently found guilty of assaulting a police officer and received a twenty-one-day jail sentence.[4]

Meanwhile, Mosley was extricated without a scratch and the next day he held a press conference where he publicly announced the coming of his new party. A hundred reporters and photographers crammed into a small, well-furnished drawing room in Pimlico were told by Mosley that the Union Movement would be formed 'early in the New Year'. As for the organisations it would replace, Mosley told those present that there were fifty-one such organisations and that all had 'offered to close down when the new movement is started'. Of course, the journalists in the room had far more interesting questions they wanted to press Mosley on.

On the matter of whether his party would accept Jewish members or candidates, Mosley responded that 'Jews would not make suitable candidates for us,' and that his movement was open 'to all parties but not Jews'. To a question concerning anti-Jewish legislation Mosley responded that he wished to put forward sensible solutions and believed that a Jewish homeland was necessary, even though Palestine could not hold all the world's Jews. 'Does that mean that you would get rid of the Jews out of this country?' someone asked. 'Jews who have not been a long time in Britain would certainly have to go,' Mosley responded. 'How long?' someone asked. 'If a Jew's family had been here for several generations it has to be considered,' Mosley replied. 'If, on the other hand, he has just come in and not got his roots here, he obviously must go.'[5]

Then the journalists began to ask for his thoughts on the Holocaust, and once again Mosley pioneered many of the arguments used by later Holocaust deniers and revisionists, suggesting that the ovens were most likely explained by typhus outbreaks within the camps, and adding: 'Buchenwald and Belsen are completely unproved . . . Pictorial evidence proves nothing at all. We have no impartial evidence.'[6]

Mosley's return was of course causing a stir and led to coverage in *The Times*, *Daily Worker*, *Guardian*, *Sunday Pictorial*, and *Daily Express*. The Wilmot Street meeting was even debated in Parliament, where MPs expressed fury at the comprehensive police protection that Mosley had received; ninety-seven policemen had been deployed to protect him. When Chuter Ede assured the House of Commons that no extra funds had been spent on guarding Mosley, Scottish Communist Labour MP Willie Gallacher made clear that that was not the point:

> Are you not aware that if this large body of police were not employed there would be no disturbance, as this man would not come out unless he was assured that a large body of police was at his disposal.[7]

Police presence was a key component to Mosley's successful launch of the Union Movement, but there was another that was just as important – venues. Since the war, fascist organisations had struggled to secure venues and when they were successful, offers were often rescinded. The Wilmot Street meeting had shown that schools could be effective venues, but the majority of these in the capital were controlled by the London County Council (LCC) which, in response to the UM meeting, debated whether or not they should permit the fascists to make any future use of their properties. With a strong Labour majority it seemed a given that the LCC would vote to ban the fascists from its buildings. However, in a shocking move that appalled Mosley's adversaries, they refused to do so, clearly sharing the views of a Labour Government so committed to re-establishing post-war democratic principles that they believed anyone who wished to exercise their rights to free speech should be guaranteed the protections of the state. This self-destructive liberalism was a major boon to Mosley, as it guaranteed him both police protection and a plethora of venues around London.[8]

One thing, however, that had not gone in Mosley's favour was the historic decision made in New York on 29 November. When the United Nations voted in favour of partitioning British Mandate Palestine and creating a Jewish state in the region, the fascists lost much of their momentum, and support dwindled over the coming years. Hamm and the League of Ex-Servicemen's success had reflected nationwide anti-Jewish feelings in large part born of the conflict between the Jews of Palestine and the British troops, which had also played a role in inspiring Mosley's return to politics. However, under partition the British and the region's Jews were no longer at war with each other and much anti-Jewish sentiment soon subsided, depriving the fascists of one of their most effective recruiting tools.

The Wrong End of a Revolver

'I think that the Mosley people were very frightened of the Jews when the 43 Group had been formed,' Trevor Grundy told an interviewer. When he was a child, Grundy was sometimes allowed into the pub with his parents after a fascist meeting, where they spent 'all their time talking about beating up Jews in the 1930s'.[9] Those were the glory days; now the fascists had to be on their guard.

> My father said that after a meeting that you couldn't be too careful because the Jews would be out in force and they had formed a vicious razor gang called the '43 Group. We had to watch out for them all the time.[10]

The fascist leadership were also beginning to realise the threat the Group posed. 'You know, if we don't find a way to finish off those bastards, they'll do for us,'[11] Raven Thompson was once reported to have said. At a dinner of the West Hampstead Book

Club, Mosley was reported to have boasted, 'The 43 Group couldn't find us; we've been able to meet in peace!' The fascists, it was clear, were running scared.[12] Mosley's followers would have happily snuffed the Group out of existence at any possible opportunity, but there was no more advantageous time to do it than the end of 1947. To be the man who orchestrated the downfall of the 43 Group and cleared the way for the UM's smooth launch would surely earn the Leader's gratitude and praise, and all but guarantee the choicest position in his new movement.

In December 1947, *On Guard* reported that the fascists had made a hit list at the top of which were Gerry Flamberg and Harry Bidney. The absence of Geoff Bernerd's name is easily explained; the previous month's *On Guard* had carried the news that Bernerd had resigned. A quote from Bernerd explained his decision as 'purely personal and due mainly to the fact that for many months I have been working at a pressure injurious to the state of my health and contrary to medical advice'.[13]

The strange thing is Geoffrey Bernerd did not resign. He remained in his position for another two years. As for the reasons behind this article I can only guess, as no other sources refer to Bernerd's resignation nor did any members recall it. When Bernerd became the Group's chairman he was also working for RKO Pictures, a position he held until his name appeared in the papers in conjunction with the 43 Group and his controversy-averse employers decided to fire him. In the wake of this decision the Group decided to hire Bernerd as its only full-time employee, a position he held until he did actually leave, at the end of 1949. Perhaps this occurred shortly after this announcement appeared, meaning Bernerd resigned his chairmanship and then resumed it in a very short space of time. Certainly, we know that *On Guard* had a small fascist readership who would have been delighted to hear that the Group had lost one of its key members.

Alongside the Group's leadership another obvious target for the fascists was its HQ at 54 Bayswater Road, in premises which had some serious security flaws. Facing Hyde Park in a mostly residential area, it was all too easy for the fascists to keep a constant watch on the comings and goings; sometimes they took photographs, often they noted down car licence plates.[14] Group members had been known to suggest going to beat up these surveillance teams, but this was expressly forbidden by Bernerd, who did not want to draw attention to the goings-on at HQ.[15] Of course Group members were reminded to always be on their guard and ensure their safety as they went back and forth from HQ, and those with cars were constantly reminded to never drive home if they thought they had a fascist tail, which was not an uncommon occurrence. A member called Alec Levitt one night drove around the Inner Circle of Regent's Park six times as he tried to escape a van full of fascists that was in hot pursuit.[16]

Not being on one's guard could have severe consequences. Frank Hiller, a Group stalwart, was very badly assaulted one night after he left HQ.[17] On another occasion two of the Group's younger members failed to spot the shadows following them as they left HQ and jumped on a bus home. They climbed up to the top deck of the almost empty bus and were immediately attacked in their seats by eight young fascists who had charged up after them. In the ensuing brawl the two 43ers managed to fight their way downstairs and tumbled out onto the pavement. The fascists, seeing that they had done enough damage, ran off towards Marble Arch, leaving the two boys to stagger back to HQ. From there they were driven immediately to the hospital where it was discovered they had between them, along with cuts and bruises, a concussion, a broken thumb and a fractured cheekbone. After this incident Bernerd put strict new security protocols in place: men had to leave in groups of at least three, and women had to be driven to the nearest safe Tube station or bus stop.[18]

The people at HQ were not the only targets in which the fascists were interested. In the summer of 1947, a man appeared at Group HQ claiming to be an inspector from Scotland Yard who had reason to believe that a fascist organisation was operating from the premises. According to *On Guard*, 'By a strange coincidence, no responsible member of the Group was present at the time of this call, and the caretaker refused to let him examine the contents of the filing cabinets.' The man failed to produce a search warrant and was forced to depart, and the caretaker reported the incident to Bernerd. Figuring that the police knew perfectly well who was operating from that address he called up Scotland Yard, who assured him that no such visit to their premises had been authorised.[19]

On Wednesday 17 December the fascists made another attempt to access the Group's files, this time choosing a much more direct approach. It was 11:30 p.m. when the doorbell rang and Miss T. Pollock, the elderly caretaker of the flats above the Group's offices, went to answer. Upon opening the door, she was confronted with the sight of three men with revolvers. One aimed his weapon straight at her while the other made for the Group's rooms and tried to open the locked door. The raiders demanded that Miss Pollock open the door, but she did not have the key. When a noise was heard from a flat upstairs the clearly jittery men were spooked and fled the scene empty-handed. During the raid someone had called the police, but by the time they arrived the men were long gone.[20]

Although the raid had completely failed, the executive decided changes had to be made. First, security arrangements were improved: HQ would have twenty-four-hour protection, with at least two shtarkers on the premises at all times and a spy-hole fitted on the doors. It was also decided to move all the Group's more valuable papers off-site to a location known only to a select few. But the executive also decided it was time to find a new headquarters, preferably one in the heart of London where the comings and goings around Group HQ would blend in amid the throng of people going about their daily business.

The next order of business was to find the men responsible for the raid. Erwin Shultz, formerly of the SS, was identified as the leader. Shultz, a tall, broad-shouldered man with a shock of thick black hair, had been brought to Britain as part of a denazification programme. The course failed to improve him, and he fell in with the fascists. Not long after the raid, three of the Group's shtarkers cornered Shultz. He reached into his breast pocket. Fearing he had a gun, one of the shtarkers pierced him through the shoulder with a bayonet, pinning him to a door.[21] Another discovery of the Group's, which *On Guard* shared with its readers, was that the raid had been planned 'at a certain establishment in the Paddington area'. John Preen was the only prominent fascist who operated from Paddington and in December 1947 he was clearly determined to deal the Group a crippling blow.

It was 10:40 p.m. on 22 December when Preen walked into the Harrow Road police station in a state of great agitation, and told the on-duty Inspector Rees that someone had just tried to shoot him from a car window. Preen told Rees that he had been in his own car at the time and had been able to take down the other's licence plate, which he had scrawled on one of his business cards. He handed the card to the inspector. The inspector then joined Preen outside and examined his car, a Wolseley 14 HP saloon which had 'a clean hole half an inch in diameter in the dead centre, two inches from the base, in the nearside front window'. Back at the station Preen gave his account of events, which began with Preen driving his car from his local pub, where he had just spent the evening with fellow members of the BAP, to his garage just around the corner.

As I was about to turn, the car which was behind me drew alongside me on the nearside. I heard a loud report and at the same time something swished by my face. The car then increased its speed, and I straightened from the turn and gave chase.

At one point Preen got just about close enough to the car that with his headlights he could make out its number plate, which he scribbled down. Then the car made a sharp turn and Preen was about to follow when two people stepped off the kerb, forcing Preen to pull up dead. 'By the time I had picked up speed I had lost sight of them.'

Preen did, however, catch sight of the driver who he recognised as 'a man who attends our open-air meetings'.

He is about 32 years of age, about 5'9", slim build, sallow complexion, hair dark, brushed straight back, long face with a rather pointed chin, nose of the Jewish type and he has a protruding lower lip. I should say he was a Jew.[22]

With Preen's statement taken, Detective Inspector Sercombe was sent for and when the senior officer arrived, the crime scene was visited. Torches were produced and for some five minutes a search was conducted. 'What's this?' Preen exclaimed, bending to the ground. Sercombe went over to inspect what Preen now held in his palm: it was a bullet cartridge case.

Meanwhile, enquiries had been made into the registration that Preen had taken down, and it transpired that the car was a rental currently under the name of a Mr Gerald Flamberg of 12 Meynell Road, Hackney. A visit was promptly made. Despite the smallness of the hour Flamberg was nowhere to be seen, although his parents were at home and asked most apprehensively about what their son had been up to this time. The Flambergs promised to have their son call Sercombe; a promise which was kept the following morning when Gerry telephoned the detective inspector and promised that he would appear at the station after a trip to the hospital – a scheduled check-up on his war wound.

Also making his way to a police station that day was Jonny Wimborne; he had agreed to speak with Detective Sergeant Barker of Paddington Station, who was investigating the raid on Group HQ. Most affable on the phone, Wimborne agreed to a 10 a.m. appointment, and so when an hour later Wimborne had not arrived, Barker was most perplexed. It turned out that Wimborne had made a rather unfortunate mix-up. Instead of going to Paddington Station he had gone to Harrow Road station, where Sercombe, who was still waiting for Flamberg, had not been idle.

An informative chat with a contact at Special Branch had led to Sercombe learning a good deal about Gerry Flamberg and his so-called '43 Group', and so when he saw another gentleman of Jewish appearance enter his station, he approached him and asked if he too was a member of this 43 Group. Wimborne said that he was and Sercombe asked about his movements the previous evening; Wimborne explained that he had spent the night with friends at the Bray House Club. Clearly, however, this answer did not satisfy Sercombe, who informed Barker when he called him at 11:30 that morning that it was no longer appropriate for him to talk to Wimborne, as he was now a person of interest in another case.

Flamberg duly arrived at 12:30 p.m. in the rented motorcar and presented himself to Sercombe, who asked if he could account for his and the car's whereabouts the previous evening. Flamberg said the car had been with him all evening and he had been to the cinema, then to 54 Bayswater Road, and finally to the Bray House Club from 10 p.m. until midnight. Having taken a witness statement, Sercombe and a Special Branch officer accompanied Wimborne and Flamberg to Bayswater Road where a thorough search for firearms and ammunition was conducted. All that was found was a weighted truncheon, explanations for which the Special Branch officer demanded from Flamberg. 'That's for protection,' said Gerry. 'You won't find any gun here, we don't go in for thuggery. Preen is only small fry, a small man in Fascism, we don't trouble about him, there's bigger men than him.'[23]

Nevertheless, Wimborne and Flamberg were taken back to the station for an identity parade with eleven other men. Preen was brought in. Almost immediately he identified Wimborne: 'This man here, that is one of them.' Then things got weird: Preen pointed to a man in a mackintosh who was of similar build to Flamberg. 'I am not quite sure of the one in the mack,' he said,

'the one who was in the back of the car.' However, he gave absolutely no indication that he recognised Flamberg, although he
would surely have known exactly who he was. After the ID
parade, Sercombe was escorting Preen through the yard to his
office when Preen stopped dead. The yard had a window that
looked into the charge room where Wimborne and Flamberg were
standing. 'There's the driver!' shouted Preen, pointing straight at
Flamberg. Sercombe charged both Flamberg and Wimborne
with attempted murder and had them locked up in a cell.[24]

The arrest of Flamberg and Wimborne rocked the Group and
rocked it hard. Flamberg had by now become a hero figure
within the Group, and Wimborne was a much-loved and pivotal
founding member. Their incarceration was a serious blow; a
guilty verdict would have devastated Group morale and handed
a major victory to the fascists. First, however, there was the
matter of bail and getting Flamberg and Wimborne out of police
custody by Christmas, something Sercombe strongly opposed
during the bail hearing. Magistrate Ivan Snell agreed with
Sercombe, but thanks to the work of Group lawyer Maurice
Melzack behind the scenes, a more senior judge granted their
release, and Wimborne and Flamberg avoided having to spend
the holidays in a prison cell. Even so, a dark cloud was now
hanging low over the 43 Group.

The Nuremberg Lawyer

The depth of feeling surrounding the case was on full display in
a Tube carriage on 9 January 1948. Flamberg's arrest and
upcoming trial were the main source of material for the fascist
speakers at Rushcroft Road in Brixton, and when Victor
Cestrelli of the British League loudly declaimed in a crowded
carriage that only British boys fought in the war, 'not people
like Flamberg who were running around with guns trying to
terrorise the British people today', he provoked Julie Sloggen
to launch herself at him. There were some dozen participants
in the ensuing set-to, an even split of men and women, Jews and

fascists, but when Cestrelli and his friend Coates brought the summons against Sloggen and her friends ten days later they were clearly unsure of who had actually been in the train carriage, and so went for one of the usual suspects.

The trouble was that Harry Bidney had five different witnesses to attest to his having spent the evening with his girlfriend, and the magistrate Mr Frampton ordered the fascists to pay his costs. Sloggen never denied her presence in the tube carriage, but insisted it was Cestrelli who caused the fracas. Mr Frampton however declared himself convinced that Sloggen was the prime mover in the incident, deliberately provoking Cestrelli who she knew to be bound over, fined her £3 and ordered her to pay the fascist's costs.

The 43 Group of course always covered these costs, but really the last thing the Group needed at this point was more legal expenses. Even though prominent barristers like John Platts Mills and D. N. Pritt were happy to work for the Group at knock-down rates, legal costs were still a huge drain. As a pamphlet published around this time explained:

> Legal expenses alone cost us thousands of pounds a year. The Group has already undertaken the financial burden of more than forty-five court cases, both defence and prosecution, and it is absolutely essential that the finest brains of the legal world should be employed.[25]

The Group might have been speaking figuratively in the pamphlet, but when Flamberg and Wimborne went on trial for attempted murder the Group were determined that no expense should be spared. In 1948 that meant hiring Sir David Maxwell-Fyfe, Churchill's former attorney general who had just returned from prosecuting Nazi war criminals at Nuremberg.[26] Maxwell-Fyfe agreed to take the case, providing of course the Group could meet his fees, and so a massive fundraising drive was launched to raise the money before the preliminary hearing. Fortunately, the Group had supporters who could make sizeable donations and it managed to raise the necessary £2,000 and retain Maxwell-Fyfe just in time.[27]

When Maxwell-Fyfe walked into Bow Street Magistrates' Court on Thursday, 15 January 1948, Magistrate Ivan Snell, who would never have expected to see so high-profile a lawyer in his court, was stunned.[28] What must have made Maxwell-Fyfe's presence even more unusual was that the day's purpose was merely to decide upon whether or not there was enough evidence for the case to go to trial, something which should hardly trouble a barrister of Maxwell-Fyfe's standing. But the preliminary nature of the proceedings made no difference to the 43 Group, who wanted Flamberg and Wimborne acquitted as soon as possible.

Opening the case for the prosecution was Mr Maurice Crump, who called two police officers and then Preen himself, to give his account of the events of 22 December. Maxwell-Fyfe cross-examined him, and asked Preen why, if the bullet went through the window, neither he nor his car were marked by flying glass. 'I do not know,' answered Preen. Similarly, wondered Maxwell-Fyfe, if the bullet had gone in one window and out the other it must have ended up in one of the houses just beyond, and yet no bullet was found. 'I cannot say,' answered Preen. 'I have had no experience of them.'

Maxwell-Fyfe then brought up a newspaper article in which Preen had described the shooter as having a 'sharp Jewish nose', before moving on to the strange way in which Preen had identified Flamberg. This led the defence barrister on to the matter of Preen's politics, and while Preen admitted he was the founder of the Britons Action Party he denied being anti-Semitic and claimed he only attacked 'certain sections of the Jews. People who condone the murdering of British troops in Palestine. We attack the Jews who are the secretaries of the communist parties in Great Britain.' 'Haven't you also attacked the organisation known as the 43 Group?' asked Maxwell-Fyfe. 'I don't know how you can attack them,' responded Preen with indignation. 'They more like attack us.'

Before closing Maxwell-Fyfe made sure to ask Preen about his involvement with the BUF, his detention under 18B, and his arrest for stealing documents from the home of a military officer. By the time he was done, Preen's credibility had taken a serious denting.

The prosecution then called a number of witnesses who testified to hearing a gunshot, but who could say no more than that. Then a police officer was questioned on the matter of the two men's alibis. Both Wimborne and Flamberg had testified that in the company of Stanley Marks, Murray Podro and two other Group members, Arthur Waterman and Gerald Lyons, they had driven from Bayswater Road to the Bray House Club, where they had spent the evening. What had most baffled police about this account was how six gentlemen could all fit in one rather small car; Flamberg, however, had previously demonstrated with the assistance of six police officers that this was in fact possible. All the car's occupants testified that they had indeed been with Flamberg and Wimborne at the Bray House, although the police found none of their signatures in the club's book for that night. This might be the most compelling evidence that Flamberg and Wimborne were in fact at the club, as it was on those nights when they planned misdeeds that they were careful to sign in.

The prosecution then made its most serious error. It called to the stand Robert Churchill, one of the country's foremost gun experts, who testified that the hole in the window was consistent with the bullet cartridge found. Beyond that, however, there was not much else he could offer, and during cross-examination Churchill admitted that the evidence from the scene was far easier to explain if the bullet had been shot when the driver's door was open than it was if it was closed. The clear implication was that not only had Preen faked the evidence, but he had done so incompetently.

Maxwell-Fyfe called no witnesses for the defence. Instead he laid out the paucity and inconsistencies of the prosecution's case, the unreliability of Preen as a witness, and the watertight alibis of Flamberg and Wimborne. Following this speech, Magistrate Snell weighed up whether or not to send the case to trial. He said that while there was a case against Flamberg and Wimborne it was entirely contained within Preen's testimony, and Preen had 'made a number of statements which I could not believe to be true. I feel bound to consider he is a witness I cannot trust under oath.' Snell duly dismissed the case.[29]

Lennie Rolnick was in the courtroom that day, and remembered the scene as he and other Group members accompanied Gerry and Jonny out onto the street.

> We were greeted by hundreds of well-wishers who had been unable to get into the packed court. There were handshakes and congratulatory slaps on the back for the defendants. We were all so excited that none of us gave the photographers, who were milling around, much thought.[30]

One of the snapped photographs was featured in the *Daily Worker* and showed Gerry and Jonny standing outside Bow Street, surrounded by their friends and fellow Group members. The shorter of the two, the moustachioed Wimborne, looks as if he is giving an instruction to the cameraman, but Gerry, like the other men in the photo, is positively beaming. He occupies the centre of the picture, standing at least half a head taller than anybody else, clearly the beating heart of the Group. Just behind Flamberg and Wimborne is Lennie Rolnick, his smile one of relief and joy, perfectly exemplifying the feelings of an organisation finally comforted by the knowledge that their leader was returning to the field.

But before Gerry could do so, he had to make a trip to the hospital for a stomach problem, and it was here that a reporter for the *Daily Express* interviewed him for an article which was the highlight of the following day's paper. The article, with a photo of the pyjamaed Flamberg sitting up in bed and beaming at someone out of frame, also featured a quote from Bernerd, who boasted about the Group's growth: 'We have so big a membership – including 500 women – that we have had to suspend recruiting; 230 people are waiting to join.'

Said Flamberg: "We'll have thousands – with everybody in the provinces too."[31]

There might have been a degree of hyperbole in this, but no incident throughout the Group's existence did more for its profile than the Preen case. The national coverage the Group received gave a huge boost to recruitment. Jonny Goodman, a trooper in the British forces in Palestine, first heard about the Group from the *Daily Express* article. Having seen how the British forces were targeting the Yishuv, Goodman, who had never before had a strong sense of his Jewish identity, felt very keenly that he wanted to do something for his people. A few months later when he was demobbed and back in London he sought out the Group.[32] The *Daily Express* article also caught the eye of some of Flamberg's non-Jewish former comrades in the paratroopers and fellow alumni of his POW camp, and several of them joined the Group.[33] It was in the wake of the Preen case that the Group reached its peak membership, which some have estimated at around 2,000 members.[34]

Letters to Murray

The start of 1948 saw a surge of new members, but it was also the beginning of the end for some of the Group's original core. All ex-servicemen, they had fought in the war and they had fought when they came home; not surprisingly, some were losing the energy to go on and were considering either stepping back or leaving the Group completely. Consequently it was towards the start of 1948 that Murray Podro, who had joined about a year earlier, was hanging around at 43 HQ when Geoff Bernerd walked out of his office and caught sight of him. Bernerd pointed at Podro and then at the office of the Head of Intelligence, saying 'You, in there, get on with it', and that, Podro later recalled, 'was it, there was no training or anything'.

The group's intelligence operation, which had been vital from the outset, was now pivotal. As Mosley began to sculpt his nascent UM from the fifty-plus smaller organisations, knowing his plans and every move in advance was essential if they were to be foiled. Fortunately, when Podro started there was already an incredibly effective network of spies in place who would communicate with him via letter, telephone and even the occasional face-to-face meeting in locations around central London. Podro then collated the information and passed on the relevant details to the executive, which then decided how to respond.

Podro took his role as head of intelligence incredibly seriously. He only began to talk even in the most general terms about his work towards the end of his life, and even then refused to divulge the identities of his agents. Which is not to say that Podro alone knew their identities, as most had been recruited by Bernerd. However, when Podro recruited and handled agents of his own, he never told even Bernerd who they were. He felt that sharing their identities with one other person was a risk just not worth taking.

Nevertheless, rumours later abounded about the Group's most successful spy, who Group members took to calling Ben. Tall, blond, blue-eyed, Ben was a perfect specimen of virile Aryan manhood; he also happened to be a Jew. A former army photographer, Ben had presented himself to Bernerd at Group HQ and expressed a desire to sign up. Bernerd took one look at him and immediately knew that he wanted him undercover.

It was in the months leading up to the founding of the UM that Ben infiltrated the fascists, first joining the League of Ex-Servicemen, and then moving with Hamm and his men to the UM when that organisation was finally founded. There Ben quickly developed a reputation as one of the UM's top stewards, standing firm against the onslaught of 43 Group heavies unaware the tall Aryan they were battering was one of their own. As a result of his renown Ben was put on Mosley's detail, and the Leader quickly took a shine to the handsome blond man whose obvious intelligence made him stand out from the other stewards. Instead of smelling a rat, Mosley most likely flattered himself that smart young men were being converted to his cause. Within a few months of going undercover, Ben was being invited to Mosley's Wiltshire home, where he sat in on many key meetings; before long he was one of Mosley's personal bodyguards.[35]

'He was the most genuine person you could ever meet,' said Podro with pride about his best spy, who as Mosley's bodyguard 'wore a black shirt and stood right in front of the speaking platform and had to take the many things that were thrown at them, and he stood it in very good stead I must say. He really put himself right in the forefront of it. We used to receive on a daily basis reports on what they were doing, on what they did, on who they met, and where they got their money from. The whole bit, he knew everything that was going on with them.'[36]

Ben's effectiveness meant Podro could later boast that 'if Mosley scratched his nose, I would know an hour later'. Ben's proximity to Mosley meant that he quickly became a far more important asset than Cotter and Kaye, who remained in the orbit of the 'mini-Mosleys'. They were still very useful spics, however, especially as they continued to meet and associate with some of Mosley's most influential and trusted supporters. One such supporter was Ken Woods, who invited them to his home for a 'very special' evening, but only let them in once they had given him a password at gunpoint.

Eventually satisfied, Woods put his gun away and asked us in . . . The living room and bedroom were crowded with Nazi emblems; swastika banners, SS daggers, pictures of Hitler, Goering and Mosley hung up on walls.

. . . Waving his gun in our faces, Woods confidentially explained that he was afraid the 43 Group would raid his flat, but he 'was prepared for them', and anyway his wife was an expert at Judo![37]

But it was not just associating with crazies that kept Cotter busy; he also found himself committing frequent acts of vandalism. Thanks to Kensington District Leader Turney, who had 'a weakness for whitewashing walls', Cotter became a prolific nocturnal painter of fascist symbols and slogans across West London. Doing so ensured Cotter maintained the fascists' trust, something that regularly paid dividends. For instance, on one occasion last-minute invitations for a secret meeting in a Kensington pub needed to be printed in a rush. Cotter and Kaye volunteered to do it.

> So the cards for the secret blackshirt meeting were printed by the 43 Group from the official membership roll of the Branch – and at one swoop we had the names and addresses of all the 'hush-hush' as well as open membership of the Kensington Branch of Union Movement. And to add to it, our stock went up with the fascists![38]

This was the last instalment of Cotter and Kaye's story that *On Guard* printed. We do not know what it was that led to the fascists finally suspecting them, but the Group decided to extract them and put them on a ship to Canada, where they remained for the rest of their lives. The first account of their time undercover appeared in October 1948, probably shortly after they had left Britain for good.

A collection of letters from spies removed by a member of the Group executive in its last days sheds some more light on the Group's intelligence operation. One infiltrator, who signs his letters Guy E. Churchill, writes to his contacts Mr Crambley and Mr Murray for clarification on what they want him to do. 'Do you want me to concentrate on getting information, or on "putting spanners in the works"?' He also tries to figure out what to do if a fight with the Group breaks out: 'I think the best thing for me to do would be to look as though I'm "piling in", and make sure the first blow I get brings me to the ground.'

The letters do not show Churchill providing the Group with any interesting material, but another spy codenamed Mustapha, with the name written in Hebrew characters, appears much more useful. He too was interested in the nitty-gritty of spycraft, in particular what could be billed to the Group, but also provides detailed descriptions of fascist meetings and life among the fascist foot soldiers, not apparently the most invigorating intellectual company. 'I'm not snobbish, and I know I'm not really exceptionally intelligent, but I have found it a difficulty in general to bridge a gap in (for want of a better phrase) "level of intelligence" when talking with U.M. members.'[39]

If this was a struggle for Mustapha then it must have been agony for one of the Group's most intellectually brilliant spies, a woman named Wendy Turner.[40] Wendy was not Jewish but was convinced to join by friends who knew that she was a staunch anti-fascist who had studied the rise of Nazism in Germany. Wendy followed their advice; aged twenty, she joined the Group and became an *On Guard* seller.

On occasion she dropped in at HQ where her blonde hair worn in pigtails immediately caught the attention of Geoff Bernerd, who also realised she was a ferociously intelligent individual. Lennie Rolnick had the same realisation the one and only time he met her at HQ. After introducing himself he quickly found himself discussing politics with her, something most Group members tried to avoid, knowing Bernerd's feelings on the subject. Wendy had always been deeply politicised, as she told Rolnick in a letter many years later: 'I started in politics when I was 11, in the Junior League of Nations, and from then on I was living about 6 different peoples' lives: studying; working; writing; initiating projects which might take 30 years to come to fruition.'

Following their encounter, Rolnick remarked to Bernerd that he thought the young woman was being wasted selling *On Guard*. 'She won't be with us much longer,' Bernerd cryptically responded.

Wendy was introduced to Podro and Harry Bidney and they began the process of infiltrating her into a fascist organisation; it did not take long before she was operating as another excellent asset. Initially finding work as a UM secretary, Wendy realised that for her to really know what was going on she had to exploit the womanising tendencies of fascists like Hamm and Burgess. She went from sleeping around to becoming Victor Burgess's mistress and living with him for a time. As for how a young, highly intelligent woman could stand to put herself through such an experience, Wendy recalled to Rolnick: 'I can only say that during the whole time I worked as closely as possible with and for the Jewish people.'[41]

Wendy's proximity to the fascist leadership meant she was often privy to secrets that she shared with Podro in long, beautifully written and frequently very funny letters. But letters were not her only means of communication, and both Podro and Bidney frequently met her at cafés and restaurants around town. Jules Konopinski recalled one incident when Wendy was due to meet the latter:

'One day she was supposed to meet Harry Bidney in Villiers Street at the Lyons Corner House on the Strand, and unfortunately for her as she was walking down Villiers Street to meet Harry she came across four [43 Group] women. One was Julie Sloggen, and the others were Rita, Helen, and another one, who were all the daughters of someone we called "Fruity Dave". These girls were like men; I'd seen them throw a man through a plate glass window at a furnishing shop in Brixton. They caught her in Villiers Street and they beat her to a pulp.'[42]

Soon after this incident Wendy disappeared, leaving no forwarding address, and for years nobody knew her whereabouts. Then in September 1978, a notice appeared in the classifieds section of The Jewish Chronicle, addressed to Geoffrey Bernerd, Murray Podro 'or other members of the 43 Group'. The message continued: 'Please write to Wendy Turner (Helen Winick) c/o Myrtle Ward Library, St. Augustine's Hospital, Chartham Down, Kent'.[43] St Augustine's was a mental asylum that had been much in the news two years earlier due to rampant malpractice. Following her notice, several Group members, visited her in hospital, including Lennie Rolnick and Harry Bidney. According to Konopinski, Bidney always blamed himself for her tragic fate. Rolnick followed his trip with a brief correspondence. In a letter dated 15 January 1979, Wendy compared her previous and full and active life to her present existence:

> Now for 7½ years penned inside a mile of corridors; surrounded by sick, twisted, deformed, insane people; doing nothing, going nowhere, only longing with every cell of my body and mind and spirit for death.[44]

For almost four more years Wendy maintained this state of non-existence at St Augustine's. On 28 December 1982 she put a plastic bag over her head and took her own life. Unfortunately, very little else is known of her life and so it is impossible to say for sure whether her commitment and suicide were caused solely by her time undercover. However, it is clear that this bright, vivacious young woman was deeply traumatised by her experiences and likely never recovered from them. According to Konopinski, Harold Bidney also never recovered from what happened to Wendy.

When I asked Murray about Wendy by name, the old intelligence head's dam of secrecy broke and he spoke of her with much fondness. Murray did everything in his power to protect his spies, but at the same time they understood the risks. When Murray spoke of Wendy in our conversations, he did not betray any sorrow about what became of her, but that does not mean she did not matter a great deal to him. During her time undercover she sent Murray over fifty letters and he kept and treasured all of them. They were a testament to the intelligence, wit and bravery of an exceptional woman; unfortunately Podro lost them in a flood. From the very little we know of her it is clear that Wendy Turner was a remarkable woman who sacrificed herself in the fight against fascism. It is fitting to end this chapter with Lennie Rolnick's words of tribute:

> I will never forget dear Wendy, who sought peace of mind in her own way. I believe that she deserved far more out of life than she received. She was a woman of virtue and had the deepest concern for others. We, who live on, can ill-afford to lose such a just and caring person. When I think of her, and I often do, I feel that I went with her . . . I often tell her story to friends and that helps me to keep her alive within me, because I would never want to forget that wonderful human being.[45]

9

Fun Days Out

Three months after Mosley first announced the Union Movement, it was finally launched. 'What had most delayed Mosley's planning', Morris Beckman claimed, 'was the severe curtailment of his indoor rallies by cancellations, the direct result of Group activity.'[1] Beckman was referring in particular to the Group's tactic of informing venues that the events of innocent organisations they had booked were in fact fascist meetings, information that almost always led to immediate cancellation. The flaw in Beckman's argument is that following the decision by the London County Council (LCC) to allow fascists use of their venues, this was not as problematic as Beckman suggests.

Whether Beckman was right and the cause of the delay was Group interference, or whether it had more to do with the inevitable fascist infighting that came from jostling for position within the new organisation, by February Mosley was finally able to launch. On 8 February fascists from all over the country made their way to the Wilfred Street LCC School in Victoria. The young Trevor Grundy was among them, travelling with his parents to the venue by a circuitous route which included rides in two different vans. Eventually they arrived at the school hall:

> Suddenly there were hundreds of people, most of them laughing,
> slapping one another on the back, and talking very loudly about
> 'Commies', 'Yids', 'the good old days' and the great days to
> come now that the Old Man, The Leader, was back.

. . . There were Union Jacks and several flags with flash and circles on them set against a blood-red background. My father said, 'It's unbelievable, Edna. At least a thousand people. Two thousand.'[2]

It was closer to three thousand, protected by the largest deployment of police officers sent to guard a fascist meeting yet.[3] The JDC had learnt of the meeting's location two days earlier and passed on the details to various anti-fascist organisations, but for some reason only AJEX tried to set up a counter-meeting, which the police forced them to hold a good distance away.[4] Why the 43 Group were absent is unclear; perhaps they knew just how substantial the police presence would be. Still, the three-foot-high painted letters on the outside of the school declaring, 'MOSLEY SPEAKS HERE. INSULT TO OUR CHILDREN', which had appeared that morning, might have had something to do with them.[5]

The question of the anti-fascists' absence did not bother those in the hall who were in high spirits and chanting at the top of their voices: 'Two-four-six-eight, who do we appreciate? M-O-S-L-E-Y! MOSLEY!' Alf Flockhart got up onto the stage and barked into the microphone: 'The Reds, the Reds, we gotta get rid of the Reds!' In response, from the back of the room people chorused, 'The Yids, the Yids. We gotta get rid of the Yids!' When they began singing an English version of the Nazi hymn 'Horst Wessel Lied', Grundy's mother began to cry. 'Several of the men around us raised their right arm. I had never seen my father look so stern. He made his left hand into a fist and placed it over the centre of his chest.'

Mosley's appearance in the hall was met with a thunderous roar that he acknowledged, 'almost bowing to his followers who were chanting, screaming, and yelling their souls out of their bodies'. When Mosley spoke it was to an audience in rapt, hushed silence, except for whenever he said the phrase 'International Jewish Finance', which triggered a bellow of approval. Going over all his usual themes and once again airing his dreams of a united Europe, Mosley spoke in an unnecessarily shouty manner. Shortly afterwards, eager that the people of east London should know of Mosley's return, the UM blasted out his speech at Ridley Road using one of its most effective assets, the Elephant.[6]

The Elephant was the second loudspeaker van acquired by the fascists. It was a big, black, converted armoured lorry, with huge speakers attached to the four corners of its roof. The two speakers on the front gave the impression that the lorry had massive ears, hence its nickname 'the Elephant'.[7] Other features of the Elephant included wire meshes in front of the windscreen to protect it from projectiles, and lights and a flagstaff on its roof, meaning it could serve as a portable, unsmashable, platform. Not only did the Elephant give the UM a serious advantage at public meetings, it also allowed them to broadcast Mosley's message even without a platform speaker. Shortly after the UM's launch the Elephant was sent on a tour of the provinces including South Wales, the Midlands and Manchester, where Mosley's belief that his opponents would not turn out to shout down a van playing a tape-recording of his voice was forcefully disproved. The Mancunian anti-fascists greeted the Elephant with catcalls and brickbats, forcing it to retreat from the streets, its message unplayed.[8]

It sometimes feels like the best way to describe the 43 Group is 'organised chaos'. While Geoff Bernerd and the executive very much guided and controlled the Group, the sections, cells and gangs of friends, as Martin Block put it, all 'had their own little things going on'.[9] The Group encouraged each branch to set up its own 'special section' for such activities. According to Beckman, 'If it was damaging to the Union Movement and not too madcap, the Executive would turn a blind eye to them.'[10] The hunt for the Elephant gives a perfect illustration of how poor communication could be throughout the Group.

Murray Podro regarded the Group's inability to discover where the UM kept the Elephant as one of its biggest intelligence failures; both Martin Block and Gerry Abrahams not only recalled the Elephant but also the attempts to destroy it.[11] Gerry Abrahams remembered that he was roped into a gang of eight, including Flamberg and Wimborne, sent to destroy the Elephant, which a spy learnt was being parked on a farm.

'We got to this vehicle and one of the boys tried to break the wheel with a pick axe, but it just bounced off, we hit it with a hammer and it didn't even make a dent, it was really well armoured steel. But while we were doing it a little window opened and someone called out 'WHAT ARE YOU DOING? HELP! HELP!' We had petrol and we were thinking of putting it up in smoke, but when we saw that someone was inside we realised we couldn't burn it, we couldn't do it with someone inside.'[12]

Martin Block's story is uncannily similar. He also found out where the Elephant was being parked and recruited Ivor Arbiter, his sidekick and best friend, to help him. 'Ivor Arbiter and I got a drill from our workshop and we were going to burn it. Ivor was drilling a hole where we thought the petrol tank was and the bloody window opened and we saw someone was sleeping in it, so I hit him over the head with the drill and we ran.'[13]

'He stole my story!' exclaimed Block when I told him I'd heard a similar anecdote from Abrahams. Maybe he did, but it is equally plausible that both incidents happened exactly as the two men said, and that news just never got around that the fascists usually had someone sleeping in the Elephant.

Although the section heads were able to plan and execute their own clandestine operations, the centre for the Group's cloak-and-dagger work was HQ, where Geoff Bernerd authorised the riskiest operations. Over time Bernerd came to rely on a select group of members who could be trusted to carry out such jobs.[14] Philip Evansky was one of them, and recalled the time he was sent with a small group to destroy an East End printers that Group intelligence had learnt produced fascist literature. 'We managed to break in to the printing press and we started breaking down the machinery. In those days the letters were loose in a box, there were boxes of them so one of our friends said to me, "Can we do something with these, shall we just take them out" and I said carry what you can. They were heavy, I only managed to carry four myself; we went outside and through the drains in the street we poured the letters down into the sewers and we smashed the place up. Then a couple of boys had it in mind that we should burn the place down, but a few of us disagreed – there were two lights burning and they might have been innocent people living there."[15]

Bernerd was also prepared to authorise sneak attacks on fascists themselves; sometimes as revenge, other times to disrupt their plans. When he learnt of a UM meeting at Speakers' Corner at which Burgess was meant to speak, Bernerd suggested to Lennie Rolnick that if they could convince Burgess not to appear it would be a blow to the fascists. A few days before the Hyde Park event Burgess was due at the Wanstead Community Centre, a much smaller event the Group had no interest in attacking; Rolnick decided that would be an excellent location for his chat with Burgess. Rolnick put together a team of six which included the Goldberg twins and another of the Group's most colourful characters, Barry Langford.

The son of a former circus strongman, Barry Langford was a natural entertainer who had spent the war years cheering up the troops as part of the Entertainments National Service Association. Living in Brighton but spending much of his time in London, the twenty-two-year-old Langford quickly developed a reputation in the Group as a 'completely barmy crackpot' and a 'total messhuganah'.[16] As well as being an immensely popular figure, Barry had another excellent quality, his father's van, which although usually full of silver (after leaving the circus Lou Langford became one of the city's most successful silver merchants), could fit in half a dozen people.

Langford drove the five other Group members to the community centre, where they waited for Burgess. When people began to emerge, Manny Levene, 'short and of no particular build', got out, put a cigarette in his mouth and on seeing Burgess approached him to ask for a light; confirmation to the boys in the van that this was their target. They all bundled out and went for Burgess, whose henchmen went for Manny with their coshes. 'He was dazed,' wrote Lennie Rolnick.

> I saw blood trickle from his head. As he fell to the ground a young woman ran over and kicked him in the head. Phil Goldberg and Barry took care of Burgess while Joe and I prevented the other Fascists from protecting him. The woman who had kicked Manny began to scream for the police . . . Joe said, 'I'll stop the woman screaming,' which he did by promptly sending her over a privet.

Police sirens wailed and Rolnick told everyone to make for the van. Refusing to leave the melee until everyone else had, Rolnick got caught by two fascists. Rolnick yelled at Langford to leave but he hesitated, and though Rolnick made it to the van's open doors, it was too late. The 43 Groupers were arrested and taken to a police station, where Rolnick told the officers he was in charge. He was then made to write a witness statement, which he did, but added that he had made it under duress. The police officer tore up the statement, 'stepped around the table and punched me with all his might in the stomach. He called me a "fucking Jew bastard".' Rolnick and the others were held for several hours before being thrown out without charge. The attack had definitely gone awry, but it had at least achieved its aim. Burgess was nowhere to be seen at the Hyde Park meeting, with 'prior engagements' cited.[17]

On two other occasions it was vengeance that inspired Bernerd to authorise attacks.[18] The first of these was triggered by an incident after a UM meeting at Ridley Road, when a group of fascists threw a middle-aged Jewish couple through the plate glass window of a shop. Four nights later, six Group members stalked four fascists through Hackney following a meeting in the area. Just before they reached the station, the fascists were grabbed and thrown through shop windows; one crawled out and was promptly thrown back in again. The next day, Bernerd called Raven Thompson and told him that for every Jew who went through a window, six UM members and ten officers of the party would follow. 'We know your movements, where you live and where you work and we'll get you one by one. You can bank on that,' Bernerd told him. The warning worked.

On the second occasion, the Group went after some 'slashers' – fascists who put razor blades in their caps and attacked individual Group members near meetings. Knowing that some of the most notorious slashers would be drinking in the Mitford Tavern just before a meeting, four Group members went in one of the Group taxis to a theatrical costume supplier in the West End. 'Not you again, lads,' the Jewish proprietor reportedly said. 'Take what you want. Don't sign for them. Bring them back in good condition. No charge. Now bugger off.'

Back in the cab the Group members changed into the borrowed costumes, and when the cab pulled up in front of the Mitford four police officers got out, and strode into the pub flashing their ID cards expertly reproduced by the Group's printers. The 'slashers' were found and told they were wanted for questioning at the police station, and led to the waiting cab. The choice of vehicle must have alerted the slashers to the fact that these coppers were not who they claimed to be; suspicions that were confirmed when they were taken not to the police station but into the middle of Hackney Downs where they were discovered around midnight, 'slumped against the ornate fountain, shadowed by the tall ring of stately poplars'. According to Beckman, they immediately quit the UM and 'word of their bloodied battered state spread among the unionists and unhinged them a little more'.[19]

There were, however, some aggressions that were not authorised by Bernerd, and these could have potentially dire consequences. On one evening, Ivor Arbiter, Martin Block's sidekick, and two other Group members drove around west London on the tail of a notorious fascist called Captain Hamer.

Cotter met him while undercover, describing him as 'well built and well dressed', with the 'florid complexion that goes with far-flung corners of the Empire' and sporting a 'fierce cavalry moustache'.[20] The 43 Groupers followed him for a while until Arbiter, spotting an opportune moment, jumped from the car and smashed Hamer on the back of a head with a wrench, before jumping back in the car and speeding off. Unfortunately, a witness had the presence of mind to take down the car's licence plate, and Arbiter and his friends were arrested and went on trial at the Old Bailey. Luckily for them two female Group members insisted that the boys had been with them in Hammersmith all night, and all three were acquitted.

Attacking someone with an iron bar in the middle of the street was not, in fact, the stupidest idea that Group members came up with. That award goes to the gang of enthusiastic youngsters who concocted a plan to kidnap Mosley and dump him naked in the middle of Piccadilly Circus. They had got so far as staking out Mosley's Dolphin Square flat before Bernerd caught wind of what they were up to and strictly forbade them to execute their plan.[21] Another idea that occasionally got floated around was assassination, and one member of the East End section was not joking when he said if someone gave him a gun he would shoot Mosley himself.

Bernerd and the executive had a strong sense of what the Group could and could not get away with. Street fights and vandalism were fine, assassination and arson not so much. To be allowed to function, the Group had not only to avoid getting into serious trouble with the authorities, but also remain an organisation that wealthy supporters in the Jewish community could continue to back without discomfort.

To Panton Street

In the past we have had to fight two enemies. One Fascism and the other, the Jew without the courage of his own convictions, who says, 'It can't happen here.'

A glance at our Aims and Objectives will show you that WE of the 43 Group do not intend to let 'it happen here'. We are peace-loving citizens, who love our peace so much that we give up our leisure hours and lend our good name to the movement, and your presence here proves to us that you are on our side and for that I offer my sincerest thanks.

So wrote Jack Myers, the chairman of the Group's social committee, in the programme for the 43 Group's Premier Ball, held on 28 February 1948 at Grosvenor House in Park Lane. The ball, with music from the Joe Loss Orchestra, the Oscar Rabin Band with Harry Davis, and Don Carlos and His Rumba Band, was primarily a fundraising affair. Although Group members were welcome, the aim was to attract wealthy community members and their chequebooks. Flicking through the programme these potential benefactors would have seen not only Myer's welcoming message, with its heavy implication that not siding with and funding the Group implied one was a Jew 'without the courage of his own convictions', but also 100 messages of support and best wishes. These messages, which came from a wide array of individuals and businesses, including Marks and Spencer, demonstrated that not only had support for the Group in the Jewish community flourished but its improving reputation meant that many were prepared to offer public support.[22]

The Group's executive also invited their wealthiest benefactors to private affairs where more direct entreaties could be made to the liberalities of their wallets. One evening Bernerd invited Beckman and three other Group members to a small dinner, held in the private room of an expensive restaurant. Also present were twenty of the Group's wealthier backers who ordered the finest things off the menu. Knowing full well who was footing the bill, the Group members, who sat at their own table in the corner, ordered the same.

During the meal Bernerd announced he had something he wanted the gathered men to hear, and played for them a recording of Oswald Mosley. It was obviously a recording obtained in secret as this was Mosley unfiltered, with the most appalling anti-Semitic epithets and invective pouring from his mouth. Once it was done, Bernerd addressed the men and told them that this was the sort of hate they were up against; by the end of the night around £20,000 had been pledged. Decades later, Beckman asked Bernerd how he had managed to get hold of the recording. He hadn't, revealed Bernerd. That wasn't Mosley on the recording. It was actually Sydney Tafler, a Jewish star of stage and screen and supporter of the 43 Group, doing an uncannily accurate impersonation of Mosley.

In March 1948 a new expense for which the Group had to raise funds was the rent for its new central London headquarters. Located on Panton Street, a side street that lies behind Leicester Square, the Group's comings and goings around HQ blended in with the hustle and bustle of central London life, as did the couple of men the Group now always had stationed outside HQ. Standing outside the building, chatting and smoking, they ensured that everyone who came into HQ was 'kosher': spying fascists could be swiftly moved along, with any minor commotion disappearing into the normal comings and goings of the street. Panton Street's location had one other excellent advantage: being right in the middle of town it was much closer to all the tea houses, restaurants, dance halls and clubs that Group members frequented and it was also just a hop, skip and a jump away from the Group's favourite haunt and alibi spot, the Bray House Club.

Seeking to make their new HQ as secure as possible, Martin Block had a couple of his builder friends install a 'great big steel panel inside the bottom door, with a sliding thing so we could see who was outside'. Anyone who was allowed in then entered into a narrow hallway with a horrible flight of stairs that led up to the ramshackle and dreary premises on the first floor.[23] There they would find a few offices, which included some larger rooms suitable for the various committees to meet, and a few smaller rooms for those like Podro and Bernerd who needed to conduct their business in secret; there was also plenty of space for the secretarial pool. As no room was set aside for socialising, the entire HQ became the social space. 'Panton Street was the social centre,' recalled Gerry Lewis, a young *On Guard* reporter who spent lots of time there. 'People came in, they smoked, they hung out, it was a hanging-out place. Stuff must have been happening at the same time, but God knows what it was.'[24]

Another major change that befell the Group in 1948 was that it went from being a purely London-centric organisation to a national organisation. This was a consequence not of the Group's efforts to set up regional branches but of ex-serviceman in other cities wishing to emulate or affiliate with the Group. For example, in Newcastle a Jewish ex-serviceman called Geoffrey Rossman had set up an organisation called the Anti-Defamation Group, but following a trip to Group HQ in 1948 he decided to turn his organisation into a branch of the 43 Group. The Newcastle branch had around 100 members, even though there was hardly any fascist activity in that city.[25] Meanwhile, the Manchester Union of Jewish Ex-Servicemen (MUJEX) was so much more in line with the 43 Group's approach than with AJEX's that it decided to unofficially affiliate with the Group and sent delegates to the Group's AGMs, while Group leaders frequently went to Manchester to give speeches to MUJEX members. A large regional branch of the Group was also set up in Leeds, and smaller branches were set up in numerous other cities. The Group would also receive petitions from local residents of areas in which they had no presence, asking them to come and drive the fascists out.[26]

The Group's expansion came at the right moment, as for the first time it was up against a truly nationwide fascist organisation. Having brought together fifty-plus different organisations and book groups, the UM had branches all over the country and in the spring of 1948 it went on the road. Speakers such as Hamm and Raven Thompson spoke at popular meeting places around the country and all members of local branches were instructed to turn out, help sell the UM's new paper *Union*, and lend their vocal support to the speakers. Where the Group had a local presence or allies they were relied upon to supply most of the opposition. Anti-fascists turned up to meetings in Sheffield, where Hamm was given short shrift in front of city hall, Derby and Nottingham, where fights between fascists and anti-fascists broke out. Meanwhile in Manchester MUJEX began selling *On Guard* near the regular UM pitch on Market Street. On one occasion the two sides came to blows, and six fascists and three anti-fascists ended up in court; the UM subsequently abandoned the pitch.[27]

In those areas where the Group had no regional presence they did have another asse – former comrades who were only too happy to reunite with their old brothers-in-arms to fight fascism once again. When the Group learnt that the UM was planning a big meeting in Newport, South Wales, Len Sherman volunteered to go there and reach out to his old comrades in the Welsh Guards. On the day of the march the fascists arrived at the forecourt of the Newport train station and were setting up their procession when a troop of massive Welshmen turned up. One of them approached Raven Thompson, who was leading the march, and offered him a choice of leaving the town 'vertically, on your feet, or horizontally'.[28] The fascists weighed up their chances and decided to beat a retreat.

Meanwhile, to the anti-fascists and spectators of the London street meetings, the advent of the UM meant almost nothing. The speakers were the same, the stewards the same, the message was mostly the same, and, having inherited the pitches from the organisations it had consumed, the times and locations of the meetings were the same. Only Hampstead saw any marked difference, with a boost in activity; on 29 February weekly meetings recommenced at Whitestone Pond, and there were five arrests to mark the occasion. In subsequent weeks UM speakers in Hampstead trialled a new tactic, of limiting their own hateful rhetoric while placing throughout the crowd fascists who were instructed to shout anti-Semitic remarks in order to give the impression that the audience was deeply anti-Jewish.[29]

Over in Dalston things pretty much picked up where they left off, with the UM preceding its first meeting in the area on Sunday 7 March with a three-day special drive of meetings throughout the East End. Of course, come Sunday and Ridley Road had been jumped by the communists, forcing the UM to set up on John Campbell Road. The meeting began around 6:30 p.m. and for the first hour the turnout was pretty dismal, with those few in attendance hugging the walls in a vain attempt to avoid the downpour. Raven Thompson mounted the platform at 7:25 p.m. By this time the rain had stopped, and he invited everyone to come closer; a crowd of around 200 gathered to listen to him fairly peacefully.

This was not to last for long, as five minutes later Group member Gerald Jacobs began heckling: 'What about the Isle of Man?' This was obviously the key phrase, as moments later four groups comprised of eight to ten 43 Groupers appeared at different ends of the street, yelling 'Down with Fascism'. As one they charged towards the platform, easily cutting through the small crowd; only speedy police intervention saved Raven Thompson from being smashed off the platform. Fighting followed, and the police made numerous arrests before closing the meeting.

Seven Group members were detained, including Gerald Jacobs and Jules Konopinski. At Dalston Police Station they were found to be carrying between them an assorted range of weapons including light bulbs, razors, a piece of iron encased in rubber, a radio valve, and even a horseshoe. On 10 May the seven men came up for trial at Bow Street Magistrates' Court, in front of Learned Recorder Sir Gerald Dodson. Four of them were found guilty on counts of threatening behaviour, assaults on police and possession of weapons, and were fined small amounts. Jacobs, identified as the ringleader and instigator, was found guilty of unlawful assembly and fined £20. Jules Konopinski and one other boy had the good fortune to be acquitted; however, before dismissing them, Dodson had some words of advice.

Do not attempt to right what you think are wrongs or grievances by taking things into your own hands. The law will take care of that. You may not like fascists, whatever they may be, or their meetings, but leave the law to look after them.[30]

But the notion of leaving the fascists up to the law was anathema to the 43 Group, especially as the law seemed completely unwilling to actually do anything about them. At least that was the case until the spring of 1948, when Chuter Ede finally realised that steps had to be taken and it was well past time to rain on Mosley's parade.

May Day

In the spring of 1948 Mosley was making plans to speak outdoors for the first time since his return, an event that naturally required a good deal of stage management to ensure the proper levels of pomp, circumstance and sense of occasion. No day would be more suitable for Mosley's return than May Day, and no location made more sense than Ridley Road. However, in 1948 May Day fell on Saturday, a market day, meaning Ridley Road was not an option. Nevertheless Mosley still wished to hold the meeting in Dalston, and so Hertford Road, a long side road half a mile to the south of Ridley Road, was selected in its stead. The meeting was to be held at 3:30 p.m and then the men and women of the Union Movement would form a procession and march west, via Mosley's wartime home of Holloway Prison, to Camden Town, where a second meeting would be held. As such a procession required substantial police protection, official permission had to be sought. It was here that Mosley's plans hit a major snag.

On 29 April Chuter Ede informed the Cabinet of Mosley's intentions, and of the police commissioner's request to temporarily prohibit processions in east London under the Public Order Act. The Cabinet agreed with Ede to implement the ban, which he announced with immediate effect, thereby stopping

Mosley from marching. This was a major blow to the UM, but it was far too late in the day to relocate the meeting, which had been advertised throughout east London.

In the small hours of May Day morning, the Elephant trundled on to Hertford Street. On the off-chance that a bleary-eyed resident, woken by the massive vehicle's arrival, had no idea what was about to occur, the hoarding on the lorry's side would have left them in no doubt: 'MOSLEY SPEAKS!' The Elephant parked right in the middle of the street, and a convoy of cars stopped behind it, out of which emerged UM stewards, dressed in suits or in high-collared black raincoats zipped up to their chins. Smoking and chatting quietly, they stood guard through the night.

In the grey and miserable May Day morning, more stewards began to arrive and help set up. The microphone on top of the Elephant was rigged up and checked and the various flags and banners of the UM were brought out and held aloft. The Union Jack was displayed beside the new banner of the Union Movement, which had exactly the same lightning flash and circle design as the BUF's old flag.[31] Signs saying 'Union or Chaos' and 'Communism Means War' were also brought out and held aloft. Joining the UM's 150 stewards was a sizeable party of G Division's finest, who, as the day wore on, were found not only on Hertford Road but throughout the entire area. Adding a further buffer between Mosley and anyone who might wish to attack him were the few hundred Mosley loyalists and UM members who arrived many hours before the meeting was due to begin. They ensured not only further protection for the platform but also that the sounds which would ring loudest in Mosley's ears were cheers and applause.

Around 11 a.m. Hertford Road began to fill with anti-fascists, journalists, photographers, and those hoping for a good punch-up. By midday, tides of Dalston locals were streaming into Hertford Road hoping to get a glimpse of Mosley. As the crowd built, so did the tension and the police had their work cut out keeping the peace and putting an end to the scuffles between the fascists and anti-fascists; a few arrests were made. By 1 p.m. Hertford Road was full to the brim, so the police formed cordons preventing anyone else getting into the road. Those unlucky enough to miss the main attraction were entertained by the many communist speakers who had set up platforms in the surrounding streets.

Eventually the meeting started with the usual bunch of support acts: Hargreaves, Pile, Moran and Raven Thompson were each allotted ten minutes to strut their stuff and play the old favourites. It was during the warm-up acts that things began to kick off, and the police moved to push the vast majority of the crowd out of the road, before reinforcing the cordon at either end with a strong mounted contingent. Only about 400 people were left in Hertford Road, the majority Mosley supporters, but a number of 43 Group members and other anti-fascists also remained. At 3 p.m. the roar of a motorcycle cavalcade was heard signalling Mosley's arrival. As he and Lady Mosley emerged from the green saloon car they were greeted with a storm of cheers and a roar of 'Sieg Heils'. Mosley climbed onto the Elephant's roof and allowed his small audience to gaze upon him.[32]

A photograph taken of Mosley speaking atop the Elephant that day depicts a man deep into middle age, wearing not the striking black shirt and trousers of his pre-war years, but a dark, conservative, three-piece suit. Gone too, it seems, are his famous Hitler-like gesticulations: instead, with one knee casually bent, he points his right hand straight ahead of him as he holds his left behind his back, as if casually giving directions to tourists. But according to *On Guard*, there was another, far more startling, change:

> Gone was the arrogant swashbuckler of the old, blackshirt days.
> In his place stood a middle-aged weary civilian, puffy of cheek
> and eye, drooping of shoulder. Gone too was the fiery orator
> who inflamed passions and swayed vast audiences. Instead, we

heard dull, often incomprehensible, rantings and a rambling discourse, lacking inspiration and even conviction.[33]

In the photograph the almost entirely male crowd that surrounds him also seems fairly placid, and Beckman recalled that 'no one heckled him, even his opponents were keen to hear what he had to say', at least at first. Soon Mosley's less than mesmerising performance drew heckles, which the stewards attempted to violently quell. The police did not step in and scuffles broke out. Beckman for the most part recalled a desultory affair:

> Group members sensed an underlying resignation in Mosley's subdued manner. They were far from impressed, and it was noticed that even some of his old cronies from the heyday of the Thirties were looking unhappy at his performance. The outbursts of 'Sieg Heils' and 'Hail Mosleys' were ragged, half hearted. It was like fresh milk turning sour as you watched.[34]

Outside of Hertford Road things were much more lively and much more dangerous, as mounted police tried to control the thousands of people that were squeezed into the neighbouring roads. The situation was getting out of hand and the police were not responding well. *On Guard* reported the particularly horrendous incident of a mounted policeman almost running down an old woman with no obvious connection to proceedings; she was saved only by the intervention of a man who grabbed the horse's reins and managed to pull it around. He was immediately arrested.

After rambling on for forty minutes on all his usual themes, Mosley began winding up and informed the audience of the home secretary's ban and the change in plans this had necessitated. He told his listeners that Ede's ban covered only east London, and so they were still able to march on part of the planned route. His followers therefore should make their way west to Highbury Corner, where the procession would form up for the march to Camden.

With the meeting over, the police relaxed the cordons and much of the crowd began trickling down the various parallel roads that led to Highbury Corner. Had Mosley been allowed to march the entire way the police would have only had one route to steward; now they had up to five, and it was all the boys in blue could do to keep the two sides apart. Scuffles and fights broke out all along the route, and even when the police were able to form an effective barrier between the fascists walking in the middle of the road and the anti-fascists on the pavement, there was little they could do to stop the barrage of rotting fruit that the 43 Group began hurling at the Mosleyites.[35] It was a dejected bunch of increasingly assailed fascists who headed west, and besides it was beginning to rain.

Around 1,000 people arrived at Highbury Corner, evenly split between fascists and anti-fascists. With the two sides squeezed together in one small area it was like a pressure cooker, and only the vast police presence that was keeping the antagonists apart allowed the fascists to form up and begin their procession. This too was accompanied by a massive police presence which included motor-cyclists, police cars and mounted police. Holloway Road, which formed the first leg of the march, was completely closed with cordons placed along the pavements protecting the marchers from their foes and from hostile locals. By this point the rain was bucketing down. *On Guard* described the scene:

> In contrast to the uniformed constabulary, Mosley's followers made an even poorer showing than they might have done if marching alone. The Fascists in the march were a motley and pathetic crew. Dressed for the most part in an odd half-uniform of black shirts or dyed battle-dress blouses, black sweaters or black ties; out of step the whole way, notwithstanding the efforts of the drum and fife band at their head.[36]

A decision was made against marching all the way to Camden Town, and Mosley agreed to end proceedings outside Holloway

Prison. It was thought that an inspection by Mosley of his men outside his wartime home was an apt way to finish, but this failed to take into account their condition following several hours of scrapping with the 43 Group. Sodden, bruised, bloody, many with clothes ripped or stained with rotten fruit, the UM stalwarts were hardly an impressive sight. Still, outside the prison they lined up and tried to make themselves as presentable as possible. Mosley's inspection was perfunctory; he returned salutes, but was careful to ignore any Sieg Heils that were forthcoming, while also endeavouring to evade all the rotting fruit the 43 Group were continuing to chuck at him from behind the police cordon.[37] Then he was back in the warmth of the car with Diana Mosley and speeding away from the city, the scene of such a shambolic return to the streets.

Once Mosley had departed, the police cordon, which had mostly done its job in keeping the 43 Group at bay, began to slacken, and the Group charged full pelt at their fascist foes. It was not a large contingent, however, and the police were just about able to rein them in. Then the familiar roar of 'Down with Fascism!' was heard as a stampede of Group members, who had been lying in wait at Camden Town, came charging towards Holloway; all hell broke loose. Jules Konopinski was right in the middle of the fighting and found himself in an incredibly precarious situation. Being charged at by mounted police, Konopinski and his friends sprinted away but realised they were heading towards a house with a massive drop next to it. 'We were either going to jump or get run down by a police horse,' Jules told me. 'But then Reggie Morris turned and hit the police horse straight on the nose; the horse went down on its haunches, and our lives were saved.'[38]

Even for an old hand like Konopinski the violence that day was intense, but for Jonny Goodman, who had only just joined the Group, it was a baptism of fire: 'I found myself with two other guys, cut off from everywhere, some people were running away, and the whole thing was chaos. I was jammed in a doorway with these two guys with about thirty or forty guys coming at us, with bottles and that, and I can tell you that I wasn't Sylvester Stallone, I crapped myself. The guy with me had a bit more going on in his brain, picked up a milk bottle, hit the first guy and he fell back into the others. But just at that moment through this heaving mass of humanity came blue, so the police grabbed me and the other two guys and threw us into a van; still petrifying because outside the mob were now rocking the van trying to overturn it.'

Goodman was taken to the police station, where more chaos reigned. Eventually they let him go, but he was told to turn up at court on Monday morning. First, however, there was another nerve-wracking confrontation, as the fascists 'were hanging out on street corners trying to pick off people as they came out the police station'.[39] Although twenty-seven Group members were arrested on May Day – a number far higher than any Sunday during the Battle of Ridley Road – it was a clear victory for the Group and a disaster for Mosley. To make matters even worse for the UM, five days after the march Chuter Ede announced a three-month ban on all political marches in the capital, thus depriving the UM of their major recruiting tool.

On 11 May, Goodman came before Magistrate Herbert Malone, along with Arnold Leigh and Harold Joseph, the two Group members with whom he was arrested. All three were bound over by the magistrate, who during proceedings informed the court that he had recently received a death threat from the 43 Group.[40] This was vehemently denied by the Group, claiming the letter was a forgery; even the JDC reckoned the Group was not stupid enough to threaten a magistrate.

The Battle of the Level

The week after May Day, at the regular Sunday morning meeting at Hereford Street, the speaker was talking about Palestine, which, with the partition about to come to an end, was very much on everyone's mind. 'Well, the mandate ends on May 15,' yelled Harry Bidney from the audience. 'You have nothing to talk about after that!'

'I demand the police arrest this Jew Bidney!' shouted the speaker in splenetic response. The call was taken up by the fascists in the crowd. 'Is Bidney immune from the law?' someone shouted. Realising he was in a somewhat precarious situation, Bidney retreated towards the back of the crowd, where he was jumped by a man named Arthur Sheppard. They fought, the police intervened and wrestled Sheppard off Bidney. Sheppard was arrested while Bidney managed to disappear back into the crowd, but a few minutes later, as he tried to get away from the crowd again, another fascist called James Smith launched himself at him. A crowd encircled the men as they duked it out before the police could intervene and arrest them both.[41]

'Only six days left to live!' Smith taunted Bidney as the two men squared up to each other. This was an unmistakable reference to the Arab armies that were preparing to attack the new State of Israel, the moment the British Mandate officially came to an end. It was a situation that was very much on the Jewish community's mind, for it was presumed that the new state stood little chance of surviving. To that end recruiters for the new Israeli army, with Major Weiser chief among them, sought out young Jews who would be willing to go to Palestine and help give the Yishuv a fighting chance.

As an organisation filled with fit and fearless young Jews, the 43 Group had a wealth of men that could be sent to fight, and the Group permitted recruiters to come and speak to its members. Particularly enticed by the idea of going to fight for a Jewish homeland were those younger men who had not fought in the Second World War and believed they had a duty to fight for their people and their new homeland. The volunteering Group members were sent to be interviewed and have their health checked by the Jewish Agency, which had secretly set up at a Marks and Spencer in town; all those who were approved were told to stand by until the Agency was ready to get them out the country.[42] For young men raring to go this delay might have felt frustrating, but it did at least mean they would still be in England to witness the 43 Group's greatest victory.

Chuter Ede's three-month ban on political marches in the capital forced the UM to change its tactics. Mosley, who condemned the ban as 'the end of real free speech', proposed a new method of 'permeation'. By this he meant UM members should join organisations like athletic clubs and pre-existing political parties, and try and take them over.[43] The UM were not completely willing to abandon old methods, though, and since the ban on marching only applied to the capital they decided to look to the provinces.

While several towns and cities had large Jewish populations, in Brighton there was also a determined UM organiser, Leslie Jones, who had successfully developed a UM cell, upon which the fascists believed they could build.

It was from David Spector that the Group first learned of the UM's plan for a march in Brighton on 5 June. Spector had been one of AJEX's most senior leaders, but had grown very disillusioned with that organisation's strict policy of non-violence. He felt increasing sympathy with the Group's methods, and so when he caught wind of the UM's plans to march in his home town of Brighton it was to the Group that he reached out. It was agreed that Spector would rally all the area's Jewish ex-servicemen, and would coordinate the counter-demonstration. The Group would send down from London as many people as Spector needed.

Meanwhile, Barry Langford, one of the few Brighton-based Group members, told his father about the march. Lou Langford was a prominent member of the Brighton community and on excellent terms with the head of the Brighton police, with whom he spoke about the UM's plans for the procession. The police chief told Langford that his hands were tied: the law required him to give the march adequate protection. Of course, how many officers constituted adequate protection was entirely at his discretion.

The day before the meeting, the Group's field commanders came down to Brighton where they were briefed by Spector in his temporary HQ set up at the back of a shop. Based on intelligence shared with him by the Group, Spector told the gathering that several hundred UM members would be travelling down to Brighton the following morning. Their plan was to march from the train station, along the seafront and up to the Level, a central park area which was Brighton's equivalent to Speakers' Corner. There, Leslie Jones and his Brighton chapter would be waiting to greet the march and all would come together for a meeting that would be addressed by Hamm and Raven Thompson; Mosley would not be in attendance. Spector then laid out his suggestions for a response. After the briefing had concluded, the 43 Group leaders went out and had a lovely day by the seaside.

Next morning, somewhere between 150 and 300 people from both sides boarded trains or clambered into their cars and headed south. One 43 Group member remembered driving down in a large open van owned by the Lipman brothers, who were both professional wrestlers, when they saw that the van behind them was full of fascists. 'Shall we make it here? Or shall we go on?' asked one of the brothers, neither of whom were among the Group's intellectuals. 'We'll carry on,' someone responded, 'we'll deal with it when we have to.' The brother drove on but made the others uneasy as he kept saying, 'What a place to kill 'em! What a place to kill 'em!' 'We're not here to kill,' someone corrected him. 'We're here to maim.'[44]

Upon arrival the 43 Groupers were posted along the march route, while the fascists headed for the train station, outside of which they formed up their procession.

The march was led by a troupe of five drummers, one of whom was Erwin Shultz, the ex-SS officer rumoured to have participated in the raid on the Group's HQ. Behind the drummers walked the UM's flag-bearers, followed by Hamm, Raven Thompson and other UM leaders. Then came the foot soldiers who marched smartly in rows of four; the Elephant brought up the rear. This was a set-up very similar to May Day, but there was one major difference. On May Day the UM were surrounded by police officers, but in Brighton there were hardly any police at all.

The march set off and at first progressed without incident, even though the local onlookers were palpably hostile. It was not long before the heckling began. As the march came to the sea and turned to walk along the seafront the first projectiles were thrown. Whether this was planned or just the pebbles of Brighton's beach calling out to be hurled is unclear, but throughout their promenade along the seafront the UM endured a constant barrage of stones and rocks.

Eventually the fascists reached the corner that took them away from the beach and up to the Level, and it was there that the 43 Group attacked. Charging right into the middle of the procession the anti-fascists split it in half and all hell broke loose, as they were joined not only by their ex-servicemen allies but also by Brighton locals, including a number of pensioners who went at the fascists with their walking sticks.

Those at the front of the march escaped the first wave of attacks and hurried towards the Level. There, Jones and his Brighton branch were proudly waiting, albeit restlessly as the procession was running late. When news came of events at the seafront, Jones and his pals abandoned the Level and ran full pelt towards the carnage.

The march had by now completely fallen apart and all-out battle was raging, stretching from the Level down to the seafront and into the many side streets and alleyways of Brighton. The fighting lasted for well over an hour, and while those policemen who were there did try to stop it, they had no desire to make any arrests. 'An inspector got me by the back of my coat, took me off,' recalled Gerry Abrahams. 'I thought I was going into the van, but he took me to the end of the Common, he smiled and let go, and I went back again.'[45] Len Shipton, a Jewish lad who lived in Brighton, turned up in the middle of the fight and witnessed the tumult:

It was quite a sight, because there were all these fascists with flags and drums being attacked and barracked by a big crowd of anti-fascists with only a handful of coppers trying to keep them apart. I'd no sooner taken this in, when another load of blokes rushed out of the park and there was a massive punch-up. There was fighting all over the place with a lot of people charging backwards and forwards across the Level and the streets.[46]

The fighting was fierce and there was only one clear winner. 'We pulverised them,' recalled the Group member who had been driven down by the Lipman brothers. 'We cut them into two groups; we went down to the first part for the leaders to be hacked and then we cut them in the middle, so they didn't know where they were and they just had to run. And the Lipman brothers, I saw them crack heads like nothing.'[47] There were weapons in abundance, coshes, knives, razor-blades, knuckle-dusters, projectiles flying everywhere; someone even grabbed an abandoned peanut barrow and started whacking the Elephant with it. When Leslie Jones appeared on the top of the lorry and went for the microphone, he was met with a volley of projectiles and went plummeting to the ground. Jones was not only the UM leader who got roughed up; several Group members cornered Hamm, who ended up in hospital with a broken jaw.

A few Group members were also hospitalised, including Jules Konopinski who was stalking the Elephant when he saw and went for 'a guy there looking about five foot tall by five foot wide, with a big roll-neck sweater, no neck, bald head, flat nose, and all of a sudden he hit me, he knocked me stark out and broke my nose . . . My whole face was wrecked, I had to have it rebuilt after that.'

What made this incident particularly absurd was that the man later apologised to Konopinski, for this was no UM heavy but the one-time circus strongman, Lou Langford.[48]

Eventually police reinforcements arrived, separated the two sides, put an end to the fighting, and herded the now bloodied and bruised fascists back towards their vehicles. One of the fascists' vans accidentally reversed into the crowd and almost ran down a policeman who had to cling on to the van's side to avoid injury. Furious at their defeat, local fascists were out causing a nuisance well into the night, starting a brawl at a local dance hall and roaming about the streets looking for anyone with whom they could pick a fight.[49]

Being one of the few times the 43 Group were really able to rout the fascists, the Battle of the Level, as it became known, stood shining in the memories of so many Group members. That afternoon and evening, while some returned to London, others enjoyed a fine day out by the sea, basking in the warm glow of victory. Of course many of them were bloodied and filthy, so it was fortunate that a couple of people had hired rooms at a local hotel; around fifty Group members squeezed in as they waited their turn for a nice hot bath.[50]

10

Things Fall Apart

The Battle of the Level was the beginning of the end for Mosley's Union Movement and the post-war fascist revival. Although the party stuttered on for a few more years, various factors in the late 1940s, other than the 43 Group, contributed to its failure to capitalise on the success of Hamm's League and the hype surrounding Mosley's return. These factors included the slow improvement in the lives of the people of Britain as the worst impositions of austerity and rationing began to subside, and the end of the British Mandate in Palestine, which meant the Jewish community there was no longer at war with Britain. But if 1948 lowered the curtain on one fascist recrudescence, it raised it on the next.

On 21 June 1948, 802 migrants from the Caribbean disembarked the *Empire Windrush* at Tilsbury in Essex. They had come to Britain to pursue work opportunities following the 1948 British Nationality Act, which gave UK citizenship to all members of its colonies. This was the beginning of mass migration to Britain, and the birth of a diverse multicultural and multi-ethnic nation. For the far right it meant the arrival of fresh new targets, ones which found it far harder to blend in than the Jews did.

By a strange twist of fate, one of the first areas the West Indian migrants began moving into was also the home of one of the country's most notorious racists, and Jeffrey Hamm's hounding of the new immigrants began almost immediately after their arrival.[1] For a couple of years such attacks were rare and sporadic, but in 1951, when immigration from the colonies really got going, the UM launched its campaign against 'the coloured invasion'² and switched the focus of its efforts from the Jews to the 'coloureds'. In 1958 Hamm was one of the most vitriolic instigators of the Notting Hill Race Riots. By that time the 43 Group were long gone, but in the 1960s, as racial tensions escalated further and new fascist and racist organisations appeared on the scene, the 43 Group's successor organisation rose up to meet them.

Jules Konopinski would be one of the founding members of that successor organisation, but in the summer of 1948 he had no idea if he would even be alive at the end of the year. Jules was one of the 43 Groupers who had been accepted by the Jewish Agency to go and defend the new Jewish state. 'Son, go do your duty,' replied Vidal Sassoon's mum when he told her he was going to fight; she fully understood the impact that fighting fascism alongside Jewish ex-servicemen had had on her son, who believed it was now his turn to step up to the line for his people.

'We left London one at a time,' recalled Sassoon, 'as we were aware we were being watched by the British authorities, who knew we were going to Israel and took a dim view of it.' Sassoon went first to Paris, where he was thoroughly vetted, and then to a displaced persons camp in Marseilles where he waited to be transported to Israel. There he met survivors of the concentration camps, which further convinced him of the importance of his mission. He remained in the Marseilles camp for five weeks before he and Jules got a place on the same plane to Israel, and to war, where Vidal joined the Palmach.³

Another 43 Grouper who went to fight in Israel was Nat Cashman. Almost all the 43 Groupers who went to the Holy Land had been too young to serve in the War; Cashman, who served in the RAF, was the exception. Short, and with a high-pitched voice, Cashman's appearance was deceptive; he was a very good boxer and one of the Group's toughest fighters. During the Battle of Jerusalem against Glubb Pasha's Arab

Legion, Cashman became the only member to lose their life during the Group's existence; his death was a devastating loss.[4]

Some of the Right Boys

The day after battle in Brighton was a Sunday, and back in the capital the UM's Hereford Street platform was up as normal. For the most part the meeting was pretty quiet, even though there were seventy or so 43 Groupers in a crowd of 350 that seemed mostly sympathetic to the platform. Things took a turn when Hargreaves began speaking and described how the previous day in Brighton the UM had been greeted by 'all the filth and sweepings of the ghettoes . . . of Europe'. The Group members began to boo and jeer and the two sides verbally re-fought the previous day's battle as Hargreaves tried to spin the defeat.

> We did not quite anticipate that the 43 Group had so much at stake in Brighton. Of course it has been known for a long time that Brighton belonged to people other than the British. There are very few places in England not claimed by these opponents of ours . . . They are all very arrogant in Brighton but the time will come when they won't be so arrogant because there won't be a Brighton for them to live in.[5]

It is fair to say that few if any political parties have come to power promising the destruction of a popular seaside resort. Brighton had the UM reeling.

A couple of weeks later the Group learnt that the UM was planning a recruitment meeting in Romford, Essex, a town and area that had mostly escaped their attention. On 19 June a small squadron of Group members, including Lennie Rolnick, Jerry Kaffin, Manny Levene, Harry Kaufman and Wolfe Wayne, went east to the new battlefront.[6] Having sent out the young Harry Kaufman to scout out the meetings, where the fascists had fifty or sixty men surrounding the Elephant, they assessed that though it was an unfamiliar area the UM set-up seemed fairly standard and they could proceed as normal.[7] They entered the road where the meeting was being held and went straight for the platform. This proved significantly easier than usual as not only was the crowd quite small, but the Group members met almost no resistance from the UM contingent and before they knew it, they were right by the Elephant. One minute they were surrounded by all their old friends from the UM and the next they were standing in front of the lorry, alone, with all the fascists diving away.

Whack! Whack! Whack! Blunt heavy objects began to rain down on the Group members. They looked at the ground. Potatoes. For some reason the fascists had decided to pelt them with potatoes. And then the blood started running into their eyes, their faces were cut. If any of the Group had been able to look down now they would have seen what Lennie Rolnick called 'potatoes with a difference, and that difference was that razor blades had been inserted into them':

> If you did not see them coming they could inflict serious damage. Those who raised their arms to parry the flying missiles would realise, too late, that they were being cut about their arms, faces and necks. The word got around quickly, and we were instructed to make a hasty retreat and, not to mince words, we did a runner.[8]

Most were able to regroup some distance away and patch themselves up before heading back to London, but Jerry Kaffin, his face badly slashed, got separated from the rest and found himself lost in an unfamiliar town. Fortunately he was rescued by a Jewish dentist who bandaged him up and drove him back to London.[9]

'Brighton Revenged' proclaimed the *Union* article on the Romford incident.[10] At Ridley Road, Duke Pile gloated:

Englishmen, Irishmen, Scotsmen and Welshmen, yesterday we
went to Romford and when we got to Romford some of the right
boys were there and you have never seen anybody run so fast as
those '43 Group' ran at Romford yesterday.[11]

Ironically, the 'right boys' were not British at all, but a Maltese
gang run by Joseph Marguerat, aka Maltese Joe, a Soho pimp
and nightclub owner. This was a significant development, as
never before had the UM associated with known gangsters. It
was clear that so strong was the fascists' desire for vengeance
that they were willing to turn to the underworld for help. The
evening after Romford, the Group's executive chewed on this
intelligence and considered whether it was finally time to swal-
low their pride and accept, in their turn, the help of one of
London's most prominent gangsters.

Jack 'Spot' Comer was a bookmaker, racketeer and club owner
who was the product of one of the Jewish ghettos of White-
chapel. Spot liked to portray himself as the defender of the
Jewish community – he claimed, for instance, that his nickname
referred not to the mole on his left cheek but to the fact that he
was always on the spot to help his people out when there was
trouble. He also frequently bragged of his fascist-bashing antics
at Cable Street, a doubtful claim as the Jewish community and
fascists hardly came into contact that day.

Spot's boasts about being the protector of his community
belied the opposite. 'Jack Spot was a ponce who preyed upon the
Jewish community,' recalled Jules Konopinski. 'He went round
the East End for protection money, and if you didn't have it you
got a smack in the teeth. He was bloody out for himself.'[12] There
have been suggestions that Spot was one of the main financiers
of the 43 Group, but this seems very unlikely. Beckman recalled
the evening Spot with 'three large men, well-dressed in raglan
coats and trilbies, came into HQ and demanded to see "the
guvnor".' 'Now listen,' Spot told Bernerd, 'if you ever need
money or the help of my lads, let me know.'[13] Bernerd thanked
him but declined the offer, knowing full well the dangers of

accepting assistance from a man like Spot. It was therefore a mark of how shaken the Group were by Romford that when Lennie Rolnick suggested reaching out to Spot, and volunteered to seek him out, the executive gave its approval.

Rolnick, who often frequented the same drinking clubs as some of the gangsters, made enquiries and discovered that Spot had plans to go to Ginny's, a club in Soho. Rolnick arrived early, ordered a scotch from Ginny and waited. 'It wasn't long before "The Firm" arrived.' The Firm, as Rolnick put it, included Jack Spot and a number of his known associates including Hymie Jacobs and Tony Schneider, two gangsters who had made a name for themselves beating up Blackshirts in the BUF days.[14] Also accompanying Spot were two fierce-looking fifteen-year-old twins called Ronnie and Reggie. Rolnick knew Schneider, so when he came to the bar Rolnick offered to buy him a drink; Schneider declined, but the interaction was enough to show 'The Firm' that he was a friend. Rolnick went over to Spot's table:

> Jack, sitting with his Crombie overcoat and Trilby hat still on, asked, 'Do I know you?' I replied, 'No, but it's possible you might of heard of the people I represent.' . . . 'Who are they?' I mentioned the 43 Group, which brought a smile to his face . . . 'You lads are doing a good job. What do you want with me?' I explained what had taken place at Romford and how unpre-pared we were for our confrontation with the Maltese gang.

They began talking and as Spot and the others expressed their admiration for the Group's efforts, Spot began to relax. Then Spot asked how much money the Group had, and Rolnick forgot whom he was addressing, and began to rant about how the Group was always struggling for funds. This brought over several people, including the twins, one of whom asked Rolnick what the trouble was.

> 'Oh, it's nothing. I am sorry to have bothered you.' The twin looked me straight in the eye and repeated in an even louder

tone, 'What's the trouble?' I repeated what I had said to Spot . . .
Imagine my delight and surprise, not to mention my relief, when
one of the twins said, 'The Maltese team interfering with you?
Forget money. Let us know when and where. We will be there!'
I could have kissed him with relief. On second thoughts, it's just
as well I did not. It might have been Ronnie Kray!'[15]

A few days later Rolnick reported back to Bernerd and some
executive members and they debated the merits of associating
with Spot. Rolnick was fairly convinced the Group should push
ahead, until someone raised an excellent point. If the Board of
Deputies learnt that the Group were associating with gangsters,
they would be sure to immediately publicise this intelligence,
leading to the Group's respectable backers withdrawing their
support; the Group would be left destitute. Rolnick conceded
the point and no more was done to foster an association. Clearly
the fascists had reached a similar conclusion to the Group –
either that, or they only ever intended to hire gangsters for
Romford – and Maltese Joe's gang was never seen at a UM
meeting again.

Deciding against working with Spot did not mean that the
Group were not still smarting over Romford. So when they
discovered the UM were going back there three weeks later, they
decided to set up an ambush. They knew the fascists would
mostly travel to Romford from Mile End on the Green Line bus,
and so planned to jump on them as they emerged from Mile End
Underground Station. One hundred and fifty Group members
split into four groups, each waiting on one of the side roads
around the station. Meanwhile one 43er was waiting for the
fascists in the station, when they emerged he would dash out
before them and cross the road; this would be the signal for the
ambush. The Group waited, and waited, and waited. No one
came. Whether it was a setup or bad intelligence is unclear, but
Harry Kaufman, who was waiting in one of those side streets,
thought the UM's non-appearance was the best thing that could
have happened. 'In a way I'm not sorry because I think

somebody might have been killed that day, the boys were so pent-up waiting for revenge for Romford.'

New Friends

Defeat at Brighton took the sheen off Mosley's return and in the weeks that followed, UM members began openly criticising their leader. In particular, Mosley's very hands-off approach annoyed them, as he rarely put in appearances and seemed oblivious to the hard work of his followers.[16] They were not imagining it: Mosley was quickly losing interest in his own party as his ambitions became more international.

Europe-A-Nation was not just a philosophy. Mosley was covertly building contacts with fascists around the world, and to that end had set up a clandestine European Contact section within the UM. Mosley believed that rebuilding this network would lead to the resurrection of a European fascist movement, which, Mosley took for granted, he would lead.

On Guard frequently kept its readers abreast of Mosley's international ambitions, reporting in January 1948 that he was making contact with fascists and racists in the USA and South Africa, including Oswald Pirow, the leader of the pro-Nazi New Order Movement, who visited London in spring 1948 and held a joint press conference with Mosley.[17] Then in August *On Guard* revealed its biggest ever scoop: Mosley was fundraising for a German wing of the UM and financing and producing a German-language version of *Union* called *Deutsches Flugblatt* for secret distribution. This news got picked up by several national newspapers and led to the government declaring a ban on all of Mosley's publications within the British Zone, even though they had learnt about Mosley's plans from the Group a whole month earlier.[18]

Also impeding Mosley's international ambitions in 1948 was his inability to leave the UK. Upon his internment the government had confiscated his passport, and five years from his release from prison and three years after the war they were still holding onto it. Mosley appealed for its return but the Foreign Office denied his request. He then made an attempt to run his operations from Jersey, and so towards the end of July he slipped out the country on a yacht and was spotted in the harbour of St. Brelade's bay two days later. The security services were well aware that he was there, but decided to take no action. Around the same time Mosley was also looking into the possibility of acquiring a passport from a Central or South American country by purchasing some land. It is fortunate for Mosley that he did not succeed, as the British government would have almost certainly stripped him of citizenship and he would have lost all credibility with his followers.

Some of Mosley's foot soldiers were beginning to feel neglected, and told the 43 Groupers that they wanted out. Morris Beckman recalled a couple of occasions when he was approached by fascists after meetings who told him they were done with Mosley and the UM. Beckman recalled one incident when he and another Group member found themselves in a pub with three fascists who told them that not only did they want out, they wanted to join the 43 Group. Sure, said Beckman jokingly, but you will need to get circumcised first.[19]

It was not just the rank-and-file that were growing increasingly disillusioned; some of the UM's senior organisers were thinking about walking away. John Webster, Bristol's leading fascist, had already left in January, before the UM had even formed, and six months later his Birmingham counterpart was giving serious consideration to doing the same. In 1932, Mosley founded the BUF and a sixteen-year-old Michael Maclean signed up, and for the next sixteen years remained a devoted Mosleyite. Maclean managed to avoid internment and joined the armed forces After the war he formed his own small fascist party in Birmingham, the State Progress Party, which soon merged with Hamm's League. So when Hamm merged the League into the UM, Maclean automatically followed suit and was made the UM's Birmingham organiser. In the pre-war days Maclean had only seen the leadership on special occasions, 'where they were on their best and most impressive behaviour', but now as regional organiser he was coming into the inner circle.

> Because the movement was but a shadow of its pre-war self, it was inevitable that provincial organisers should be more closely associated with the national officials of headquarters staff. I knew several of them intimately, and soon got to know the others . . . They had no sense of loyalty to the high spiritual aspirations that they talked about so glibly, being concerned for the most part with their own petty advancement.[20]

But it was a falling-out with Mosley himself that drove Maclean out of the UM. In June 1948 he reached out to various Jewish organisations, including the JDC, AJEX and the 43 Group, telling them that he wanted to come out publicly against Mosley. Lionel Rose of AJEX interviewed him and tried to ascertain the trigger for his decision. Maclean, a devout Catholic, claimed that it followed an interview with the Leader in which he asked why Mosley permitted 'widespread immorality' among Party members and in particular the extra-marital affairs of men like Hamm and Moran, 'who were openly living with female Party members', despite being married. When Mosley responded that leading Nazis had not been 'squeamish morally and that sexual morality had nothing to do with Party politics', Maclean was disgusted and he started to seriously doubt Mosley and his movement. Rose, however, was not convinced by this argument and thought Maclean was actually motivated by a 'spirit of revenge', possibly after a quarrel with Tommy Moran, in which Mosley had taken Moran's side.

When Maclean asked Rose if he could speak from an AJEX platform, Rose turned him down. He was sceptical of Maclean's motives, thought him too controversial a figure and suspected he was in the midst of a nervous breakdown. But the JDC very much wanted AJEX to find a way to work with Maclean and stop him falling into 'the hands of extremists',[21] which is exactly what happened. Geoff Bernerd shared none of Rose's qualms about having Maclean up on a platform, and since the Group had decided at their June AGM to start holding public meetings of their own, they were delighted to have a real star attraction to draw audiences to what would be their first public platform.

On Sunday 11 July, Basil McGlory mounted the 43 Group's platform near the UM's Hereford Street pitch in Bethnal Green, held under the aegis of *On Guard*, and addressed the growing crowd. Upon a platform fronted by the sign 'Mosley Fooled Me', McGlory, another former fascist who would become one of the Group's most popular platform speakers, regaled his audience with impressions of fascist leaders so brilliantly and with such wit that, according to *On Guard*, the neighbouring UM audience was reduced to just half a dozen people.

Around McGlory the growing crowd was almost entirely friendly; the Group had heavily advertised the meeting, passing out handbills and even interrupting Jewish dances in the run-up to the meeting. But there were interruptions, especially from a few fascists at the back who greeted every new speaker with choleric shouts of 'You fucking traitors, we'll bloody get you!' Some tried to start fights, but they were swiftly and none too gently dealt with by Group stewards. Midway through the meeting an ambulance arrived, followed shortly afterwards by a fire engine. Then the Elephant turned up, blasting Teutonic music. The interruptions did little to ruin the mood and by the time McGlory introduced Maclean, an audience of around 1,000 had gathered to hear his blistering denunciation of Mosley and the UM.[22]

No transcript of Maclean's remarks exist, but an article he published in *On Guard* called 'I Choose Freedom' probably featured most of his big talking points. In the article Maclean began with an explanation of Mosley's strategy, which had 'by Mosley's own admission' little to do with electoral success, and was instead focused on establishing 'scattered groups of tough stormtroopers' who would be capable of exploiting the 'economic crisis that he considers would be his opportunity' when it inevitably arose. Mosley's anti-Semitism was a part of this campaign, for Mosley and some of the fascist leadership 'neither hate nor love the Jew; they do not consider him except as a tool to create the sort of striking force that they need in order to accomplish their own selfish ends.'

For Maclean, who had always, he claimed, 'tried to resist the policy of unrestrained anti-Semitism', this 'artificial' anti-Semitism among the fascist leadership was abhorrent. Just as bad, however, was their complete lack of morality and interest only in their own advancement. 'There is about as much unity between them as there would be in a room full of starving cats when a piece of fish was thrown amongst them,' Maclean wrote. Of Mosley he was even more damning:

> Mosley is a self-seeker without feeling for others. This ambition is sufficient to justify any abandonment of duty, or of principle, he has thrown away . . . as he will do again . . . the services of men who have, in his opinion, 'served their purpose'.
>
> Under his influence the grandeur of our ideals in 1932 have been reduced to a mockery and degradation. I am not ashamed that I hailed Mosley sixteen years ago, but today I would be ashamed were I not to say . . . farewell.[23]

Sunday 11 July 1948 was not a good day for Oswald Mosley. Not only was a former follower denouncing him in the strongest possible terms while being cheered on by his Jewish enemies, he also discovered that his home in Wiltshire, the base of all his operations, had been burgled.[24] There were persistent rumours among the 43 Group that they had broken into Mosley's home, but it was only decades later that Beckman learnt from Bernerd that the rumours were true. It was all thanks to their undercover bodyguard, Ben, who had become such a regular feature at Ramsbury that no one noticed him taking the measurements of rooms, doors, windows, and so on, which he began posting to Group HQ. There, the Group's budding architects began producing a blueprint based on the information, and a plan was made to raid the house.

On the grass verge next to Mosley's estate, overhanging trees gave cover to the nine 'commandoes' as they emerged out of three taxis. They went over the walls and subdued the few heavies who were patrolling the grounds. They then headed into the house and, following Ben's plans, found Mosley's filing cabinets, which Ben had left unlocked. They filled four bags with letters and documents and made their escape. In case they were being followed, the cabs split up and headed to different parts of the country. Once all the sacks were back in London, the secretaries went through the documents – which included letters between Mosley and a few sitting MPs – copied them, and sent selected copies out to trade union leaders and friendly members of parliament.[25] Meanwhile, as per Bernerd's instructions, Ben went on a very long holiday; soon after, everyone in the UM was told to keep an eye out for the now very much wanted man.[26]

Next Time a Bomb

A further sign of the UM's malaise in the summer of '48 was its decision to close many of the regular pitches it had opened in the spring, as they were now attracting paltry crowds. By contrast, buoyed by the success of their first outdoor meeting, the Group, under the auspices of *On Guard*, was now holding regular meetings around the city. Speakers were predominantly former fascists such as Basil McGlory, who would reveal the Mosleyites' sordid truths in the hope of drawing more of the rank-and-file out of the UM.[27]

Meanwhile the UM platforms were hosting new speakers who did not know, or probably care, where the uncrossable lines were. The day after Romford, twenty-one-year-old Doreen Cooper was introduced to the platform at Ridley Road and told the audience of how she and her aunt had been recently assaulted by a gang of Jews in Brixton. Cooper then exhorted her listeners:

What are you English people going to do about it? Do something about it! Don't stand around! The damn Yids want throwing off British streets altogether. We are all going to turn up at Brixton next Friday and we want everyone to come along to help us break this dirty filthy Yiddish rabble down off the streets of Britain. We don't want any more of this Yiddish rabble, kill them, do anything, get rid of them. It is a pity we don't have the concentration camps in this place.[28]

Cooper was immediately arrested and charged with using insulting words, but her unrestrained invective was not a million miles away from the sort of language veteran speakers were employing regularly. The day after Brighton, Duke Pile was at Ridley Road describing the actions of the 'Jewish thugs armed with razors, iron bars and stones' and their co-religionists, the 'dirty filthy Jewish murderers in Palestine'. Two months later, these remarks forced Mr Blake Odgers to bind Pile over for disturbance of the peace. Pile finished with a promise that there would be a return to Brighton:

Brighton is not very far off, you can easily get there, and we are going there again and next time if these Jewish thugs attack us we are going to take the offensive in the same way the Arabs have taken the offensive in Palestine.[29]

That is not what occurred. The UM mustered a much smaller force for their second trip down to Brighton where they were greeted by, as *On Guard* put it, 'Jewish-controlled weather'. As around eighty UM members began their procession in the pouring rain, they found they were being led by the police away from the Level where, they learnt, an anti-fascist meeting was ongoing. Held under the auspices of *On Guard* and addressed by Flamberg and Basil McGlory, this meeting had a good turnout despite the weather.

By contrast, when the fascists arrived at their designated meeting spot, well away from the Level, they were addressed by a 'a damply dripping Jeffrey Hamm' for about twenty minutes, before they decided to pack up the meeting and head back home.[30] 'Damp Squib' was how *On Guard* summed up the affair, and in the late summer of 1948 this could have described most of the UM's meetings. According to a Home Office report,

> the audiences are normally apathetic to Union Movement themes, unless there are some members of the Jewish anti-fascist '43 Group' present, when vigorous heckling develops but seldom results in any grave disorder.[31]

The 43 Group would have disputed this assertion, making the case that even though they were present it was fascist-hating locals who generated most of the heat. This had particularly been the case in south London, where the UM had been concentrating most of its efforts, holding up to five meetings a week.[32] The focus of their energies was Brixton, where locals turned out on the regular not only to jeer and heckle the UM's speakers, but also to provide them with a guard of dishonour back to their buses, 'in order to let them know just how unwelcome they were in Brixton'.[33]

On one occasion in August the fascists had a particularly bad time of it, when the 43 Group stole their normal pitch on Station Road – forcing Victor Burgess, who was leading the meeting, to set up on a nearby side road. Having his pitch nicked clearly did no favours to Burgess's mood, as he issued threats towards the *On Guard* paper sellers: 'If the sellers of opposition papers do not stop at once . . . we will not be responsible for the consequences.' Burgess then dismissed the angry comments coming from his audience as coming from 'the 43 Group imported to the district'. This, according to *On Guard*, roused the people of Brixton 'to fury'.

> Events that evening should put an end to Fascist stories that their only opponents are the 43 Group. Any members of the Group present in Brixton on that occasion were too busy supporting

the anti-Fascist platform to bother with Blackshirt propaganda. Protests came from local Brixton people, roused to anger by the Fascist speakers' disloyal and provocative statements.

Burgess eventually brought his meeting to a close with a playing of the National Anthem, which he decided to accompany with a Nazi salute. This gesture did not further endear him to the good people of Brixton, whose cacophony of yells chased Burgess and his men back to the train station, while the police kept a close guard around them. Finally bundled into the train station the police held them for quite some time, before eventually letting them take a train back to Victoria, where an anti-fascist welcoming committee awaited. Jeers and heckles quickly gave way to a series of skirmishes, before enough police arrived to clear up the fighting.[34]

Not all local opposition was violent. In July, Hamm was addressing a meeting in North Kensington when a fife and drum band appeared out of a nearby church, where they had been playing to the Kensington Girls' Brigade. Catching a few words of Hamm's speech, the pipe major lined up his band and started marching past the meeting, with drums and bagpipes being played as loudly as possible. According to *On Guard*, the music completely drowned out Hamm's loudspeakers.

The crowd flocked away from the meeting and followed the band, cheering and laughing, until Hamm gave up trying to make himself heard.

As soon as the band had passed, Hamm endeavoured to speak again, but then it was swung round and marched back and once more his remarks were completely swamped.

The band went on marching up and down until the police, apparently worried about the success of the meeting, asked if by any chance they could be doing it on purpose.[35]

In comparison to what Hamm was getting thrown at him a month later, one imagines he would have taken a fife and drum band any day of the week. On 26 August, Hamm and Alf Flockhart took the Elephant down for a meeting in Mile End, where they were joined by Mrs Toni Moran, who was even more virulently anti-Semitic than her husband. Soon after Mrs Moran began addressing the crowd from atop the Elephant she found herself in a shouting match with some 43 Group girls. A small volley of projectiles followed, and the police ordered her to get off the platform. Alf Flockhart told Hamm to take her place. He did so and as he launched into a speech, a large band of 43 Groupers rushed on to the scene and clashed with the UM membership.[36] From behind the van, a police inspector yelled an instruction at Hamm to close the meeting, threatening arrest if he disobeyed. Hamm knew that the officer was unlikely to want to clamber up and chance the projectiles, so he tried to stall him. Then the inspector's insistence began to annoy Hamm, and he turned around to argue. 'It was then', wrote Hamm, 'that I forgot the golden rule of any ball game: never take the eye off the ball.'[37]

In among the Group members that day was Murray Podro, who as head of intelligence had to ensure that he stayed well out of the action and avoid any and all trouble with the law. But Podro heard Hamm say something that really riled him up. 'I'm a very mild kind of bloke really,' said Podro, describing what happened next: 'I picked up this piece of concrete, it must have been about that big I should think, quite heavy, and this piece of concrete seemed to have a life of its own. It left me and propelled itself right up on top of Jeffrey Hamm, landed on the top of his head.'[38]

While the UM stewards clambered up the Elephant to retrieve their unconscious leader, widespread fighting broke out. After waiting an age for an ambulance, the stewards decided to drive to Bethnal Green hospital, with Hamm still lying on the roof. A 43 Group car drove after it in hot pursuit. A fascist called Fred Bailey was riding in the back of the Elephant and as its rear doors were open he grabbed an object and hurled it at the car with such force that he threw himself out, almost landing underneath the chasing car's wheels.[39] Meanwhile the police were struggling to contain the escalating fighting, arresting five belligerents before peace was restored.[40] As for Murray Podro, he managed to avoid being arrested, but the following morning two burly police officers found him at his mother's shop and took him to Old Street Station, where he was charged with grievous bodily harm. Afterwards he went to Panton Street to explain to Flamberg and Bernerd what had happened. Furious that their intelligence head had been stupid enough to get himself into such trouble, they nonetheless promised they would get Platts-Mills, their best lawyer, to represent him.

Meanwhile, Hamm spent several days recovering in hospital and took the opportunity to write an article for *Union* entitled 'My Answer to the Hooligans':

> The writer had planned this article before he became the latest victim of Jewish violence, and it is only a coincidence that it is written with some difficulty, from a hospital bed. This attack merely reinforces our indictment of the Government's failure to declare the notorious '43 Group' a criminal organisation, to confiscate its funds, and to imprison its leading members.[41]

And yet, when Hamm had the opportunity to do just that he refused. At Podro's trial the police superintendent claimed it was Hamm who had brought the charges, which Hamm denied; the judge threw out the case.[42] One possible reason Hamm backed out from bringing charges was that the Group had finally spooked him. As he lay recuperating in his hospital bed, he received an anonymous letter written on 43 Group–headed paper: 'This time a brick – next time a bomb. If you speak at another meeting you will end up in the morgue.'[43]

Hamm did keep on speaking; but as a Special Branch report observed, he was overworked, looking very ill and clearly falling apart.[44] He was not the only one. When Maclean left the UM, he had looked tired, hungry, in desperate need of some money and on the verge of a nervous breakdown; Victor Burgess, who always looked dishevelled, was also in a bad way. 'Wash your bloody shirt!' Podro had shouted at Burgess at a meeting in Kensington earlier in the year. He continued:

> When did you have your shirt washed last? Did your mother wash your shirt, Victor? Why don't you get Lifebuoy and wash your bloody shirt? Why don't you fall down and break your neck?[45]

Clearly Burgess's situation only worsened, as some time later, when the 43 Group were planning on jumping the UM's Notting Hill pitch, Martin Block and Reg Morris took him out for breakfast. Another organisation had beaten both the Group and the UM to the pitch, so both sides were at a loose end. Block and Morris found themselves standing next to Burgess. 'Long straggly hair and a ragged overcoat and hungry-looking ... We might have started with some banter you know, "Nice, isn't it, someone's got our pitch," and it went from there. I think Reg probably said to him, "Fancy a cup of tea?" and we found a caff and we had breakfast.'[46]

By autumn things really were going badly for the UM, with recruitment at paltry levels as members left in droves, and Mosley struggled to work out how to plug the gap. The situation was so bad that, according to an intelligence report, 'Mosley feels that Union Movement as at present constituted carries insufficient appeal even to persons who are anti-Semitic and anti-Communist.'[47] John Warburton, a fascist and intimate of Mosley's, admitted that this was the fault of a leadership that was still stuck in a post–First World War mindset and had failed to understand how their ideology was so at odds with a population that was beginning to say 'never again'.[48]

But never mind the wider population, Mosley failed to understand his own supporters. On 16 October he addressed a UM meeting at the Wilmott Street School and bored his audience with a speech focused on European union. Then he made an even bigger mistake. Having asked the press to leave the hall, he informed his followers that it was against UM policy to attack Jews or Winston Churchill: their attacks should instead be focused on the communists.[49] When Duke Pile asked why he was changing this policy about a man they regarded 'as the greatest war criminal in the world', Mosley explained that it was now 'not diplomatic to attack him directly'. He continued: 'Now we must concentrate on the principal enemy, Communism, and after all Churchill is also fighting it.'[50] It was Mosley's hope that this decision would make his movement more palatable to a wider audience and boost recruitment. It did no such thing, but only led to more and louder grumblings from a dissatisfied membership.

Towards the end of 1948 an opportunity arose for the UM to capitalise on a brief spike in anti-Semitism. The Lynskey Tribunal was called to deal with allegations of corruption and the bribing of ministers and civil servants. At the heart of it was Sidney Stanley, a Jewish Polish spiv and conman. The allegations against Stanley led to newspapers making anti-Semitic jokes and the country saw another small surge in bigotry. *Union* and UM speakers heavily milked the tribunal and made frequent attacks on Jewish spivs,[51] but even this failed to arrest the UM's continuing decline.

The Duel of the Dictators

Throughout 1948, the Group's evident successes against the fascists had helped improve its standing within the Jewish community. For Louis Hydleman and the JDC this was a galling state of affairs, as their campaign to freeze the Group out of the community and starve it of resources was losing traction. Every time a local defence association or synagogue considered giving the Group a platform, Hydleman sent a very strongly worded letter, but increasingly these were ignored. Even more frustrating were the prominent businessmen who continued to back the Group, while the willingness of some members of the Board of Deputies to speak in the Group's favour had Hydleman spitting with rage.[52]

By 1948, the Group had established too strong a foothold in the community for Hydleman to force it to close unilaterally, but there was still a chance he could negotiate it out of existence. This was not actually anathema to the Group's executive, who, being far from certain about their long-term survival, were keen for the Group to have a meaningful legacy. If as a condition of its closure and merging with the official defence structure the Group could get its leaders into positions of influence, it would be able to change the way the Jewish community defended itself. For an organisation that was only created in reaction to official defence policy, that would be a meaningful result.

In August 1947, Bernerd and Hydleman met on a couple of occasions and according to Bernerd had 'agreed *in principle* that there should be unity'.[53] However, the two men clearly had very different ideas as to what this actually meant, with Hydleman telling a correspondent that Bernerd was ready to close the Group and turn it into a sports club. To mark this agreement Hydleman arranged a dinner party at the Trocadero for the Group's leaders 'to give a respectable "funeral service" to the 43 Group and to give a feeling of solid confidence in the genuineness of my assurance that the Defence organisation will make good use of every one of their members'.[54] The dinner took place and was perfectly pleasant. It was only in the meeting afterwards that the Group learnt the JDC wanted it to fully disband before 'any detailed discussion of policy and programme' would take place.[55]

Negotiations recommenced in the summer of 1948 and got much further, with a verbal agreement being reached that the Group would merge with the JDC and have a say on policy and planning, along with representation on committees on the national and local level, and licence to continue printing *On Guard*.[56] Within a month, however, talks had broken down and in September, Hydleman took to the Letters page of the *JC* to lay the blame solely on the Group who, he said, had 'no desire to conform to communal discipline' and had introduced 'pretentious claims and impossible demands' into the discussion; their only objective was to turn 'the limelight upon themselves'.[57]

Unsurprisingly Geoff Bernerd felt the need to respond, and duly accused Hydleman's 'iron wall of dictatorship' of being the principal obstruction to any accord. Hydleman, Bernerd claimed, said he wanted 'co-operation' but his real goal was the 'complete subjugation and disbandment of our organisation and machinery', an organisation which, unlike the JDC, did not 'hide inactivity and lack of a positive policy and programme behind a cloak of secrecy and officialdom'.[58]

One week later, Hydleman was taking aim at the Group's leadership who, he said, were incapable of putting 'the welfare of the community before their personal leanings'. Bernerd once again penned a vigorous response, insisting that the Group's leadership had the full support of its members, although he wondered if the same could be said of the JDC. It was clear, however, that Bernerd was getting as fed up with this protracted public tiff as everyone else, and so he tried to land a knockout blow, informing the paper's readers that

> Mr. Hydleman's recent attack on the 43 Group was received with great glee by the Fascists themselves, who, ever seizing an opportunity, have taken full advantage of 'dirty linen being aired' by splashing it both in their journals and on their platform. I can, in fact, state, that the only definite support that Mr. Hydleman has so far received in his efforts to end our existence has come from within the Fascist ranks.[59]

Hydleman this time chose not to react and the conflict receded from the *JC*. Meanwhile, the Group's unofficial affiliation with the communists was as strong as ever and two weeks after Bernerd's last letter, the Group sent its members to protect one of the country's most famous communists. On 25 October the Hackney Trades Council organised a peace conference at Stoke Newington Town Hall, where the senior churchman Hewlett

Johnson, known as the 'Red' Dean of Canterbury, was to be the keynote speaker. Johnson, one of the worthies who wished *On Guard* well in its first issue, was a controversial and outspoken figure and a popular target for the fascists. When Group intelligence learnt that the UM were planning on disrupting the meeting, their offer to protect it was gratefully accepted. For Jonny Goodman it was an event he was unlikely to forget, starting as it did when the 'bus went two stops past the bloody town hall'. Goodman and two other guys from the Group got off and walked back up the long street. 'On every corner Fascists started shouting at us, and I wanted to go for it, to run for it, to the town hall. And one of them said don't run, because that would be the catalyst that sets them off, so we strolled, it was quite nerve-wracking as they were getting closer. We got to the town hall and manned all the windows and doors.'[60]

Gerry Abrahams was also present that day: 'We were told there were about thirty or forty Blackshirts coming and so we had thirty of our boys inside the town hall by the doors. As they came in, into the parking area, we came out and met them and they had the fright of their lives, as they didn't expect us, and they disappeared.'[61]

For a short while at least. When Group members identified twelve fascists who had borrowed the Group's tactic of forging tickets, they were asked to leave. A v ensued, but the fascists were finally evicted. However, their reappearance outside the building triggered the fascists' raid and over a hundred of them charged, with some wielding petrol-filled bottles, fireworks and bricks which they proceeded to hurl at the hall. A huge fight broke out on the steps, and 'van-loads of police' were required to break it up. Quite a few people were taken to hospital with injuries, and a large number of arrests were made.[62] Martin Block's recollection was that so many people were arrested that the officer on duty gave up and just shouted, 'Get the fucking lot out of here!'[63]

In total just two fascists were charged, and both were subsequently let off by Magistrate Herbert Malone, who opined: 'You are entitled to hold your views and express them in public, and anyone who stops you will be punished.' This, *On Guard* observed, was a far cry from the advice Malone usually gave to anti-fascists, whom he never failed to warn away from fascist meetings. *On Guard* also pointed out the inconsistencies in the actions of the police, for whereas they always offered protection to fascist meetings, none had been provided for this meeting.

This lack of police protection for left-wing anti-fascists was the norm, which is why they often had to request protection from the Group, who were happy to oblige. When a large trade union meeting was to be held in York Hall in Bethnal Green, the Group were turned to once again. The Group sent about fifty members down, and they guarded all the entrances while the meeting progressed without interruption. The Group waited until all the leaders and trade unionists had left before departing themselves and heading to the train station. It was at the corner of Victoria Park Road that the Group came face to face with 100 fascists, one of whom was brandishing the Union Jack. The Group were outnumbered two to one, but stood their ground. Then a chap called Cyril Kearns picked up a bottle and threw it at the flag-bearer and all hell broke loose as the two sides rushed together. Harry Kaufman was in the middle of the melee:

'I got pushed in the back by someone and I landed on top of somebody and I was hitting them, I hope it was a fascist. There weren't streetlights, so it was dim lighting, it was pot-luck. I was hitting this guy and suddenly a police sergeant comes up and he says, "Right, I've got you, you're coming with me, son." As he put his hand around me and stood up, Reggie Morris, who was wearing a white raincoat with flaps and epaulets, put his hand in his pocket and he pulled out a card, which I didn't see, and the police sergeant didn't see, and said, "I'm Special Branch, I'll take that man, sergeant." He grabbed me and said, "Fuck off!" and I ran to the station.'[64]

In December 1948, Group members worked with the communists again, this time to help disrupt a meeting Mosley was to hold at the Roman Road school in east London. When the fascists arrived, they discovered that there were already sixty people in the building who had barricaded it from the inside; in effect they had jumped the school.

Newspaper reports at the time stated that this invasion had been led by the communists, which prompted an indignant *On Guard* editorial on the subject of the press's insistence on identifying all anti-fascists as communists, heavily suggesting that the invasion was led by the Group.[65]

The police managed to break through the barricades and demanded that the invaders leave at once. In response they lay on the ground and locked arms, forcing the police to violently wrestle them apart. Eighteen-year-old Group member Arnold Erlick was so badly injured, he had to be rushed to hospital to get his head injuries X-rayed. 'I don't know why the police hit me,' he told *On Guard*. 'I was not fighting – I was lying on the floor when I was kicked all over my body and one constable took my shoe off and started to beat me over the head with it.'[66] Eventually the police managed to clear the hall for Mosley and his followers, who were finally able to commence their meeting.

Outside the hall both the Group and the Stepney Communist Party set up platforms, and Mosley was forced to compete with the sound of slogan-shouting anti-fascists and orators with loudspeaker equipment, one of whom was Harry Bidney.[67] Around him churned a large cluster of young Jewish lads, who were far more violent than the ex-servicemen who had founded the Group. These youngsters were gradually becoming the majority. The 43 Group was undergoing a fundamental change.

11

Cornered Animals

At the start of 1949, Stanley Marks went to his doctor, as the chest problem he had picked up in Burma was getting worse. His doctor diagnosed him with tuberculosis and told him to take things easy. Marks knew he would have to leave the Group, and so became yet another of the Group's early wave of members to say farewell. The principal cause for this exodus was that by 1949 most had been arrested and bound over at least once, and they knew what would happen if they were caught again. Recalled Marks:

'I can remember towards the end of the Group where I'd look around the room and we had a few of our hardliners but we had lost a lot. We had lost a lot of our good people because they knew the next thing that would happen would be they go to jail, now the situation with the fascists hadn't reached the degree where they looked like they were going to really obtain power . . . Then we would have probably all reconsidered that it probably was worth going to jail.'

The diminishing threat meant that many of those who had given all their spare waking hours to the anti-fascist cause were beginning to wonder if such sacrifice was now necessary. Many wanted to get on with their lives, focus on their careers, and start families, while others were simply burnt out.

The Group's work could exact a huge psychological toll on its members. Alexander Hartog was one of those who realised his 'character was being affected'. He later told an interviewer,

I couldn't get on a bus or a train or walk in the street as I do today. I was very much on edge. I was always watching who was a Jew and who was a Christian, and who was for me, who against me. I was on guard like the name of our paper. I was living on my nerves. I was like a saboteur. We had broken up so many fascist meetings that we were having to hide, we could no longer come out into the streets.[1]

If this was the cost of Group membership after two years, it was hardly surprising many of the original members were calling it a day.

In their stead a new wave of young Jews was entering the Group. These were boys still in their teens who had never fought in a war and lacked the military discipline of their predecessors. Moreover, while the founding members had had their fill of fighting, which they thought of as a necessary evil, these younger members were very eager to mix it up wherever and whenever. Of course, the Group had always had its younger, more pugnacious members, especially in the East End section, but by the start of 1949 they were beginning to look like the majority. One such newcomer was seventeen-year-old Martin White. 'I was fighting against anti-Semitism since I was five,' said White, who on his first day at his school in Forest Gate had had his hand shut in a desk and been kicked by the other boys for being a Jew. 'My older sister said to me, "You've got to go and fight. You've got to go back tomorrow, find the boy, and hit him." And that's what I did, and I've been fighting every day since.' When still a teenager, White started frequenting Soho bars and nightclubs, frequently getting into fights with American servicemen who called him a Jew-boy, or worse.

In many ways, White was the perfect fit for the Group: a tough, young, man who was willing to fight for his people. But he also exemplified the unrestrained violence and blindness to sensible tactics that the ex-servicemen found so troubling in the younger generation. 'Let's just throw bombs at them?' White loudly suggested on numerous occasions.[2] In an attempt to turn

White and his ilk into more useful members, the Group began holding talks at Panton Street to educate the youngsters on the Group's aims, objectives and methods, but White found these dismally boring.

Even more frustrating, the Group had in recent months pivoted towards holding their own street meetings rather than constantly attacking the fascists'. Originally the main purpose was to give a platform to ex-fascists, but once it decided on holding weekly meetings of its own it encouraged its own members to try their hand at speaking. After a brief period of success when Group meetings could attract an audience of up to 1,000, however, the pulling power petered out and towards the end of 1948 meetings were being closed early on account of the low attendance.

This was hardly surprising. The Group thrived when its enemies were active and full of fight, but at the start of 1949 fascist energies were depleting, and fast. Mosley, fuming at the government's continued refusal to return his passport, was now more than ever convinced that his future lay overseas, and even put his Ramsbury estate up for sale. But some of his grandiose dreams for the UM remained, and he gave the go-ahead for the party to lease new headquarters at Vauxhall Bridge Road, premises far larger than the party currently required.[3] He was also looking ahead to the upcoming municipal elections for which the UM was planning to field candidates, whose names Mosley planned to announce at a meeting at Kensington Town Hall.[4] With a capacity of 700, this was by far the largest venue the UM had successfully booked, and the leadership were delighted to learn they would fill it to capacity.

By the beginning of 1949 the fascists were pretty confident that they knew all of the 43 Group's tricks, including its penchant for infiltrating meetings with forged tickets, and they pulled out all the stops to ensure this could not happen. They need not have worried, however, as the Group had decided not to attack the meeting but instead hold a mass protest and wreath laying ceremony at the adjacent war memorial. The Group's leadership knew full well that Mosley's presence meant a massive police turnout that would nullify any violent attack; far better to hold a heavily advertised, peaceful protest which would draw attention to the goings-on in the hall and hopefully attract anti-fascists who normally stayed away from the Group's more violent encounters.

On 31 January, attendances both inside and outside the hall exceeded expectations. Mosley was gratified that not only was the venue filled to capacity, but for once many of the more upper-class fascists were in attendance; an audience that had heretofore shunned UM meetings. Even better, a strong police presence ensured that none of these good people had to endure the harassment of the 43 Group. With nothing to interrupt the meeting, Mosley was able to launch into his speech, which along with his usual spiel on European union featured attacks on both Churchill and 'International Financiers'. This was because his most senior lieutenants had told him that the new policy of refraining from attacking these targets was alienating large parts of the UM's membership, many of whom were considering leaving to join a movement connected to the virulently anti-Semitic Arnold Leese. Former League speaker Ronald Hargreaves had already left, and Duke Pile was grumbling very loudly.[5] Mosley's speech was therefore a signal that it was open season on Churchill and the Jews once again.

At the war memorial, 700 Group members had been joined by approximately 3,000 others, including many communists. Signs and banners were held aloft and the laying of a wreath was carried out in reverential silence. According to *On Guard*, the most popular of the speakers was Reverend B. E. Peake, Minister of Golborne Road Congregational Church, who told the assembled that everyone, 'irrespective of their religion, should unite together to fight this curse of Fascism'.[6]

One person who did not think much of this protest was Martin White, who, having sold his tickets for a boxing match, had come along with his friend Brian hoping for a fight. Such hopes were dashed when they arrived and were met by Jackie

Myerovitch, who told them to grab a placard and join the other Group members marching in the road in front of the hall. The trouble was, only placards without poles were left. Reluctantly, White took one and holding it aloft joined the march. 'Where's your fucking pole, Jew!' yelled one of the fascist stewards. 'It will be up your fucking arse when I come round next time!' yelled White in reply. The next moment he had Myerovitch in his face. 'No!' he warned. 'I told you, no!' Angered that he had missed the boxing for this joke of a protest, White decided to cut his losses. He and Brian headed back to a coffee shop in Swiss Cottage, which, because it had a club with a dice game in the basement, was a favourite Group haunt. They ditched their signs, went to play dice, and missed all the fun.

It started during Mosley's speech when a tear gas canister was thrown into the hall, leaving several hundred members of his audience struggling to breathe. Mosley, up on the stage, was unaffected and kept going despite many people rushing from the hall, and an impromptu first aid facility had to be set up in the basement. After the meeting broke up, the mounted police struggled to keep the two sides apart and fights broke out all over the neighbourhood.[7]

The first Martin and Brian heard of this was when Harry Bidney and a half dozen others arrived at the coffee shop, told them about what had happened and started ranting about how once again the police had only arrested the Jewish boys. Everyone was agitated and full of energy, and before long they had squeezed into a couple of cars and sped away. Kensington reached, the cars slowed down as the 43ers kept a look-out for their prey. White was the first to spot one: 'He was wearing a black-and-white checked scarf; I pointed him out, so we stopped. One car stopped in front, one car stopped behind. Bidney and somebody else got out; that should have been enough, but no, our men were getting good hidings because they [the fascists] had these knuckle-dusters, so I got out.'

In his hand White was holding the handle of a small dumb-bell which had been given to him by his brother. White had knocked the ends off, and the metal handle gave him 'a little bit extra':

'I turned this guy around and he hit me with a knuckle-duster and I could see the flashing of the metal and I could feel the blood in my mouth and that really upset me. I got hold of him, I put him against the wall, and I smashed, I really smashed his face. It was completely broken. He was unconscious. I left him on the floor.'

In the distance a police siren wailed, someone shouted that they needed to scram. They rushed back to the cars and sped away into the night.

A few days later Martin White received a letter on official 43 Group–headed paper, telling him that as a result of his actions he had been banned from the Group with immediate effect.[8] White might very well have killed his victim and so he had to go, but he was not very different to plenty of the youngsters who were allowed to stay, and whose presence in the Group was making the older members feel deeply uncomfortable. Gerry Abrahams recalled: 'When it got too bad, I think that's when we left, because a different type of person came in who just wanted to come in and scrap and use knives, and that wasn't for us. We all left about the same time; we did the job and then these youngsters came in who were stupid and who weren't doing it for the same reason, and most of us left.'[9]

Ironically, this change in the membership was happening just as Bernerd and the executive were trying to frame the Group as a respectable and mature anti-fascist organisation. As Bernerd put it in a letter to the *JC*, in which he defended the Group's tactics from Hydleman's criticisms:

It is high time he realised that he is not dealing merely with a few naughty school-children, but with a body that is fully alive to its responsibilities and one that has proved its value to the vast majority of the community.[10]

Waiting at the Regent

The Union Movement made the infighting in the Jewish community look like amateur hour. From its inception Mosley's organisation had been plagued by his lieutenants' perpetual jostling for power, and as Mosley grew more removed from the running of his organisation, this agitation intensified. This was beginning to rankle with the members, who were also growing disillusioned with the UM's inability to build a membership or gain any political traction. When rumours spread in late 1948 that a new British League of Ex-servicemen had formed within the UM and was about to split away, Mosley sent Tommy Moran to investigate and smooth things over.

However, even Tommy Moran – who up in Derby should have been away from most of the internecine conflicts – was embroiled in the infighting. His wife Toni had recently left the UM following a massive row with Alf Flockhart, and so Moran already had an axe to grind when he reported back to Mosley; an axe which had been made all the sharper as he listened to the members' grievances. Moran informed Mosley that the unrest within the UM was caused by goings-on at national HQ, with the membership being dissatisfied with the inefficiency of the leadership and the perpetual position-seeking among Mosley's lieutenants. Taking this as a direct criticism of himself, something he could not brook, Mosley immediately threw the charges back at Moran, who stormed out of Mosley's home. It was not until he was denied entry to the Kensington meeting that Moran realised he had been completely expelled from the movement.[11]

On Sunday, 13 February, Michael Maclean introduced the Morans from a platform at Speakers' Corner, and Tommy and Toni took it in turns to attack the UM, Mosley and the fascists' cynical use of Jew-baiting. While some in Hyde Park appreciated these attacks, others were struck by the opportunism and cynicism of these notorious anti-Semites who were now walking a well-beaten and very predictable path. The exchanges between speaker and crowd grew hostile and the police were forced to escort the former fascists away. An AJEX report blamed 43 Group members for instigating the unrest;[12] however, the chances are it was AJEX members who were causing the ruckus, as the Morans were in fact speaking from a Group platform.[13] Subsequently Moran began holding his own meetings at Hyde Park, although Toni did not approve. On one occasion, she chased him off his own platform and closed down his meeting.

Concurrent with the Maclean and Morans meeting, 200 UM members were marching from Bethnal Green to Dalston in smart military fashion, all wearing, *On Guard* reported, the unofficial uniform of the UM: 'Black-dyed battle-dress blouses and black roll-neck sweaters marked with flash and circle badges'. The march was led by the UM's Drum Corps.[14] They were out to mark the end of the ban on public processions that had been in place since May Day, but were met only by the attention of some apathetic locals; their enemies had decided on this occasion to completely ignore them.[15] Certainly the Group saw little point in attacking a Mosley-less, poxy little march that was not deliberately provoking a Jewish population. No need to throw fuel on the fire unnecessarily, especially not if it might help an organisation that was so clearly struggling.

By March 1949, MI5 assessed that the fascists posed so small a threat to national security that they no longer warranted any extra investment in surveillance. Subconsciously the fascists were coming to a similar realisation, and grew slacker at hiding their Nazi proclivities. Post-1945, the fascists were careful to hide their affinity for their European cousins and strove to avoid using any Nazi signs, symbols, gestures or phrases, especially in public. However, in the early months of 1949 this was starting to slip. During their procession through the East End, the marchers had sung an English version of the 'Horst Wessel Lied', and UM members were beginning to perform Nazi salutes with some frequency. Even Mosley, who had been assiduous in his avoidance of the salute since his release, had been seen to use it. Raven Thompson, clearly realising that gaining popular support was now deeply unlikely, argued that a return to pro-Nazism was a good thing as it would have a 'strong influence' on the party and bring back 'the best of the pre-war membership'. Once again the opposite was true, as the more politically savvy members began abandoning the UM, believing it was the organisation's pro-Nazism that was holding it back.[16]

Predictably, this descent into Nazism was accompanied by more overt anti-Semitism. Anti-Semitic remarks were becoming far more prevalent at fascist meetings, and there was another flurry of anti-Semitic attacks. On 12 February the Philpot Street synagogue in Stepney was broken into, a Sefer Torah was destroyed, prayer books were torn up, and ceremonial wine was poured out all over the building. Five days later in Mile End, fascists walked into a Jewish fish restaurant, started fights and smashed the windows. Not long after, a synagogue in Brighton was defaced with anti-Semitic slogans.[17] In March the fascists decided that once again they were going to march through the heart of one London's most Jewish areas.

Stamford Hill, just north of Dalston, had for the most part remained unaffected by the violence. This was clearly an omission the UM wished to correct, planning a procession on Sunday, 20 March from Dalston to Tottenham, a route that took them straight through that neighbourhood. As with Cable Street thirteen years earlier, this was a route designed to provoke the local Jewish community; the 43 Group were determined that it should fail.

For Harry Kaufman, this march would be a last hurrah. Now eighteen, Kaufman was waiting to do his National Service in the RAF. A couple of Group members had been arrested at fascist meetings while still serving, and their punishments had been far more severe than normal; Kaufman had no intention of making the same mistake.

As per usual, the day began with the East End section's briefing, this time held in the Sidney Street dress factory of Joel and Sylvia Holder. This was followed by a trip to the Regent cinema, a massive Art Deco movie palace which just so happened to be right next to the planned march route, in the heart of Stamford Hill. A hundred or so Group members jumped off the bus, bought tickets, and trooped into the auditorium. A whistle from outside was their signal to rush out and charge into the passing fascist march. Until then, they could enjoy the regular Sunday programme.

A whistle blew. A hundred young people were on their feet and running towards the exit. 'It was like it caused a panic attack,' recalled Kaufman, especially for the cinema's regular Sunday afternoon patrons who had absolutely no idea what had caused the sudden rush out of the cinema and on to a completely empty street. The march, the lookouts told them, had been diverted.

An hour earlier, 600 UM members had gathered at Ridley Road for an initial meeting. The Communist Party also tried to hold a meeting, and the constant chanting, heckling and scuffles meant the speakers could barely be heard over the din. Also protesting the UM's march were delegations from the local Labour Party, Liberal Party, and trade unions. The UM brought their meeting to a close and half of those present lined up for the march, while the other half slipped through the crowds and posted themselves along the march route, ready to lend a hand if violence broke out. The marching fascists carried no weapons, but those waiting along the route carried coshes, razors, knives and knuckle-dusters, which they fingered as they waited. And waited. And waited. For like the Group members at the Regent Cinema, as well as thousands of other anti-fascists stationed along the road to Tottenham, they too were caught out by the last-minute route change.

As the UM tried to leave Dalston they come up against 2,000 protesters blocking the road, making it almost impossible for the fascists to leave the neighbourhood. A cordon of police-men separated the two foes and did their best to force back the anti-fascists, who charged at them in waves. In response, the protesters threw fireworks under the police horses and mass panic ensued. Then, to guarantee the fascists were not able to march along their chosen route, the protesters overturned a tram. The original route clearly impassable, the police told the march leaders they would have to get to Tottenham via Green Lanes and Manor House, just to the west.

Back up in Stamford Hill, the 43 Groupers were trying to figure out what to do when the Elephant, which had somehow managed to skirt around the blockade, drove into view. Reacting without thinking, Harry Kaufman picked up a stone from the street and hurled it straight at the windscreen of the vehicle. The protective wire mesh did its job; the stone bounced right off and the lorry drove out of sight. Unfortunately for Kaufman, he had been spotted in the act by a constable who immediately arrested him, and took him off to the police station. The other Group members split up, some going towards Manor House, where several hundred comrades were lying in wait for the diverted march, or towards Tottenham, where chaos reigned.

Thousands of protesters had gathered around West Green, Tottenham, where the march was to finish. Scores of speakers were denouncing fascism from platforms, while protesters blocked the streets. A bus was boarded, its radiator unscrewed, and the air let out of its tyres; yet another obstacle for the march to overcome. When news came that the march was approaching Tottenham Town Hall, thousands of protesters rushed to meet it. The police tried to disperse the tide of people, but were met with concrete and stone projectiles, while mounted officers had to deal with ball-bearings and marbles thrown at their horses' feet. Lennie Rolnick was right in the middle of the fighting when he saw a mounted policeman charging at one of the Group's female members with a truncheon. He and Manny Levene rushed forward and grabbed the truncheon, hoping to yank it from the policeman's hand, but he did not let go. The policeman came flying off his mount, one foot still stuck in the stirrup. Rolnick and Levene freed him and then rushed back into the melee, but Rolnick was grabbed by several policemen and taken to the police station.

Harry Kaufman was already in the waiting area when Lennie Rolnick arrived; the two men gave each other a quick nod of recognition but did not speak.[18] Sat opposite his friend, Kaufman watched as Rolnick shook his sleeve and a cosh slid out, which he quickly stashed under the seat. Rolnick was taken to a cell, and deciding to act contrite and claim he was only acting in self-defence, he agreed to accept a charge of insulting behaviour and was let go around 1 a.m.[19] Kaufman had managed to get out a few hours earlier, thanks to his Rabbi having witnessed the stone-throwing incident as he looked out the window of a popular bar mitzvah venue. A few phone calls later and the Rabbi located Kaufman's parents at his aunt and uncle's house in the middle of a game of canasta, and Kaufman's father went quickly to the station to bail him out.

Back by Tottenham Town Hall, the police had decided it would be quite impossible for the UM to hold its second meeting, and the fascists were ordered to disperse. It was not until well into the night that the police were able to restore peace to the area. Thirty-four arrests were made during the day, including the detention of half a dozen Group members, and ten members of the police force sustained injuries. Unsurprisingly, Chuter Ede declared another three-month ban on all political marches in the capital.[20]

A week or so later, Harry Kaufman was on trial at Tottenham Magistrates' Court, and, following his barrister's advice, pleaded guilty, hoping the magistrate would take his imminent call-up to the RAF into consideration. This the magistrate said he would do, and yet still fined Kaufman the very hefty sum of £20; it was immediately paid by Kaufman's father, who was subsequently reimbursed by the Group. Stamford Hill was Kaufman's last meeting with the 43 Group; a month later he received his call-up papers, and joined the tide of people leaving the Group.[21]

Out of Date and Out of Fashion

On 15 April 1949 the *JC* carried a small notice: 'Mr. Gerald Flamberg M.M. has resigned his offices as Joint Chairman of the 43 Group on grounds of ill health.'[22] *On Guard*, in its report the following month, quoted Flamberg's letter of resignation in which he assured the members of the 43 Group that 'in the event of any emergency both you and the Jewish community can count on my complete support.'[23]

While Flamberg's health issues, including a chronic stomach condition and on-going issues with his war wound, almost certainly played a part in his decision to resign, so too did the unexploded incendiary device that was pushed through the letterbox of his home. For a while Flamberg's fiancée had been making it clear that she would not marry him while he remained in the Group, and this incident made painfully clear the extent to which Flamberg was endangering his loved ones.[24] As well as leaving the Group, Flamberg moved home, changed his surname, and left Bernerd as sole chairman of a Group whose profile was continuing to grow.

On 25 March, Geoff Bernerd and other Group leaders were welcomed to the Cardiff United Synagogue, where they received an ovation and a large contribution to the Group's funds. In his welcome speech, the synagogue's president mentioned a letter he had received from the JDC, an 'obsolete body with a pamphlet-eering psychology', asking him to have nothing to do with the Group, who he praised for not burying their head in the sand and standing 'erect and four-square to protect Jewish inter-ests'.[25] This endorsement was a triumphant moment in the Group's perpetual battle for communal recognition. If that was not bad enough for the JDC, some of its own regional sub-committees were expressing a desire to invite speakers from the Group – something they were absolutely forbidden from doing.[26] Outside the community the Group was also gaining more and more recognition, and officially affiliating with the National Council for Civil Liberties.[27]

Also endorsing the Group in the spring of 1949 was the great African-American singer, actor and civil rights activist Paul Robeson. Robeson was on a European tour speaking against fascism and racism, and so he was more than happy for Gerry Lewis to come and interview him for *On Guard*. The interview primarily focused on the African-American struggle in the Deep South, but Robeson was keen to point out the link between this and struggles against prejudice and fascism all around the world. He had personally witnessed not just the horrors in the American Deep South but also the impact of fascism in Europe. 'I was in Spain during the civil war, and I saw the growth of Fascism in France. I was in Dachau and other camps, and I saw some of the ashes.' As for the solution, he was unequivocal: 'I want to see Fascism rooted up and smashed in every part of the world.'[28]

Of course, growing prominence in public consciousness – the Group had even been mentioned in Parliament following the protest at Kensington Town Hall[29] – meant that it also attracted more negative attention. First, in March, Hampstead Town Hall banned it from holding meetings there, fearing it would lead to disorder.[30] Then in April Sidney Stanley, the man at the centre of the Lynskey Tribunal, escaped the country and fled to Israel. The *Daily Mail* claimed that the arrangements were made and the pilot provided by the 43 Group. It was a false claim for which there was no evidence, and the Group took out a writ against the paper claiming damages for libel.[31]

The irony of this growing attention was that it came at a time when the leadership were seriously beginning to wonder whether or not the Group could sustain itself post-victory. For if there was any doubt that victory had been achieved, then May Day 1949 laid that to rest. Mosley was supposed to speak on a platform at Ridley Road; instead he remained inside the local pub addresseding a small number of supporters, while his lieutenants were left to talk to the crowd of 500 outside.[32] While Mosley cowered inside, some 2,000 anti-fascists gathered to hear 43 Group and AJEX speakers – sharing a platform for the

first time, much to the JDC's fury.[33] At the time the two organisations were involved in productive negotiations concerning a
possible merger; a few days later an AJEX speaker appeared on
a panel hosted by the Group on the topic of 'The Menace of
Fascism'.[34]

This might have seemed an odd title when the movement was
so obviously in retrograde, but the fascists had responded to
failure by becoming even more violent. Although clashes around
meetings were becoming rarer than in previous years, the
fascists fought with heightened ferocity, and almost all of them
seemed to be armed. 'God, I was scared. They were out to kill,
I'm sure of it,' Beckman quoted one young Group member as
saying, while another veteran suggested the lack of fatalities
was 'more by luck than judgement',[35] and this violent upsurge
was spilling out from the meetings and endangering the Jewish
community.

On 30 April, two sixteen-year-old Jewish boys, Raymond
Keene and Henry Freedman, were about to leave their Boys
Club in Clapton and head to Keene's house. As Keene lived on
Colvestone Crescent, next to Ridley Road, his club leader was
concerned. He knew of the plans for the UM meeting the following day, and a recent spate of attacks on Jewish lads had him
particularly worried.[36] He decided to call the police, and they
assured him that all was calm around Ridley Road and it was
safe for the boys to head home.[37] The journey occurred without
incident until the boys approached a street corner in Dalston,
where, according to the *JC*, 'they passed a group of men who
hurled insults at them.' Two of the men, armed with sticks,
began to follow the boys as they ran to Keene's house.
Unfortunately, there was no one home:

> As the youths stood at the door, a car with two men on the
> running board and four inside drew up. The boys were so
> savagely attacked with empty beer bottles and chair-legs, and
> so severely kicked, that they sustained grave head and facial
> injuries.[38]

The attack on Freedman and Keene gave the Group the opportunity to show how it might function as a communal defence organisation, something it had always aspired to be. Bernerd announced at a meeting of the Bayswater Jewish Centre that the 43 Group would begin to patrol the streets if fascist attacks on Jews continued.[39] Four days later, another Group leader told the Hackney Trades Council that the Group had discovered the attackers' identities and passed these on to the police, with the warning that if nothing was done within a month they would take matters into their own hands.[40] The trouble with such idle talk – the Group never did 'patrol the streets' – was that it was fodder for *Union*, which claimed that the Group was doing just that, and sending carloads of thugs to beat up isolated fascists, as they had recently done to Victor Burgess near Paddington.[41]

Just over a month after the attack, a twenty-one-year-old fascist called Francis William Shaw was charged with assaulting Keene and Freedman.[42] That only Shaw was charged, when he so clearly did not act alone, was a source of anger to many in the 43 Group and the wider Jewish community. When Shaw went on trial in September he was found guilty and given a twelve-month sentence by the recorder, Sir Gerald Dodson, who described Jew-baiting as 'out of date and out of fashion, and never will be in favour in this country, and what is more, is against the law.'[43]

Although the Group might have had ambitions to turn itself into a community defence force, it had never really been set up for such a purpose. Despite the various goals of the Group's founders, it had taken shape as an organisation that could successfully fight fascism in its more political and public manifestations: street meetings, marches, and so on. Here the Group's success was undeniable, and that was the problem: without an ascendant fascist movement or the pull of the weekly fights, the Group struggled.

The Group's 'Guide to Branch Leaders', published in the spring of 1949, showed that it was struggling to keep its members busy. 'BOREDOM is highly dangerous', warned the guide, declaring that 'INTEREST must, and can be maintained – training and rehearsals pay in the long run.' It also recommended branch leaders encourage their members to 'attend discussions and become acquainted with current world positions', and 'take part in Sports and Social activities'. It advocated building a 'healthy competitive and inter-Branch spirit'.[44] By mid-June, though, it seems that for many of its members the Group was turning into nothing more than a social club. At a dance at Wembley Town Hall, Bernerd railed at the 900 people in attendance whom he accused of being happy to come out for a social occasion but not when there was a 'spot of work to be done'.[45] But what work was there to do? Fascist activity continued to dwindle, and there was not even an *On Guard* to sell, since funds were so low. Only three more issues of the paper would appear.

At the JDC, news from their sources that the Group's disbandment was now inevitable would have been music to their ears. This was slightly tarnished by rumours of a 44 Group, coalescing around Harold Bidney and Reg Morris. According to the JDC's sources, while a 44 Group would probably be more radical than its forbear, its chances of surviving were slim, with Bidney and Morris having attracted a mere handful of young followers.

It was the Group's dire financial situation that convinced the JDC it would surely close. It had been running low on cash for a while, which had led to rumours of financial impropriety. Alexander Hartog recalled that money was still coming in from wealthy backers, but members were no longer getting their expenses covered.[46] Jonny Goodman heard a rumour about who was responsible: 'I didn't know the details but Bernerd seems to have something to do with funds that went awry, and I think actually at one stage he was given a very good hiding by somebody in the group . . . I think there was some talk of financial misdeeds.'

If such an event had occurred, it had done no lasting damage to Bernerd's position. Earlier in the year, when Flamberg had been abroad, Bernerd had unilaterally decided to halve the executive and got his way despite strong objections. When Flamberg quit shortly afterwards, there was no doubt that Bernerd was the Group's sole leader – but by the summer even he was beginning to question how long his position could be maintained.[47] Bernerd had for some time relied exclusively on his salary from the Group to support himself and his young family, but knowing the state of its finances, he knew this couldn't continue. Considering his options, he began looking into the possibility of investing in a restaurant or café.[48] Most in the Group had no idea of this, and at the AGM in June he was confirmed as its sole chairman and leader.[49]

The Old Man and the Yacht

While Bernerd, publicly at least, had shown himself to be firmly committed to the 43 Group, his opposite number had already skipped town. For months Mosley had been planning a summer cruise of the Mediterranean to meet European fascist leaders, even though he was still without his passport. Continuing to petition the foreign secretary for its return, Mosley was now thinking of just leaving the country without it. When the Foreign Office got wind of his plans, they decided to return it to him – better that than to be made to look like fools. On 26 May, nine years after they were first confiscated, Oswald and Diana Mosley's passports were returned. Sixteen days later they were aboard Mosley's yacht, the *Alianora*, with their two sons Max and Alexander, setting sail from Southampton.

Mosley left behind a political party in terrible shape. During the London Municipal elections, the UM had fared poorly. *On Guard* gleefully carried a photograph of a UM meeting at Whitestone Pond where the speaker, prominent Hampstead fascist Douglas Peroni, addressed an audience of one boy and a dog.[50] In the LCC elections the three UM candidates received just over 600 votes apiece, while in the local council elections the twelve UM candidates received a grand total of 1,993 votes; the UM came bottom in all eight boroughs in which it stood.[51] These were humiliating numbers – the Communist Party received almost 50,000 more votes[52] – and meant that only a small proportion of even hard-core anti-Semites could have voted fascist.[53] *Union* tried to put a positive spin on things, but it was clear that this was a disaster for the UM, and was a major factor in Mosley's decision to not field candidates in the following year's general election. Electoral failure was compounded by the continued exodus of fascists out of the party, while sales of fascist newspapers fell by three-quarters.[54] Meanwhile, the persistent infighting among Mosley's lieutenants had claimed another victim.

Although Jeffrey Hamm had brought the strongest and most active following into the newly formed UM, he had never been a popular figure among the leadership. One person who had long hated Hamm was Victor Burgess, who had never forgiven him for forcing him out of the League. Burgess, with his Bohemian airs, was far more popular and regarded as the UM's 'lovable rogue'. When the UBF and League had joined the UM the two men had been forced to work together, with Hamm's large following putting him in the much stronger position, but as the UM's numbers dwindled, Hamm's followers faded away and he became an easier target. As a notorious womaniser, Hamm was particularly vulnerable to attacks on moral grounds, and in November 1948 a complaint was brought to Mosley about him and Alf Flockhart, whose homosexual tendencies were well known. Mosley remarked that he had no interest in interfering with a man's private life and he certainly had no interest in interfering in the lives of his loyal lieutenants.[55]

Six months later, following the humiliating defeat at the polls, things had clearly changed. The hatred between Hamm and Burgess was out in the open, and even Mosley realised such fervent antipathy could not be tolerated. In June 1949, the discovery of yet another of Hamm's extra-marital affairs gave

Mosley the excuse he needed to sideline him. The UM's Manchester organiser had just left the party for a radical splinter group, and so Mosley ordered that Hamm be sent to take his place.[56] The assignment was couched in complimentary terms – they wanted Hamm to recreate his east London success – but it was obvious to all he was being demoted. Hamm refused to see this as a betrayal, and remained loyal to the leader he had always revered.

Hamm would not succeed in recreating his previous success. By his own admission, his time in Manchester was a 'total failure' that left him severely depressed.[57] As for the other morally questionable members, Flockhart remained as assistant secretary and organiser, essentially running the UM, and Burgess remained in the UM while continuing his side business of selling American pornographic magazines. This venture was no secret for his fellow fascists – after all, Burgess often stored the literature in the back of the Elephant.[58] For the fascists, moral concerns were only to be acted upon when it enabled one to stab a fellow in the back.

In July, Chuter Ede decided against extending the marching ban that had been in place since Stamford Hill, and, seizing the opportunity, the UM held two marches in quick succession. The first, a procession from Shoreditch to Highbury, met with no opposition;[59] but the second, a march through east London four days later, had company, with a hefty police presence just about keeping the 250 Group members away from the seventy UM marchers. By the time they got to Victoria Park Square, the police had decided the situation was untenable and forced the UM to disperse.

Since the police had come out for a lovely day's marching, the 43 Group were good enough to step in and form their own procession, which headed via Aldgate to Ridley Road and finally to Stamford Hill; it must have made a pleasant change to see the police for once protecting them. The police themselves were somewhat confused as to which organisation they had found themselves protecting.[60]

For the rest of the summer, UM activities ranged from the lacklustre to the fiasco. The East End street meetings and marches still occurred, but drew almost no attention from anti-fascists and locals, and the UM were made increasingly despondent by the apathy with which they were met.[61] In the provinces, matters were even worse. A march through Banbury in Oxfordshire, organised by David Barrow, so infuriated the local population that it had to be abandoned halfway through. Meanwhile, in Hastings on the south coast a march led by Alf Flockhart was ripped apart by a large anti-fascist turnout; Flockhart was dragged off the UM's loudspeaker van and had his head cut open.[62]

At the end of August, Mosley returned to the UK.[63] In a trip that had taken in Spain, Portugal, Italy, Tangiers, Antibes, Monte Carlo and concluding in France, Mosley met with several prominent fascists and Nazis including Mussolini's exiled former foreign minister, and the leader of the fascist Italian Social Movement (MSI). General Franco in Spain had, however, denied him an audience.[64] While on tour Mosley made new friends and established new connections, but he also displayed his knack for infuriating and alienating those he should have been keeping onside. E. H. Batt, the captain of Mosley's yacht, had been warned by Arnold Leese about taking the commission, and subsequently wrote to Leese full of regret, describing Mosley as 'the biggest liar I have yet come in contact with, and he's a fraud and a charlatan'. Batt continued: 'I have had one or two terrific rows with him and yesterday I was going to leave him flat and return to England – unfortunately I am bound by contract for a year.'[65]

Another individual with whom Mosley fell out in 1949 was Francis Parker Yockey, an American fascist intellectual who had been working in the UM's European Contact Section while he waited to see if Mosley would help him publish his 600-page treatise, *Imperium*. In this epic tome, Yockey argued that America was a far greater threat to European culture than the Soviet Union – a view that was anathema to Mosley, who saw no greater threat than communism. For months

Mosley failed to give Yockey an answer, and by mid-1949 the American had grown so desperate that he offered to let Mosley publish *Imperium* under his own name. To Mosley, such a suggestion made Yockey seem weak and pathetic, and he began to treat him with disdain. Yockey responded with absolute hatred and shared his feelings with Guy Chesham, a young Oxford-educated lawyer from Sheffield with whom he worked in the European Contact Section. Yockey and Chesham agreed to quit the UM, and four days after he returned from his cruise Mosley received a 'Memorandum of Disassociation' from Chesham that began with a survey of the failings of the UM:[66]

> In Britain, the membership is now an irreducible minimum of 2–300, all of which is of the lowest intellectual, spiritual and political calibre, as you well know. The journal 'Union' is fortunate if it exceeds a thousand circulation; it is without the slightest influence in British public life . . . there is no evidence of any support at all for you or your writings.

Chesham, like Yockey, was far more radical, anti-Semitic and pro-Nazi than Mosley, and he saw Mosley's lack of ideology as the cause of both the movement's failings and all the defections it had experienced:

> The revolting aspect of this disintegration was not so much the high incidence of desertion, but the ease with which the deserters betook themselves to attacking you from Jewish-sponsored platforms.
>
> This is the most striking evidence of my persistent complaint that there is no ideology in your group. These people were never more than 'Mosleyites', i.e., political morons whose loyalty was to your person, and whose subsequent disaffection led to purely ad hominem attacks from enemy platforms.
>
> Where flattery and ability to bring good news only are the sole tests of loyalty, it is quite simple for enemy spies and agents

to operate freely within you [*sic*] group, although it is probably no longer worth their while.[67]

Chesham and Yockey went off and formed their own splinter organisation, the European Liberation Front, along with John Gannon, whose resignation as the UM's Manchester organiser had precipitated Hamm's move up north.[68] Also leaving the UM at this point was John Preen, who moved to join his local Conservative Party, and Duke Pile who joined the more radically anti-Semitic National and Empire Unity Party.[69]

Desperation

On 11 September, the 43 Group and their communist allies had occupied the area around Hackney Town Hall in order to forestall a UM march to Ridley Road which was due to set off from there. It was a partially successful intervention, with the police forcing the UM to set off from a side street, and then keeping them away from the main roads as they headed to Dalston.[70] It was ironic then that it was on the steps of the town hall that Geoff Bernerd came face to face with the scariest opponent he would ever encounter as leader of the 43 Group: Jules Konopinski's mother. Jules had recently returned from fighting in Israel and had immediately thrown himself back into the 43 Group, and his mother was completely fed up. Jules watched in red-faced horror as his mother, in her thick Central European accent, berated Bernerd on the town hall's steps, blaming him for everything her son had got involved with over the past three years, while Bernerd, with maximum futility, tried to protest that he had no more influence over her son than she did.[71]

Everyone's parents reacted differently to their children being in the Group, of course. Many were proud to see their children standing up for themselves and their community, while others would have shared the view of the Board of Deputies and taken a dim view of what they considered violent hooliganism. Mildred

Levy's mother reacted with horror. 'You what!' she yelled, when she discovered her daughter had been down at Ridley Road. 'You fought the fascists!'

'Well who do you think was going to fight them, mum!' her daughter yelled back. 'You couldn't have come out to do it!'[72]

Of course, anger was a product of fear, the justified fear that their children could end up hurt or in serious trouble. 'My father was quite proud of it,' Harry Kaufman told me, 'but my mother was quite upset that I got arrested obviously, you know what Jewish mothers are like.'[73]

Geoff Bernerd certainly did, as Mrs Konopinski continued to scold him, but this embarrassing moment was a small price to pay for the safe return of the much-loved Jules, Vidal, Mo Levy and all their friends. Relief and joy were greatly dampened by the news of the death of Nat Cashman, but overall, just as the boys' departure came with the trepidation that they might never be seen again, their return was a cause for huge celebration. Similarly, the victory of the new Jewish state was not only a source of pride for the Group but also proof that they were not outliers but part of a new generation of global Jewry, ready and willing to stand up against any aggressor.

But this came at the moment when the 43 Group's role in the fight was coming to an end, and the clash at Ridley Road that followed the fascists' march through the side streets of east London would be the last time the two sides met in open street battle. Twelve arrests were made that day, including Philip Goldberg who was charged with assaulting an officer.[74] No one knew this would be the last clash, of course; another major confrontation was expected on 3 October, when the UM announced a march through the East End to mark the seventeenth anniversary of the founding of the BUF.

Chuter Ede had other ideas, though, and on the day before the march the home secretary announced another three-month ban on marching in the capital. The fascists were furious, blaming the ban on the secret backdoor machinations of Jewish and communist organisations. They quickly arranged a meeting in Victoria Park Square, where Victor Burgess burnt copies of the *Daily Worker* in protest. Watching him do so was a crowd of barely 1,000, and as half of those present were UM members, it was obvious that not even evoking the memory of the BUF, which once boasted thousands of members in east London, could help the UM's cause.[75]

The UM subsequently went into a downward spiral of desperation. On 10 October, a small gang of fascists led by Victor Burgess turned up at an AJEX meeting and started hurling abuse at the platform. 'The Jews ought all to be put into gas chambers. Lampshades should be made out of their skin,'[76] one man apparently shouted. This was a far cry from the coded anti-Semitism of 'international financiers' which Hamm and Burgess had been careful to employ four years earlier. Meanwhile Alf Flockhart had decided he was not going to let Ede's ban hobble the UM, and he got to work on what he dubbed 'Operation M', regarding which he was determined to keep the rest of the UM leadership in the dark. There was good reason for this: he knew what he was planning was illegal and would almost certainly be stopped by Mosley if he was to learn of Flockhart's plans.

Operation M was a three-part event which took place around the capital on the evening of Saturday, 15 October. The first two parts happened simultaneously. Ede's ban, Flockhart had realised, only covered the London Metropolitan Police District, which does not include the City of London, the capital's financial district. Therefore, when eighty UM marchers, led by ten drummers, began smartly parading through the City they knew they were flouting no laws. The problem was, this was a Saturday evening in the business district, and there was barely anyone around to watch them. Meanwhile, all over the boroughs of Kensington and Chelsea in west London another seventy fascists were trying to sell UM literature to passers-by; again, this was in breach of no laws.

At 10 p.m. the 150 UM members who had been involved in the previous two parts quickly converged on Piccadilly Circus, and formed a procession. Then, much to the horror of the pleasure-seekers enjoying a night on the town, the fascists began to parade around the area singing and shouting. As no anti-fascists had any inkling of the plan there was no one to oppose them, and it took a while for the police to muster up a large enough presence to disperse the march, which they did near Leicester Square, making seven arrests in the process.

What made this so distinct from all previous fascist marches was that not only had the UM not informed the police of their intentions, they had also knowingly and publicly broken the law.[77] Police licence for fascist activity arose in part out of the fascists' careful practice of trying to appear on the side of law and order. By deliberately disobeying a ban, the fascists had abandoned the strategy that had served them so well and revealed the levels of desperation to which they were sinking.

Two days after Operation M, Mosley addressed a capacity audience at Kensington Town Hall. This was the first time he had spoken since his cruise which had made him even more enthusiastic about Europe-A-Nation, a topic which he spoke about at length.[78] His return had given a slight morale boost to the UM leadership, but this did not translate into new activity or enthusiasm, and outdoor meetings continued to only attract a handful of people. Then, in the second half of October, Mosley returned to east London for two meetings at LCC schools, with the UM leadership hoping that a rumble with the enemy might give the party a much-needed publicity boost. On both occasions, 200 fascists turned out, but their Jewish and communist enemies were nowhere to be seen. Their absence had the fascists miffed – in particular Alf Flockhart, who had anonymously called Communist Party HQ and provided the times and dates of the meetings.[79]

In December 1949 Geoffrey Bernerd resigned as chairman of the 43 Group and was replaced by Vice-Chairman Cyril Barcan, one of the few remaining members of the original 43. In a letter to the *JC*, Bernerd explained that he could 'no longer devote the time necessary to fulfil this office' and that he wanted to 'make it clear that there are no other reasons apart from this for my action'.[80] In far more tragic circumstances, the man who had been Bernerd's principal sparring partner also departed the story. In October, Louis Hydleman died in a car accident;[81] it was a cruel irony that the man who would have most rejoiced at the Group's demise would not be around to witness it.

12

Into Memory

In December 1949, a new issue of *On Guard* appeared for the first time since September. Its different typeface and layout suggested that this would be the start of a new era for the paper; instead this was to be the last ever issue, and one that indicated a volte-face within the Group; Previously *On Guard* had avoided any overt link to the Group; now its masthead declared, 'ON GUARD: THE ORGAN OF THE 43 GROUP'. Beneath this was a front page–dominating editorial, which began: '*A Call to the Jewish People:* LET'S HAVE DONE WITH APPEASE-MENT', and called out the 'official leaders of Anglo-Jewry' and their 'stale policy of appeasement and timid effacement'.

This, the editorial noted, was a new departure for the paper which had previously ignored 'the struggle in the community' for 'the larger issues outside', by which it meant British and global fascism. However, as the Group had now decided 'to work within the Jewish community for support and understanding of its policy of militant anti-fascism', there was a need for *On Guard* to become 'its official propaganda weapon, ready to defend it against mud-slinging and opprobrium'. This move to work within the Jewish community signalled a clear realisation that the Group could no longer do without mainstream Jewish support, but as the Group had no intention of changing its stance it had to convince the community that 'a minority group does not gain respect by taking things lying down [but by] standing up to the enemy, fighting back, and showing it is a force worthy of consideration and esteem.'[1]

This new willingness to confront the community had already begun to emerge, often in ways that did not show the Group in the best light. Recent failed negotiations with AJEX had soured relations between the two organisations and led to open hostility from the Group. In October, 43ers turned up at Speakers' Corner to heckle the AJEX platform. 'Isn't the Board of Deputies fascist?' shouted a Group member, while another accused AJEX of being controlled by the Board. 'At least the 43 Group fight back, that is more than you do!' called out a third.[2] On another occasion Group members, including some in the executive, hijacked the stage at an AJEX reunion and made an appeal for funds. A request to leave was refused and the police were called.[3] Perhaps it was hardly surprising that the Group was beginning to turn on its own community, when its natural enemy was almost nowhere to be seen.

By 1950, the fascists had pretty much given up. A general election was in the offing, but UM resources were so low that the party announced: 'To fight an election at this time would be a gesture without reality. Our time has not yet come. We have no money to waste on gestures.'[4] Meanwhile, Mosley was continuing to arrange his departure from Britain, convinced that he would have far more success fighting for the fascist cause on the Continent, and was preparing to leave the running of the UM to Flockhart and Raven Thompson.[5] So it was completely against the run of play that in February 1950 the fascists scored a small victory.

Shot in 1949, *The Sword in the Desert* was the first feature film made about the conflict between the Jews and British in Palestine. Filmed in California, the plot centred on an American freighter captain who has been paid to smuggle Jewish migrants into Palestine and decides to fight along with his passengers against a British patrol boat that tries to intercept them. 'Not for the eyes of Britons!' declared the *Evening Standard*, when during the film's production the British press got wind of the plot. Nevertheless, a British distribution deal was agreed, with a premiere date set for 2 February 1950 at the New Gallery Cinema on Regent Street.

With four screenings scheduled, there were plenty of opportunities for fascist skulduggery, and both the police and 43 Group had large presences around the cinema that day. At first there was little to occupy either force, with the 1:40 and 4:50 p.m. screenings passing without incident. In the late afternoon the crowd began to gather for the 6:25 p.m. showing; in among them were Alf Flockhart and a band of UM members, who tried thrusting leaflets into the hands of passers-by until the police moved them along. Flockhart probably did not mind, as he already had his people on the inside.

One of these insiders was Ernest Heaton, a member of the UM Drum Corps who was sitting up in the circle waiting for the evening's final performance. Heaton had been assured by Flockhart that the signal he should expect, shouts of disruption, would come towards the beginning of the final screening, but the film had started and no such disruption had occurred. Heaton, who had been nervous from the outset and had spent the period between screenings hiding in the toilet, was sitting and fidgeting nervously, his fingers constantly running over the smoke bomb that was hidden in the pocket of his raincoat.

It was not until 10:20 p.m., when the film had reached its final act, that Duke Pile got to his feet and began loudly excoriating the work. The police reached him fast and escorted him out, but whether or not Pile was the man Flockhart had designated to give the signal, his followers went right ahead. From his seat up in the circle Heaton heard a crack and 'saw a trail of smoke travel from the right-hand side of the stalls and towards the centre of the screen'. A moment later, another 'huge cloud of smoke rose up from the floor' and the cinema became a 'mass of smoke'. The crowd was on its feet and struggling to get to one of the exits as panic set in. Even worse, some people in the audience were getting hit with things that were soft and furry, and moving, and then scurrying about. The fascists were throwing live vermin into the smoke! Attempts by the usherettes to restore order were met with indignation, as audience members demanded the lights be switched on.

Meanwhile, up in the circle Heaton was still in a bind. People were rushing out of the cinema, but he had not yet thrown his bomb. A year later, while being held in an Irish prison, he explained to the police: 'I was a loyal fascist at the time and under orders, my bomb had to be thrown in such a way as to be effective.' Heaton followed the audience out of the auditorium, down the stairs and through the swing doors towards the foyer. This was his chance: he 'darted round the corner of the stairs' and threw the bomb up the stairs, which quickly began to fill with smoke, causing even more panic as it drifted up towards the circle. Heaton ran, but a 'short stout man with a chubby face' spotted and chased after him, grabbing him just as he was about to leave the cinema. The man dragged Heaton over to the police and accused him of throwing a bomb, Heaton denied it and was searched, but the police found nothing incriminating on him and let him go. Outside, Heaton bumped into two female UM members, who joined him in watching the people and smoke stream out of the cinema, before they went in search of a public telephone so they could report to Flockhart.[6]

Back in the cinema, both the 43 Group and the police were working to restore calm and clear the smoke, and, one hopes, the rodents. Eventually the audience was able to return to the auditorium and the film was resumed with no further incidents. Outside, however, the remaining 43 Group and UM contingents loitered until well after the film had finished, and the police had to move both organisations along.

It was the view of the chief superintendent of C Division, expressed in a report that was forwarded to Special Branch, that *The Sword in the Desert* should be banned to prevent any further trouble; the Public Control Committee of the LCC agreed, and banned all future showings.[7] The UM and all of its numerous splinter movements proclaimed a major victory, but those proclaiming it were by this point no more than scattered clusters of extremists. One of the very few intelligence officers left watching the fascists wondered whether banning *The Sword in the Desert* would lead to similar incidents, but in reality this was a movement that had just run out of steam.[8] Mosley went off to Europe again in March and forbade Flockhart from engaging in 'sensational activities' in his absence, and so, except for a few lacklustre and poorly attended street meetings, the fascists did nothing.[9]

In April Mosley returned, and the UM announced his intention to speak at Ridley Road on May Day. Other than a failed attempt by AJEX to steal the platform that led to some controversy, Mosley's first outdoor speech at Ridley Road met with little incident but plenty of opposition. The meeting was opened by Hamm, down from Manchester for the occasion, who introduced Raven Thompson and then Mosley. A crowd of just 1,200 gathered around the Elephant to listen to Mosley, demonstrating just how little pull he now had. Even worse, anti-fascists outnumbered Mosleyites two to one and Mosley had to contend with boos and heckles throughout his speech. As for violence, there was hardly any. No injuries were reported and only one arrest was made during the entire day. Hamm brought the meeting to a close and the crowd dispersed peacefully. The meeting had gone off without a hitch, and as a result hardly anyone noticed.[10]

Also hardly noticed that May Day was the 43 Group. Loitering among the market crowds, Group members, led by Harry Bidney, kept a watch on the fascists throughout the Saturday as they held the pitch, but that was the only time they came to the attention of the police. G Division could have been forgiven for thinking that the 43 Group no longer existed.

Like Having Your Leg Off

The 43 Group was a victim of its own success. The disappearance of the fascist threat had several consequences that jeopardised the Group's continued survival. First and foremost was the swift exodus of much of the original membership, with the majority of those remaining being pugnacious youngsters. This in itself was a problem, as without an enemy against which violent passions could be directed, destructive behaviour could result. This was recognised by the most loyal backers, and even they began withholding funds and pressuring the executive into closing the Group down. The executive, however, did not want the Group to simply go out of existence, at least not without making a real and lasting change to the way the Jewish community defended itself.

In 1949 a proposal for a way the Group might close with dignity had been devised by an unlikely source, Louis Hydleman. After his failed attempts to get the Group to dissolve in 1948, he came up with a far more elegant solution: the creation of a single united Ex-Servicemen's Association, to be formed by AJEX, MUJEX, the Leeds Association and the 43 Group. As the Leeds and Manchester associations had strong relationships with AJEX and the 43 Group, it was to them that Hydleman turned to propel his idea, and they were successful in getting all parties to come to the table for a conference where a united ex-servicemen's association was in principle agreed upon. The 43 Group leadership were particularly on board with this proposal, and it was as a result of these productive negotiations that the Group and AJEX began to publicly collaborate with each other in the spring of 1949. In the end, AJEX scuppered the negotiations, refusing to see why, as the largest association, it should close down, and demanding the smaller organisations merely merge into it.

Long after the negotiations had collapsed, the 43 Group held out hope they could be restarted, as was made clear from Geoff Bernerd's resignation letter sent to the *JC* where he called on all Jewish ex-Service men and women to assist in the immediate establishment of a united ex-Service front.[11] But distance between the 43 Group and AJEX remained, and the willingness of Group members to heckle AJEX speakers was unlikely to lead to a rapprochement.

By March 1950, however, the Group was willing to try and restore relations with AJEX and they requested a meeting with the JDC, which they hoped would help to bridge the gap. Lieberman of the JDC met the Group's representatives, who he found were 'anxious to close the rift' between the ex-servicemen's organisations and asked him if he would 'use his good offices to recall the conference of the various organisations which had been held some months ago'. They also informed him that the Group 'was ready to disband and come into the Ex-servicemen's organisation on an individual basis'. Why, Lieberman inquired, did the Group want to recall the confer-ence if it was going to disband anyway? Explained the chair Cyril Barcan, the Group 'wished to disband in a systematic way'. He also claimed to 'have material which would be of use to a national organisation'.[12]

Lieberman, who continued to support the idea of a united ex-servicemen's association, promised to relay the Group's request to AJEX, but they never received a response. According to Group secretary Wolfe Wayne, the Group had heard nothing from AJEX since October 1949, when they had last requested the conference be recalled. Since then the Group had sought to reach out to AJEX through intermediaries, but 'AJEX remained firm to the principle of non-co-operation.'[13]

With no response from AJEX it was becoming clear that the Group only had one option left: unilateral disbandment. Murray Podro, who was still serving as intelligence director, recalled that once the decision had been made by the senior members of the executive, the rest of the officers were made to go along with it. 'We all had to agree there was nothing more to do,' recalled Podro. As for the rank-and-file members, by the spring of 1950 they could be forgiven for thinking that the Group had already closed without anyone telling them. Jonny Goodman was in the Group until the end, but all he remembered about the closure was a fizzling out. The fact that the Group did have a final meeting, which Goodman had no memory of, shows just how inactive it had become in its final days.

At 2:15 pm on 4 June 1950 at the Holborn, Gray's Inn Road, Cyril Barcan called the Extraordinary General Meeting of the

43 Group to order. A paper was passed around to all those in the hall, entitled 'Disbandment of 43 Group Resolution':

> In the interests of the Jewish community, as the ultimate proof of our sincerity in this desire for unity, and because we consider that Jewish ex-servicemen can and must play a leading role against all forms of reaction, it is hereby resolved by the membership of the 43 Group of Ex-servicemen that this organisation shall forthwith disband, and that all those eligible should immediately join and take an active part in the work of the Association of Jewish Ex-servicemen.
>
> We call on the members of the 43 Group to take with them into AJEX the great spirit which won the admiration of the Jewish community, and to continue the fight there against fascism and anti-Semitism.

The mood in the room was fractious and disruptive. 'A lot of people who were very angry about the decision to close the Group,' remember Jules Konopinski. 'There were many there who had been beaten up or who had been sent to prison, and they thought that it was wrong to end a campaign right in the middle of it.'[14] Konopinski himself was so furious at the decision to close the Group that when he got to his feet to say his piece he refused to stop, and was thrown out of the meeting hall.[15] In his eighties, Jules still felt that the decision was the wrong one: 'The only major failing of the Group that I can think of, is if the Group hadn't disbanded then, if it had stayed together, even as a social club, then we would not have had the problems of the '60s.'

Konopinski's view was typical of the youngsters, but the older members believed that closure was the correct move. Even if they themselves believed they could go on fighting, they realised that the Group had done its job, it had crushed the fascists' attempts at a revival and had sent Mosley packing: what more could it actually achieve? The debate was brought to an end, the motion put to a vote, hands were raised – the motion carried.

'It was like having your leg off,' recalled Murray Podro, for whom, like so many others in the room, the Group had been his life. From its most committed members, the Group had demanded and enthusiastically received their time and dedication, and potentially their freedom, health and lives. But now all it wanted from its most involved members was that they help pack up.

Without an agreement to merge with AJEX, there was a question of what should happen to the records and sensitive files. Gerald Anthill, a member of the executive, was afraid the CPGB would get its hands on them via one of its operatives still in the Group. In the dead of night, Anthill, who had a key to Panton Street, let himself in and removed some of the most sensitive material, including letters from spies and the massive card index of known fascists. He would hold onto these for decades before handing them over to Gerry Gable of *Searchlight*. His paranoia saved an extraordinary record for posterity as other Group leaders, likewise fearing their files would fall into the wrong hands, fed them to the flames.

New Beginnings

One year later, Harry Kaufman finished his National Service and began working as a travelling salesman. Kaufman sold his wares all over London and one day was driving back home from south of the river when he passed the UM's headquarters on Vauxhall Bridge Road. Compelled by forces unknown, Kaufman got out of his car and walked into the bookshop that fronted the HQ. 'They knew who I was but they didn't know my name, I don't think.' No one said anything to him but just watched suspiciously as he perused the literature before buying a paper. It became a ritual for Kaufman, every few months for six or seven years: whenever he was driving back from south London, he would stop, go into the shop and buy a paper. Occasionally he saw members of the fascist brass, including Hamm, and he once caught a glimpse of Mosley walking down the stairs before disappearing into a corridor. When I asked Kaufman what drove him to keep going back, he insisted that he was not there to cause a fight: 'Listen, they were all six foot tall, I'm five foot two. I just went there, call it chutzpah. I just wanted to let them know that I wasn't scared and to tell them we're still here.'[16]

Kaufman was not the only Group veteran who kept tabs on the fascists; Jules Konopinski and his old East End section friends all kept their ears to the ground, and turned out whenever anyone, normally the ever-vigilant Harry Bidney, learnt of a fascist march or demonstration. While most of the Group's veterans felt like they were done with the fight, should they ever chance upon an old enemy in the street, well, then instincts might force their hand . . . or foot. 'I kicked Raven Thompson off a bus once,' boasted Martin Block. 'I had just got married, the Group was over, I was living a normal life. We lived in Battersea and we used to come regularly on the bus to Chelsea to go to the pictures; we were upstairs because we smoked on the bus, came down the stairs and, standing on the platform, holding the bar and waiting to get off the bus, was Raven Thompson. I automatically kicked him off the bus, and he went rolling into the road. His daughter was screaming her head off and I got hold of my wife and we ran into the cinema. It was just instinct, pure instinct.'[17]

Opportunities to confront the fascists throughout the 1950s were few and far between. Mosley left England for good in 1951, splitting his time between France and Ireland, and became one of the founders of the fascist European Social Movement. Following Mosley abroad was Jeffrey Hamm, who, Mosley was told, had succumbed to crippling depression due to his work in Manchester and would quit the movement if not given a new role. Heeding this advice, Mosley put Hamm in charge of his publishing company and, following the death of Raven Thompson in 1955, made him his private secretary, a role in which Hamm served until Mosley's death. When he was not abroad working with Mosley, Hamm was back in London encouraging his small band of UM thugs to target, sometimes violently, the new 'coloured' migrants, many of whom were settling in Hamm's neighbourhood of Notting Hill. In the late 1950s when the Teddy Boys began targeting the new immigrants, Hamm fanned the flames and was one of the main agitators of the 1958 Notting Hill Riots. Up on his soapbox, egging 'the Teds' on, Hamm hoped that these young men would join the UM and lead to a resurgence for his organisation, but it was not to be: this subculture had no interest in fascist politics.

The most successful far-right organiser in the 1950s was A. K. Chesterton, who had returned from Africa to found the League of Empire Loyalists in 1954. Chesterton did not share Mosley's belief in a fascist state, and instead shaped his movement around principles of nationalism, patriotism, anti-Semitism and a furious opposition to the break-up of the Empire. The Empire Loyalists primarily consisted of 'retired military gentlemen, ex-colonial administrators, anti-communist and anti-Semitic Roman Catholics, alienated scions of the Conservative establishment and energetic upper-middle-class ladies'.[18] These were hardly the sorts to run dangerous street movements, and they mainly resorted to publicity stunts such as gatecrashing Tory conferences, or striking journalists who insulted the monarchy. Nonetheless, in Chesterton's League were the next generation of far-right leaders, including John Tyndall, John Bean, Martin Webster and Colin Jordan,[19] whose politics were far more influenced by Chesterton's nationalism than by Mosley's European fascism.

In 1956 Colin Jordan became the first of these young men to split with Chesterton, forming his own, strongly Nazi, organisation: the White Defence League. The following year, Bean and Tyndall founded the National Labour Party, and three years later the two organisations merged into the British National Party, based at the Notting Hill home of Jordan's most significant mentor, Arnold Leese.[20] However, two years later, infighting led to Jordan and Tyndall breaking away from Bean to form the virulently pro-Nazi National Socialist Movement (NSM).

On 1 July 1962 Jordan and Tyndall held a mass meeting for their new movement at Trafalgar Square. The meeting was well publicised and one 43 Group veteran, who had never stopped watching the fascists, caught wind of it and started to ring round a few of his mates, some of whom were also Group veterans. Arriving at Trafalgar Square they saw that the NSM had erected two massive signs, reading 'Britain Awake' and 'Free Britain from Jewish Control'. Jordan and Tyndall must have been encouraged when they saw the crowd was thousands strong, but the moment they started speaking it was obvious they were outnumbered, as the boos and jeers drowned out their voices and a barrage of projectiles were hurled at them. A 43 Group veteran has given his account of events:

> Then it went off. Fights were breaking out all over Trafalgar Square. The papers said there were 5,000 there, of whom about 800 were the enemy . . . The police shut the NSM meeting down and when we got our hands on the Nazis we really laid into them, but it was disorganised.

Following that rally, many of the Jewish anti-fascists in the crowd began discussing the possibility of setting up a successor organisation to the 43 Group. Some had been in the older organisation; others were younger and new to the fight. One such youngster was Gerry Gable. Now twenty-five years old, he had been just twelve when he witnessed the fascists' attempted march on Stamford Hill and tried to join the fight before being pulled away by Harry Bidney.[21] Now Bidney, the most prominent 43 Group member involved in these discussions, was encouraging Gable and everyone else to throw themselves in.

A few weeks after Jordan's rally, it was discovered that Mosley was planning to hold a rally of his own in Trafalgar Square, and preparations for the anti-fascist organisation went into overdrive with the hope that it could be brought into existence before Mosley's meeting. It was not to be, but really it did not matter. According to the 43 Group veteran:

We had 17,000 people waiting for Mosley and I can assure you they were not his friends. Only about 300 of them had crawled out of their rat holes that day.

I remember they all were up on the plinth of Nelson's column putting up huge placards with slogans on and a tannoy system. Before they got around to testing the sound, some bright spark in the crowd had lassoed the loudspeakers and dragged them into the crowd. The placards and the Mosleyites followed in quick succession.

The following month, the 62 Group came into existence. Although it was actually called the 62 Committee and named after the year it was founded, not the number of people in the room, the 62 saw itself as the successor of the 43. Among the 62 Committee's founding members were Jules Konopinski, Jonny Goodman and Harry Bidney, who became its head of intelligence. On the whole it was the 43 Group's younger members who joined its successor organisation; 43 Group luminaries such as Flamberg, Bernerd, Sherman and others were all approached and asked to join, but manifested little interest: they were all much older by this point, had jobs and families and felt their fascist-fighting days were behind them.

For thirteen years, the 62 Group fought fascists. At first its main target was Mosley and the Union Movement, who once again focused their activities around Ridley Road in an attempt to stage a comeback.[22] For four years the 62 Group targeted UM activities with a level of violence that equalled, and even surpassed, the 43 Group's. In 1966, Mosley tried and failed to run for Parliament, but by this point the 62 Group had almost completely smashed his organisation off the streets, and after 1966 the UM and Mosley were hardly ever heard from again. With Mosley gone, the 62 Group focused most of its attentions on Jordan, Tyndall, Bean and their organisations, including the NSM, BNP and the nascent National Front. Not that there was an active far right throughout the 62 Group's existence, but unlike its predecessor, it did not need one to survive.

The 62 Group never sought to grow into a large organisation, which meant that in periods of inactivity it did not need to worry about satisfying the demands of a large membership. Another key difference between the 62 and 43 was that the 62 was only ever open to Jewish members – although it was constantly seeking to work with other anti-fascist and anti-racist organisations, especially those within immigrant communities vulnerable to the far-right threat. Two concerted efforts were made by the police to close the 62 Group, first in 1963 and then in 1969, when the police ordered that leading members be arrested on sight – but both failed to deter the Group.

In the end, the 62 Group decided to shut itself down in 1975 when its members realised they had grown too old for the fight.[23] In that same year, *Searchlight,* an anti-fascist magazine intermittently published by Gerry Gable and others attached to the 62 Group, became a monthly publication. Like *On Guard*, today it keeps a close watch on the far right and ensures that it is always forced to live under the bright lights of scrutiny and constant observation. Also created by veterans of the 62 Group is the Community Security Trust (CST), whose founding chairman is the 62 Group veteran and business tycoon, Gerald Ronson. Started in 1994, the CST is responsible for protecting the Jewish community and its places of worship, and also keeps tabs on anti-Semitism and threats from the far right. When the 43 Group aimed to form an organisation 'capable of communal defence', they were probably envisaging something very much like the CST. In the Group's day, the leaders of the Jewish community baulked at such a notion, but today the CST is one of the community's most valued and necessary organisations, and it traces its lineage all the way back to the 43 Group.

Lives

For those activists who were members of both the 43 and 62 Groups, both are part of their proud anti-fascist stories.

However, anti-fascism is just one glowing element of the often extraordinary lives of the 43 Group veterans.

The most famous of those veterans was of course Vidal Sassoon, who became the world's most celebrated hairdresser, helping define the look of the 1960s with his iconic 'Bob Cut'. Sassoon went on to build a hairdressing empire, but he never forgot his anti-fascist roots, and in 1983 he founded the Vidal Sassoon International Centre for the Study of Anti-Semitism at the Hebrew University in Jerusalem. Sassoon left England for California in the 1970s, but he made sure to stay in contact with his old friends, many of whom became increasingly jealous of his Californian tan and apparent immunity to the ageing process.

Sassoon was not the only Group member to make iconic contributions to popular culture. While Martin Block remained a musical instrument restorer for his entire life and repaired the instruments of many of the jazz greats, Ivor Arbiter, his sidekick who had followed him into that line of work, quickly realised he lacked the required patience; besides, he had dreams of running a major company. Arbiter's first company was the UK's first specialist drum shop, Drum City, located on Shaftesbury Avenue. It attracted all the world's best jazz and rock drummers, including in 1963 a young Ringo Starr, for whom Arbiter designed the famous dropped-down T logo and printed it on Ringo's drum; Arbiter would become the main supplier of the Beatles', and many other bands', gear through his second shop, Sound City. In the late 1980s, Arbiter made another massive contribution to music in the UK when, at a Japanese trade show, he spotted a machine that allowed people to sing along to the music of their favourite songs. With a hunch that this could be an incredibly popular form of entertainment, he ordered a large consignment of these machines and introduced karaoke to Britain.[24]

Also present at the beginning of numerous famous musical careers was Barry Langford. He had first followed his father into running the London Silver Vaults, where he deployed his considerable flair for publicity to attract such patrons as Liberace and Elizabeth Taylor. Langford's PR talents and his magnetic personality brought him to the attention of director John Boorman, who featured him in his 1963 television documentary series, *Citizen 63*. This experience gave Langford a taste for the silver screen and he became a successful producer and director, making the music shows *Juke Box Jury* and *The Beat Room*, through which Langford helped launch the musical careers of, among others, Tom Jones and the Who.

After *The Beat Room*, Langford produced another music show called *Gadzooks! It's All Happening!* where he ran into a bunch of long-haired lads called the Mannish Boys. Langford told them they had to cut their hair before going on air, but the boys refused. One of the Mannish Boys was a young chap called David Robert Jones, whose talent for self-promotion eclipsed even Langford's. In response to Langford's request he formed the Society for the Prevention of Cruelty to Long-Haired Men, and was interviewed by the BBC's *Tonight* Show: that's how Britain was introduced to David Bowie. In the 1970s, Langford moved to Israel, where he was instrumental in developing its TV industry and became one of the country's first TV stars.

Staying firmly behind the camera was Jonny Goodman, who had started working in the TV industry as a page boy when he was just fourteen. When he returned from his service in Palestine, he went back into the business and slowly made his way up the ranks, until he became the production supervisor on *The Saint* with Roger Moore. When *The Saint* finished, Goodman helped create Moore's successor project, *The Persuaders!* which starred Moore and Tony Curtis. Goodman produced many other hit shows, including *Quatermass* and *Minder*, and from 1987–89 he served as the chairman of BAFTA.

Gerry Lewis, *On Guard*'s young journalist, also ended up in the entertainment industry. Ditching journalism in the 1950s, he was hired by the PR company of another former journalist, Frederic Mullally. Although the two men never met when the

Group was active, they quickly established the connection and Mullally became Lewis's mentor and lifelong friend. In the 1950s, Mullally's was the pre-eminent celebrity PR company, whose clients included Audrey Hepburn, Frank Sinatra and Douglas Fairbanks Jr. His semi-autobiographical novel, *Looking for Clancy*, became the basis for the BBC's mini-series *Clancy*, and in the 1970s and 80s he wrote a long-running satirical cartoon for *Penthouse* called *Oh Wicked Wanda*. Lewis meanwhile specialised in movie marketing and PR, and ended up working directly for Steven Spielberg; he was responsible for the European marketing and distribution of films including *E.T.*, *Schindler's List* and *Jaws*.

Success for 43 Group veterans did not, of course, come only within the entertainment industry. Gerry Flamberg (now Lambert) worked with his aunt to expand their door-to-door jewellery sales business into a very successful chain of dress jewellery and gift shops. Gerry's life remained rich and colourful and he often found himself in the company of noted celebrities and sportsmen – his daughter Barbara once walked in on the great boxer Joe Louis lying in the family bath – and even some well-known New York gangsters.

When Geoffrey Bernerd became the Group's chairman he was employed at RKO Pictures, but after being fired from the studio following his work with the Group he decided to have a career change and went into the hospitality industry. In the 1960s, Bernerd became the landlord of the Grenadier pub by Hyde Park, which has a reputation of being one of the most haunted pubs in England, something he attested to during a Halloween programme made for the BBC.[25]

Unlike Bernerd, many of the Group veterans stayed and made successful careers out of the trades in which they were apprentices. Butcher's boy Philip Evansky went on to own a chain of kosher butchers in north and east London, while Jules Konopinski, apprenticed as a leather goods maker, acquired a successful leather goods shop near Scotland Yard – the high-ranking police officers who frequented his shop knowing nothing of his violent past. Martin White, who went into the cloth trade, continues in that line of work today and has been referred to as London's last cloth merchant. Morris Beckman, by contrast, realised that the writing in which he had dabbled during the war was unlikely to turn a profit, and so he abandoned it for the world of business, and for a time ran a rather successful clothing manufacturer. Following his retirement, Beckman returned to writing and published several historical works.

As for Philly and Joe Goldberg, they never lost their reputation for being East End toughs; ask any Group member about the notorious twins and they always said the same thing: 'Even the Krays were afraid of them.' One East End tough who did change, however, was Jackie Myerovitch. Towards the latter days of the Group, Myerovitch was stabbed in a fight in a dance hall. During his recovery he was approached by the notorious bookmaker and future owner of Ladbrokes, Maxie Parker, who hired him as one of his heavies. For years Myerovitch worked for Parker, before deciding he preferred a more sedate lifestyle and becoming a tailor. In his fifties, Myerovitch sought to gain the education he had been denied by his family's poverty and earned a bachelor's degree in literature at the age of fifty-three. Six years later, in 1986, he passed away. 'Despite his tough exterior he was a gentle man,' wrote the playwright Bernard Kops of his childhood friend. 'He had a heart of gold and helped everyone and anyone. So I sing of this unsung hero, of this sweet human being whose contribution to Jewry was incalculable.'[26]

Two years before Myerovitch died, his old East End section boss Harry Bidney passed away. Bidney never abandoned his lifelong commitment to anti-fascism, and upon his passing his friend and mentee Gerry Gable made clear just how important Bidney was to the anti-fascist cause in Britain:

> He was a man hated yet respected by the enemy and they will not sleep any easier in their beds now he has passed away,

because his work laid the foundations for the network of anti-fascist intelligence work which exists in this country today and grows steadily stronger.[27]

Over the course of its existence, the 43 Group probably had some 2,000 active members; to tell all their stories, both during and after the Group, is of course an impossibility. Some naturally told their own stories to their children and grandchildren, but many others, for various reasons, kept quiet. Then, in 1990 a number of Group veterans received a letter on official 43 Group–headed paper. The letter was from Lennie Rolnick, inviting them to the first official reunion of the 43 Group.[28] Around 150 veterans attended the event in Willesden, and were delighted to be reunited with their old comrades for the first time in forty years. Some in the room had remained close friends and become in-laws or business partners; others had not even met each other during the Group's existence; but the spirit of brotherhood united them all.

These reunions became annual affairs, and a *JC* reporter who attended the penultimate event in 2006 was impressed by how 'the mostly octogenarian old soldiers showed they had lost none of their combative spirit.' This would be Gerry Lambert's final reunion: 'Thugs were what we were fighting, and we proved we were more ruthless than they were,'[29] he told the reporter proudly. Gerry died the following year. Although 2006 was supposed to be the final reunion, enough of the Group's veterans were around in 2009 for them to decide to hold one more – but that one, all agreed, should definitely be the last. Old friends never lost touch, though, and no opportunity was missed to reminisce about old times, even if those opportunities only ever seemed to occur at the graveside of yet another comrade.

By the time Luke Brandon Field and I began our search for veterans of the Group, the vast majority of its members had passed on. We were, however, fortunate to find around a dozen who were still around and willing to share their experiences.

One brisk March day in 2015, we hired a studio in Shepherd's Bush and filmed interviews with those members who were happy to talk on camera. Towards the end of Jules Konopinski's interview, Murray Podro entered the studio; Jules, effusive and enthusiastic as ever, greeted the taciturn old spymaster. They embraced and spoke for a few minutes and then it was Murray's turn to be interviewed. An hour or so later, as we were about to finish, I recalled that moment. 'Do you think about the members of the 43 Group with love and fondness?' I asked. 'Oh yes, definitely,' Murray responded. 'I haven't seen Jules Konopinski for donkey's years, but he greets me as if I am a brother and that's . . . quite moving.' For Jules, it was this sense of brotherhood that made the Group so special: 'The camaraderie was felt throughout the group, regardless of whether someone was an ex-serviceman or not. The older members took the younger members under their wing. It felt like a very strong brotherhood, and the women were very much a part of that as well.'

Even without the spirit of brotherhood that echoed down the years, veterans felt immeasurably proud of their time in the Group. 'I don't go around shouting it from the rooftops, but I'm very proud to have been a member . . . It's part of my general makeup,' said Podro. 'It's a part of my life I will always be proud of, always,' Harry Kaufman told me. For Gerry Lewis, 'It holds a special place in my heart; I think of it very often and very warmly, and I'm very glad I was involved in it.'

I never got the chance to meet Mildred Levy, the Group secretary who often threw herself right into the thick of the fighting, but her son Simon told me that in her later years she would often say that being in the 43 Group was the thing in her life of which she was proudest. Stanley Marks, the North London section head, was another veteran I never got the opportunity to interview; fortunately, however, he was interviewed for the BBC Archive Hour's programme, *A Rage in Dalston*, and I'll leave the last word to him:

If it achieved nothing else, it gave Jewish ex-servicemen the sense of pride that we are a people, that we can defend ourselves, and we're not just running away. If it did nothing else. But I'm sure it did do more than that.

Afterword: We Fight Fascists

As the great Douglas Adams once wrote: 'Human beings, who are almost unique in having the ability to learn from the experience of others, are also remarkable for their apparent disinclination to do so.' Were Adams alive today in 2019, he would surely be shaking his head in disbelief at the sheer bloody accuracy of this statement. The far right is once again on the march around the world, and its charismatic leaders with their easy answers are once again finding support at the ballot box. Meanwhile, those who have some inkling as to why a resurgent far right could be a problem remain characteristically incapable of opposing any real resistance.

Some might say that fascism and authoritarianism are irresistible forces of history whose moments are cyclical, and there is little we can do to stop them. Similarly, it might be argued that there is little point in drawing on the story of the 43 Group, an anti-fascist organisation that existed when fascism had little chance of success in Britain, and which therefore offers no lessons for the modern struggle. What can be said in reply? Perhaps the struggle is futile, and the only logical thing is to succumb to defeatism. Or perhaps logic be damned and we fight on no matter how unlikely our success, because we believe that what the fascists seek to destroy are things which to us give life its rich colour; that we wish to live in a diverse kaleidoscopic world and the fight to maintain it is a good one. If so, we will take our lessons from wherever we can, and I believe the story of the 43 Group provides us with two essential teachings.

The members of the 43 Group chose violence. This is significant, and it is particularly significant because of who they were and what they had witnessed. Despite the perceptions of the JDC, the police and the press, the 43 Group were not political radicals. They did not share the ambitions of their communist allies to smash the status quo and bring the capitalist system crashing to the ground. Truth be told, most of the 43 Group – even those who grew up in the cauldron of radical left-wing East End politics – were by their twenties ready to reap the benefits capitalism offers to smart, dynamic, hard-working individuals. Similarly, the majority of the 43 Group's members considered themselves to be patriots and had a great respect for the institutions of the British state, even if they were well aware of the anti-Semitic attitudes that permeated it throughout. Most came from families who felt profound love for the monarchy, an expression of gratitude to the country that had taken them in as they fled the pogroms. The younger generation did not necessarily share this royalism, but through serving in the forces their sense of patriotism was reaffirmed. Throughout its existence the Group tried to cooperate with the law as far as possible and continually called for the ban of fascism. This is at odds with the more radical, and more prevalent, anti-fascist philosophy which sees the destruction of fascism as the first objective in a campaign against the exploitative capitalist state. The 43 Group was not a revolutionary organisation; it wanted to preserve the state and its democracy, and only acted because the Labour government of the day would not.

The 43 Group turned to radical means to achieve moderate ends, but all they did was pay attention to a lesson that everyone else, and especially the government, seemed determined to forget. Just as you could not appease Hitler, fascism cannot be reasoned with, and anyone who thinks you can debate someone who will happily watch you choke to death breathing Zyklon B is a fool. Fascism is a politics of violence. It rejects the norms of civilised democracy and wishes to return to a state of nature, where might is right. The 43 Group realised that to defeat the fascists you had to beat them at their own game and hit them twice as hard as they hit you, and doing so was a moral imperative. As service personnel during the war, they saw what happened to a continent where fascists held the reins of power, and as Jews they knew the sheer horror of the destruction of their community. They lived under the shadow of the Second World War and the Holocaust and, having first- and second-hand experience of these traumatic events, knew that when the British fascists raised their heads there was only one morally sound course of action. For anyone who baulks at the idea of turning to violence to preserve democracy, the 43 Group's story is essential. When those who had seen fascism unleashed on the world discovered a seed of a resurgence, they knew that a modicum of violence now (recall the journey down to Brighton with the Lipman brothers: 'We're not here to kill. We're here to maim!') is far preferable to destruction and desolation later.

And yet as I write these words I know that I for one am unlikely to heed them. I confess to a certain cowardice and, personally, do not much fancy coming face to face with fascist thugs. It is, however, not just those on the front line who can draw valuable guidance from the Group, which offered one lesson that applies to us all, whether we are out on the streets, at work, down the pub, or on social media. The 43 Group held it that so long as you were opposed to fascism you could be a member or an ally – no matter what. There is no room for claim-staking narcissism in the fight against fascism. It is vital that anti-fascists never forget they are always on the same side, and that every potential new recruit to the fight should be welcomed with open arms, no matter what their other politics are. The fight against fascism is too important for ego, and when the enemies of fascism fight among themselves, it only makes things easier for the people who would kill us all.

Those of us who believe in democracy, tolerance, and the ability of all peoples to be neighbours must be intolerant of anyone who would foment hate, suspicion and conspiracy, and whose words would lead to the targeting of individuals based upon traits inherent to their identities. We must be clear-sighted, and this means being able to tell the difference between a fascist and someone with whom we merely disagree. You might not like someone who does not share your politics, but if their views and opinions can exist in the same space as yours and everyone else's, they do not lead to persecution or victimisation; if they can accept plurality and difference, then they are on your side. This is I think the most crucial lesson we can learn from the 43 Group.

The title of this book was inspired by a phrase that appeared on much of the Group's publicity material: 'The 43 Group Fights Fascism Today'. But in stripping away the Group's name, I hope to evoke the universality at the heart of the Group's politics. For while the Group consciously identified as Jewish, alerting would-be persecutors to the news that the Jewish community would no longer be content with the roles of scapegoat and whipping boy, it was always intended to be inclusive.

Yes, *we* fight fascists, but *you* are welcome to join us.

Acknowledgements

Over the past eight years many people have helped me try and tell the story of the 43 Group, and without their contributions there is no way this book would exist.

First I must thank my wonderful agent, Zoe Ross, at United Agents. Her passion and immediate connection to the project let me know I had someone wonderful on my side. My thanks also to Zoe's assistant, Gabriella Docherty, for all her efforts. I am also beyond grateful to my editor, Leo Hollis, who from the outset has offered unstinting and excellent guidance and advice as well as plenty of all-too-necessary reassurance. Also at Verso I am very grateful to Mark Martin, who responded to my obsessional perfectionism with good humour and patience, and to Jim Caunter for his expert copy-editing.

For the first six years of working on the Group's story my focus was on developing a television show, and whenever people suggested I should write a book I resolutely declared that that was something I would never do. Therefore I owe a huge debt of gratitude to Richard Warlow, who gave me the kick up the arse I needed. I do not think this book would have happened had Richard not forced my hand – I am eternally grateful.

The vast majority of the research for this book was done when I was working on developing the TV show. Therefore, I need to thank everyone who was involved in supporting that. In particular I should like to thank Eric Webber, for his continued enthusiastic and generous support; Clifton Wiens, who though he stopped working on the project several years ago has continued to send excellent leads and information my way; and Josh Sugarman, who knows better than anyone else what an abject trial working with me can be. Josh and I have had numerous passionate disagreements about the Group over the years, and it is through those that my thinking about the subject has developed and taken shape – this book would have been a considerably inferior work were it not for those heartfelt and fervent discussions.

I am also very grateful to everyone at the various museums, archives and libraries I visited. In particular I would like to thank Kathrin Pierson at the Jewish Museum, Roz Currie at the former Jewish Military Museum, and Howard Falksohn and Sonia Bacca at the Wiener Library for the Study of Holocaust and Genocide. My thanks also to everyone who helped at the London School of Economics' Women's Library, Birmingham University's Cadbury Research Library, the London Metropolitan Archives, the National Archives, and the British Library, or, as I like to call it, my office.

By the time I started working on this story many of the Group members had passed away, and so I am hugely thankful to their children and other relatives who told me so much about them. In particular I should like to thank Barbara and Jamie Lambert, Simon and Philippa Garland, Jeremy Brull, and Monica Symonds. I am also incredibly grateful to Catherine Evans for putting me in touch with her great-uncle Philip Evans (Evansky), and to Alison Dagul for introducing me to her father Gerry Abrahams.

A huge thanks to Gerry Gable for reading an early copy of this manuscript, spotting several errors, and sharing with me his insights. I am also incredibly grateful to Gerry for trusting me with the collection of documents Gerald Anthill removed from Group HQ in its final days. My thanks also to the Anthill family for giving me permission to view them – Gerald himself recently passed away, but if I had had the opportunity to meet him he would have had my enthusiastic gratitude for holding onto these invaluable documents.

For me the greatest privilege of this work was the opportunity I had to interview around a dozen members of the 43

Group and other eyewitnesses who shared with me their stories and recollections. I am indebted to the time and generosity of Frederic Mullally, Alan Foreman, Davina Bensusan, Harold Melzack, Trudie Malawer, Gerry Abrahams, Ivor Benjamin, Murray Podro, Morris Beckman, Harvey Lubin, Martin Block, Philip Evans, Gerry Lewis, Harry Kaufman, Martin White and Jonny Goodman – several of whom have passed away since our interviews. I would, however, like to single out Jules Konopinski, who was not only wonderfully keen to share with me his stories of the Group and the East End section (every time we spoke Jules seemed to produce yet another amazing anecdote about the Group), but has since we first met become one of mine and the project's most enthusiastic cheerleaders. I have no doubt that I would have given up this project long ago were it not for the fear of letting down Jules and all the other Group veterans who trusted me with their stories.

To my grandparents Pat Sonabend and John Slome, who shared with me their recollections of the period as well as their own small connections to this story, I give both my thanks and my undying love. John passed away in 2012, only a few months after he first revealed his involvement with the Group, and it is to his memory that this book is dedicated.

If there are two real heroes in the story of this book, it is my parents. Like the good millennial that I am, I wrote the vast majority of my book while living in their home, and so a massive thank you to them for putting up with me and my horrendous habits and personality.

My final thank-you must of course go to my very dear, very old friend Luke Brandon Field, who in December 2011 got into his bath to watch a documentary about a hairdresser and got out to call his baldest friend. Luke, you have no idea how grateful I am that you thought of me. By introducing me to this story you genuinely changed my life. What's more, working alongside you these past eight years has been a wonderful, exciting rollercoaster, and I for one sincerely hope the journey still has a way to go.

Notes

Abbreviations

BOD	Archives of the Board of Deputies, London Metropolitan Archives
BOD DCR	Archives of the Jewish Defence Committee of the Board of Deputies, Wiener Library for the Study of the Holocaust and Genocide
CAB	Records of the Cabinet Office, National Archives at Kew
HO	Records of the Home Office, National Archives
LSE COLL	Collections of the London School of Economics
MEPO	Records of the Metropolitan Police Office, National Archives
KV	Records of the Security Services, National Archives
OMD	The Oswald Mosley Collection, Cadbury Research Library at Birmingham University
PREM	Records of the Prime Minister's Office, National Archives

Introduction

1. A second edition was published in 2013, entitled *The 43 Group: Battling with Mosley's Blackshirts*. References to Beckman's book are to this edition.

2. Interview with Mildred's son and daughter-in-law, Simon and Philippa Garland.
3. Morris Beckman, *The Hackney Crucible* (Vallentine Mitchell & Co. Ltd, 1995), p. 29.
4. Stephen Dorril, *Blackshirt: Sir Oswald Mosley and British Fascism* (Thistle Publishing, 2006), p. 298.
5. Tony Kushner, *The Persistence of Prejudice: Antisemitism in British Society during the Second World War* (Manchester University Press, 1989), p. 166.
6. Beckman, *The Hackney Crucible*, p. 105.
7. Lennie Rolnick, *That's What's in It for Me* (unpublished), pp. 1–2.
8. This was amplified by the government's refusal to reveal who was listed in the book. The names only became public knowledge in 1989.
9. William Joyce was also due to be arrested, but was tipped off by his old friend Maxwell Knight and escaped to Germany, where he became the infamous Lard Haw-Haw.

1 Dipping a Toe in the Water

1. Jeffrey Hamm, *Action Replay* (Black House Publishing, 1983), p. 47.
2. Ibid., p. 48.
3. Ibid., p. xx.
4. This is according to a Special Branch report; in his autobiography, Hamm says the camp was split into communists and non-communists.
5. This was particularly the case for the fascist ladies who were detained in Holloway Prison.
6. Kushner, *Persistence of Prejudice*, p. 40.
7. Just before he discovered this, Hamm had got involved in a plan to escape and had been energetically digging a tunnel for several months.
8. Kushner, *Persistence of Prejudice*, p. 16.
9. Ibid., p. 34.
10. The fund was initially founded as the British Union Dependents' Fund, but the name was changed in order to make less overt the connection with the BUF.

11. Internment reached its peak in December 1940, and in 1941 the government slowly started releasing fascists who were not thought a threat. By the middle of 1943, by which time the threat of German invasion had passed, only 429 people were still detained under 18B and by 1944 only the most rabid and dangerous remained behind bars.

12. And she was by no means the only one.

13. HO 45/25394.

14. Quoted in Nicholas Mosley, *Rules of the Game: Beyond the Pale* (Secker & Warburg, 1994), p. 501.

15. When Clementine retorted that at least Mosley was being protected 'from the fury of the mob', Lady Redesdale was furious.

16. For direct quote, see Herbert Morrison's *An Autobiography* (1960).

17. Ironically, Mosley outlived every member of the cabinet which interned him – see Anne Poole, 'Oswald Mosley and the Union Movement: Success or Failure', in Mike Cronin, *The Failure of British Fascism: The Far Right and the Fight for Political Recognition* (Palgrave Macmillan, 1996), p. 57

18. *Daily Worker*, 19 November 1943.

19. Kushner, *Persistence of Prejudice*, p. 169.

20. See Paul Willets, *Rendezvous at the Russian Tea Rooms* (Constable, 2015), p. 309.

21. *Hansard*, 1 December 1943, HC Deb 01 December 1943 vol 395 cc395-477, 429.

22. Martin Pugh, *Hurrah for the Blackshirts*, (Vintage, 2013), p. 314.

23. Mosley said that while he was perfectly fine with the government's observation, the phone tap annoyed him as it was interfering with his connection (KV 2/888 314A).

24. The way the information is presented suggests the source is either Green himself or someone very close to him.

25. KV 2/890 435z.

26. Hamm, *Action Replay*, p. 108.

27. There was a rumour in fascist circles that he was the son of a gypsy: see Graham Macklin, *Very Deeply Dyed in Black* (I.B. Tauris, 2007), p. 31.

28. Much of the information on Burgess comes from the 43 Group's own index of fascists. This index and a series of other sensitive 43

Group documents and materials were shown to me by Gerry Gable, who was given them by 43 Group member Gerald Anthill. These documents will soon be available to view at the Searchlight Archives at Northampton University.

29. Macklin, *Very Deeply Dyed*, p. 31. See also Keith Thompson, *Victor Burgess: Leadership, Idealism and Courage* (Stephen Books, 2008).

30. KV 6/3 342a. See also Dave Renton, *Fascism, Anti-Fascism and the 1940s* (Palgrave Macmillan, 2000), p. 126.

31. KV 6/3 308c.

32. KV 6/3 294b.

33. Trevor Grundy, *Memoir of a Fascist Childhood: A Boy in Mosley's Britain* (William Heinemann Ltd, 1998), p. 22.

34. KV 6/3 326c.

35. XX 0/0; HO 45/24467.

36. Kushner, *Persistence of Prejudice*, p. 35.

37. KV 2/980 444b.

38. Francis Hawkins had been a fascist even longer than Mosley, and along with William Joyce (better known as Lord Haw-Haw) had convinced Mosley to embrace anti-Semitism. He, however, played almost no part in the post-war fascist revival.

39. *On Guard*, January/February 1948.

40. He was most likely contacted and instructed via a go-between such as Enid Riddel.

41. KV 2/890 450a.

42. Dorril, *Blackshirt*, p. 546.

43. Subsequently when they learnt that Mosley had been behind the Independent Nationalists, Dunlop received several apologies.

44. For instance, Mosley had his solicitor send a letter to Fund members telling them that Mosley could have no connection 'with any political movement at present functioning', but then sent Francis-Hawkins to assure Dunlop that it was a legal letter which should not cause him any undue alarm (KV 2/890 451a).

45. HO 45/24467.

46. HO 45/25395.

47. KV 2/1366.

48. HO 45/25395.

49. See Richard Griffiths, *Patriotism Perverted: Captain Ramsay, the Right Club, and British Anti-Semitism, 1939–1940* (Constable, 1998), p. 138.
50. XX o/o.
51. XX o/o.
52. XX o/o
53. Dave Hann, *Physical Resistance: A Hundred Years of Anti-Fascism* (Zero Books, 2013), p. 155.
54. HO 45/24467.
55. Kangers is cockney rhyming slang for Jew, which rhymes with Kangaroo.
56. HO 45/24467.
57. In 1946 Dunlop did try to officially launch the Independent Nationalists but with few supporters and no funds, it was stillborn. He tried several times over the ensuing years to resurrect it, but never with any success.
58. KV 2/890 480b.
59. KV2/890 491a.
60. Much of the research and information in this section is borrowed from Graham Macklin, '"A quite natural and moderate defensive feeling"? The 1945 Hampstead "Anti-Alien" Petition', *Patterns of Prejudice* 37 (3), 2010.
61. Not much is known about Margaret Crabtree, but Sylvia Gosse was a painter and printmaker with the Camden Town Group, and her father was the writer Edmund Gosse. She had been mentored by the painter Walter Sickert, who was himself an immigrant from Germany – Clair Wills, *Lovers and Strangers: An Immigrant History of Post-war Britain (Allen Lane, 2017)*, p. 73.

2. Who's Going to Stop Them?

1. Interview with Gerry's daughter, Barbara Lambert.
2. Jerry White, *London in the Twentieth Century: A City and Its People* (Random House, 2016), p. 42.
3. Stephan Wendehorst, *British Jewry, Zionism, and the Jewish State*

(OUP, 2014), p. 38.

4. David Renton, *This Rough Game: Fascism and Anti-Fascism* (Sutton Publishing, 2001), p. 175.

5. Beckman, *The 43 Group*, p. 17.

6. Interview conducted on behalf of the author by Jeremy Brull with Len's niece Monica Symonds.

7. *A Rage in Dalston*, BBC Radio 4, aired 19 April 2008.

8. Morris Beckman, interview with author.

9. As from this point on Beckman and Sherman's accounts roughly converge, I have relied mostly on Beckman's telling. The one substantial difference is that while Beckman presents the following as spontaneous, Sherman saw it as very much planned.

10. Sixty-six years later Beckman reliably informed me, as he resumed his seat after acting it out, that this move was known as the Hackney Kiss.

11. In Morris Beckman's account he states that the attack at Whitestone Pond occurred on the last Sunday evening of February 1946, and the Group's founding meeting took place just one week later. Supporting this timeline, Beckman cites an article in the *Edgware Local* entitled '43 Group Jewish Answer to Fascists', which, he says, was published on 26 March 1946. This is an error. The article was published on 26 March 1947 and in it a 43 Group spokesman states the Group was founded in September 1946. The article does not mention when the attack on Hamm occurred, but a contemporaneous letter written by Beckman himself suggests May 1946 as the most likely date. A gestation period of several months is more in tune with the version of events as told by other veterans of the Group.

12. CAB 130/8.

13. CAB/128/2.

14. CAB/130/8.

15. Two others were Franco's Spain and Salazar's Portugal, both essentially fascist countries.

16. *Jewish Chronicle*, 22 February 1946.

17. Nigel Copsey, *Anti-Fascism in Britain* (Palgrave Macmillan, 1999), p. 83.

18. Richard Thurlow, *Fascism in Britain: A History, 1918–85* (Wiley

Blackwell, 1987), p. 304.

19. *Daily Worker*, 9 January 1946.

20. Murray Podro, interview with author.

21. Rolnick, *That's What's in It for Me*, p. 122.

22. Beckman, *The 43 Group*, p. 19.

23. BOD DCR 1658/9/1/1/2/918.

24. Beckman, *The 43 Group*, p. 34.

25. Graham Macklin, 'The Jewish Defence Committee and Its Post-War Intelligence Activities', talk given at British Fascism, Anti-Fascism and Jewish Defence Conference held at Weiner Library on 7 March 2013.

26. Hansard HL Deb, 12 March 1946, vol. 140, cc36-64.

27. Preen's defence of the charge of breaking in and stealing documents was that he was acting upon the instructions of MI5, who wanted to take possession of the documents that Vernon was allegedly passing on to the Soviets. According to historian Richard Thurlow this defence might not have been that far-fetched, as MI5 was certainly not above using BUF members for their dubious anti-communist activities. The light nature of Preen's sentence – he was merely bound over for a year – further supports Preen's claim.

28. See sussexhistoryforum.co.uk; Cronin, *The Failure of British Fascism*, p. 47; MEPO 3/2866.

29. *On Guard*, October 1947.

30. XX o/o.

31. XX o/o.

32. XX o/o.

33. KV 6/4 409b.

34. HO 45/25395.

35. *Daily Worker*, 12 March 1946.

36. According to Beckman, Albert Hall was the first action the members of the newly formed 43 Group were involved in. Although the 43 Group did not form until several months after the Albert Hall meeting, that does not mean there is any reason to challenge Beckman's assertion that a number of the Group's founding members were in the hall that day.

37. Hamm had accepted Preen's invitation to make a short speech, an

invitation Preen had rescinded at the last moment (KV 6/4 410c).

38. *Jewish Chronicle*, 15 March 1946.
39. *On Guard*, April 1948.
40. Hansard HC Deb, 14 March 1946, vol. 420, cc1260-4 1260.
41. KV 2/890 517.
42. KV 2/890 518b, 522.
43. *Daily Worker*, 1 May 1946.
44. KV 2/1351 36a.
45. BOD DCR 1658/2/1/10/85.
46. *Jewish Chronicle*, 24 May 1946.
47. Ibid., 31 May 1946.
48. One innovation the JDC had proposed was a Standing Youth Conference on anti-fascism. But this was exactly what the ex-servicemen were reacting against: all talk and no action.
49. Jules Konopinski, interview with author.
50. Gerry Lewis, interview with author.
51. *News Review*, 8 January 1948.
52. He missed Gould's speech, and neither Bernerd nor Flamberg were scheduled to speak at that first meeting.
53. BOD DCR 1658/10/23/1/2/217, 219.
54. *News Review*, 8 January 1948.
55. Len Sherman interview with Alan Dein for *A Rage in Dalston*, BBC Radio 4.
56. It is worth noting that no age limit to membership was ever considered or implemented.
57. *Edgware Local*, 9 April 1947.
58. Beckman, *The 43 Group*, pp. 23–5.
59. BOD DCR 1658/6/6/10–29.
60. KV 5/25.
61. XX o/o.
62. *Jewish Chronicle*, 8 November 1946.

3 The 43 Group

1. The sequence of events compiled here is chiefly taken from the subsequent court proceedings.

2. KV 6/5 464a; *Unity*, 17 January 1947.

3. Some sources say that it was five men, but as McGrath stated under oath that it was two men, this seems more likely.

4. Hamm later said that he could blame the attack for inducing his wife's labour, which occurred shortly afterwards. When it was pointed out that his wife was already nine months' pregnant at the time, Hamm shrugged and suggested it would make a good story and account for the bitterness of his animosity against the Jews (KV 6/5 464a).

5. It was on the following day that the JDC first realised they were dealing with an entirely new organisation, when Bernerd called Roston and revealed that 'his organisation' was gathering useful news about the fascists (BOD DCR 1658/3/10/7/1/53).

6. The young woman in question was twenty-six-year-old exotic dancer and prostitute Margaret Cook, who danced at the Blue Lagoon. The murder went unsolved until 2015, when a ninety-one-year-old man in Canada confessed to the crime.

7. Alan Dein interview with Len Sherman. Len was filmed outside of Arundel Gardens for a documentary on the 43 Group where he recounted the story. That can be found at 11:00, 'The '43 Group', youtube.com.

8. BOD DCR 1658/1/1/3/34; *Daily Worker*, 31 December 1946.

9. Blacke was also an alibi witness for Flamberg at his trial. When he appeared in the dock, Hamm tried to ask him questions about the Pile case before the magistrate quickly stopped that line of questioning (KV 2/1351 52–61).

10. KV 3/52 9a.

11. Lionel Rose, *Fascism in Britain*, Survey 1 (McCorquodale & Co., 1948); Beckman, *The 43 Group*, p. 61.

12. Macklin, *Very Deeply Dyed*, p. 39.

13. It was sometimes referred to as the Burnt Oak Task Group.

14. *Edgware Local*, 18 December 1946.

15. Ibid.

16. Ibid., 1 January 1947.

17. HO 45/24469/1.

18. KV 3/52 9a.

19. *Edgware Local*, 9 April 1947.
20. Ibid., 29 January 1947.
21. Morris Beckman, *The Hatemongers* (unpublished manuscript), p. 73.
22. *Edgware Local*, 23 April 1947.
23. This was not actually the first mention of the 43 Group in the paper. One week earlier the Group had placed a notice advertising a 43 Group Dance, to be held at the Royal Hotel on Southampton Row.
24. *Jewish Chronicle*, 7 February 1947.
25. BOD DCR 1658/10/23/2/2/15.
26. *Jewish Chronicle*, 14 March 1947.
27. Ibid., 21 March 1947.
28. XX o/o.
29. BOD DCR 1658/1/1/3/59.
30. BOD DCR 1658/10/23/4/126.
31. Ibid.
32. Gerry Abrahams, interview with author.
33. BOD DCR/1658/1/1/3/93.
34. Members of the Provisional Committee included Bernerd, Flamberg, Beckman, Blacke, and several others who do not feature as much in this account, including Vivian Harris, Laurie Curtis, Norman Jacobs, Frank Hiller, Bernie Newman and Alf Zeff. Beckman, *The 43 Group.*
35. Martin Block, interview with author.
36. Gerry Abrahams, interview with author.
37. *A Rage in Dalston*, BBC Radio 4.
38. When Hydleman heard about these recruitment meetings, he was furious. He told the Maccabi national organiser that it was 'cock-eyed' that Maccabi was offering 'scope to further the membership of a dissident group' (BOD DCR 1658/2/1/10/68).
39. There is some disagreement over the names and areas covered by each section, and it is likely that certain sections appeared and disappeared at various points during the Group's life – for instance the North and North-West London sections probably merged and split, and merged again.
40. Ivor Benjamin, interview with author.

41. Details on North London section from Gerry Abrahams,' interview with author.
42. Martin Block, interview with author.
43. Both the North and East sections covered Dalston; as this was the major flashpoint of the conflict, this is unsurprising.
44. Martin Block, interview with author.
45. *Jewish Chronicle*, 19 December 1986.
46. BOD DCR 1658/9/1/11/3/132.
47. Ivor Benjamin, interview with author.
48. Martin Block, interview with author.
49. BOD DCR 1658/1/1/3/59; Gerry Abrahams, interview with author; *A Rage in Dalston*, BBC Radio 4.
50. When Mildred applied to join the War Office, she was only fourteen, but claimed she was eighteen. When her true age was discovered some time later, she was kept on. This was in part because she was so good at her job, but also because her commanding officer had developed a thing for her and liked to chase her around the desk.
51. *A Rage in Dalston*, BBC Radio 4.
52. Simon and Philippa Garland, interview with author.
53. *On Guard*, July 1947.
54. Renton, *This Rough Game*, p. 177.
55. Copsey, *Anti-Fascism in Britain*, p. 78; Hann, *Physical Resistance*, p. 167.
56. Rolnick, *That's What's in It for Me*.
57. In fact, when I put this question to Trudie and her brother Harold, they both laughed in my face.

4 Going East

1. HO 45/24469/2.
2. Strachey was one of Mosley's earliest supporters and followed him into the New Party. However, he abandoned Mosley before the BUF was formed and moved far to the left.
3. Kushner, *Persistence of Prejudice*, p. 120.
4. Things were so bad that my grandparents, who had a grocery store on Ridley Road, enjoyed a roaring trade in cracked eggs and stale bread.

5. Simon Garfield, *Our Hidden Lives: The Remarkable Diaries of Post-War Britain* (Ebury Press, 2005), p. 266.

6. HO 45/24469/2.

7. HO 45/24467.

8. HO 45/24469/2.

9. Kushner, *Persistence of Prejudice*, p. 98.

10. A. J. P. Taylor, *English History 1914–1945* (Oxford, 1965), p. 419.

11. Kushner, *Persistence of Prejudice*, p. 154.

12. Ibid, p. 199.

13. White, *London in the Twentieth Century*, p. 127.

14. Garfield, *Our Hidden Lives*, p. 432.

15. David Leitch, 'Explosion at the King David Hotel', in Michael Sisson and Philip French (eds), *Age of Austerity* (Hodder and Stoughton, 1963), p. 57.

16. *Jewish Chronicle*, 22 October 1948.

17. Renton, *Fascism, Anti-Fascism*, p. 28.

18. *Jewish Chronicle*, 26 September 1947.

19. HO 45/24469/2.

20. Ibid.

21. Ibid.

22. HO 45/25395; BOD DCR 1658/2/1/10/86.

23. BOD DCR 1658/6/6/54.

24. Most of these new branches were around London, but an active one also sprang up in Brighton.

25. Details from Lionel Rose, 'Survey of Open-Air Meetings Held by Pro-Fascist Organisations April–October 1947' (unpublished, written 1948).

26. HO 45/24469/2.

27. *On Guard*, November 1947.

28. HO 45/24469/2.

29. Ibid.

30. Gerry Abrahams, interview with author.

31. My thanks to Len's great-nephew Jeremy Brull for sharing this recollection with me.

32. KV 6/5 438b.

33. HO 45/24469/2.

34. This is a reference to the famous opening of Joyce's Lord Haw-Haw broadcasts from Germany.

35. Beckman, *The 43 Group*, p. 76.

36. Ibid., pp. 76–7.

37. HO 45/24469/2.

38. *Daily Worker*, 24 June 1947.

39. Jules Konopinski, interview with author.

40. Kushner, *Persistence of Prejudice*, p. 123.

41. Harry Kaufman, interview with author.

42. Hamm was found guilty of 'using threatening and abusive words and behaviour' and was bound over for a year at a cost of £5. *Hackney Gazette*, 30 June 1947.

43. *Daily Worker*, 24 June 1947.

44. Black Maria was the nickname for police vans used to transport prisoners.

45. BOD DCR 1658/9/1/3/8/123; *Hackney Gazette*, 16 July 1947.

46. BOD DRC 1658/9/1/11/1/180.

47. Rebecca West, 'Heil Hamm', *New Yorker*, 7 August 1948, p. 27.

48. Renton, *This Rough Game*, p. 174.

49. Hann, *Physical Resistance*, p. 174.

50. Gerry Abrahams, interview with author.

51. Quoted in Dave Renton, *An Unbiased Watch? Fascism, Anti-Fascism and the State* (Macmillan, 2000).

52. In total, ninety-six individuals were separately charged. Sixty-four were anti-fascist, twenty-three were pro-fascist, and seven were undefined. Renton, *An Unbiased Watch?*

53. Vidal Sassoon, *Vidal: The Autobiography* (Macmillan, 2010), pp. 46–7.

54. Jules Konopinski, interview with author.

55. Len Sherman for a time worked as a police martial arts instructor.

56. Wendehorst, *British Jewry*, pp. 87–8.

57. David Kynaston, *Austerity Britain, 1945–51* (Walker, 2008), p. 270.

58. KV 6/4.

59. *The New Statesman and Nation*, 23 August 1947.

60. MEPO 2/7983.

61. *The New Statesman and Nation*, 6 September 1947.

62. Beckman, *The 43 Group*, p. 56.

63. Copsey, *Anti-Fascism in Britain*, p. 84.

64. Graham Macklin, '"A Plague on Both Their Houses": Fascism, Anti-Fascism and the Police in the 1940s', in N. Copsey and D. Renton (eds), *British Fascism, the Labour Movement and the State* (Palgrave Macmillan, 2005), pp. 46–67, 64.

65. Martin Block, interview with author.

66. Beckman, *The 43 Group*, p. 46.

67. *A Rage in Dalston*, BBC Radio 4.

68. Jules Konopinski, interview with author.

69. *Daily Express*, 16 January 1948.

70. Alexander Hartog, *Born to Sing: Memoirs of an East End Mantle-Presser* (Brick Lane Books, 1979), pp. 75–6.

71. Jules himself tried to recruit people from the Boys Club, including the playwright Harold Pinter; Pinter, however, did not join.

72. Alec Carson, interview with Alan Dein.

73. Jules Konopinski, interview with author; Monty Goldman quoted in Hann, *Physical Resistance*, p. 166.

74. Details from interviews with Jonny Goodman and Jules Konopinski.

75. Philip Evans and Jonny Goodman, interviews with author.

76. Harry Kaufman demonstrated the newspaper technique in a video for the *Guardian*: 'Jewish ex-servicemen of Group 43', YouTube, 27 January 2009.

77. Gerry Abrahams, interview with author.

78. Martin Block, interview with Alan Dein.

79. Jonny Goodman, interview with author.

80. *A Rage in Dalston*, BBC Radio 4.

5 Not Just Hooligans

1. In Bernerd's phone call to the JDC's Roston in which he first mentioned the Group's existence, he hinted at the amount of intelligence the Group had already gathered.

2. Both documents are held in the archives of the London School of Economics.

3. Gerry Abrahams, interview with author.
4. ATS stood for Auxiliary Territorial Service, the female branch of the army during the war.
5. There is in fact some debate over who first took the role of intelligence head, with both Jonny Wimborne and Stanley Marks being mentioned. However, as Marks was the head of the North London section, Wimborne seems like the more obvious candidate, even though he was officially in the Merchant Navy until mid-1947. He was definitely Cotter's handler, though.
6. *On Guard*, October 1948.
7. This number is taken from a Special Branch report on the biggest book clubs. Modern Thought was quite a lot bigger than the others. The Bethnal Green Book Club and Enfield Union Book Club had thirty and thirty-one members apiece, while the West Yorkshire Book Club had forty-seven (HO 45/25395).
8. Beckman, *The 43 Group*, p. 75.
9. In fact, so unaware was the vast majority of the Group of Cotter's identity that his face inadvertently appeared in *On Guard*, as he protected Victor Burgess at a UBF meeting in Earl's Court.
10. Beckman, *The 43 Group*, p. 93.
11. Tony died when he was just forty-four, although it is unclear if this was a consequence of his heart condition.
12. All biographical details are drawn from an interview with Roy's wife, Davina Bensusan.
13. Gerry Lewis, interview with author.
14. Renton, *This Rough Game*, p. 176.
15. *On Guard*, September 1947.
16. Ibid., July 1947.
17. Ibid., March 1948.
18. Ibid., July 1947.
19. Ibid.
20. Ibid.
21. Ibid.
22. Ibid., October 1947.
23. Ibid.
24. Ibid., July 1947.

25. Ibid., September 1947.
26. Ibid., October 1948.
27. Beckman, *The 43 Group*, p. 103.
28. Jonny Goodman, interview with author.
29. Ivor Benjamin, interview with author.
30. Beckman, *The 43 Group*, p. 74.
31. Jules Konopinski, interview with author.
32. JDC DCR 1658/9/1/11/5/113.
33. Harry Kaufman, interview with author.
34. Martin Block, interview with author.
35. Jules Konopinski, interview with author.
36. Jules Konopinski, interview with author.
37. Jonny Goodman, interview with author.
38. Beckman, *The 43 Group*, pp. 96–7.
39. Martin Block, interview with author.

6 The Battle of Ridley Road

1. *Daily Express*, 1 August 1947.
2. Tony Kushner, 'Anti-semitism and Austerity: The August 1947 Riots in Britain', in Panikos Panayi (ed.), *Racial Violence in Britain, 1840–1950* (Leicester University Press, 1993), pp. 149–68, 155.
3. Hann, *Physical Resistance*, p. 171.
4. Sisson and French (eds), *Age of Austerity*, pp. 60–1, 66–7.
5. Copsey, *Anti-Fascism in Britain*, p. 81.
6. West, 'Heil Hamm'.
7. Kushner, *Persistence of Prejudice*, p. 59.
8. Pat Sonabend, interview with author.
9. Hamm, *Action Replay*, p. 113.
10. Len Sherman, interview with Alan Dein. Jewish Museum Collection, Tape 204.
11. Alan Foreman, interview with author.
12. Raphael Samuel, *East End Underworld: Chapters in the Life of Arthur Harding* (Oxford University Press, 1981), p. 275.
13. *Sunday Pictorial*, 17 August 1947.
14. Steve Silver, 'No Regrets – Frederic Mullally Recalls His Fight

against Mosley', March 1998.

15. West, 'Heil Hamm'.

16. Copsey, *Anti-Fascism in Britain*, p. 79.

17. Frederic Mullally, 'Fascism Again in 1947'.

18. *Sunday Pictorial*, 17 August 1947.

19. Frederic Mullally, interview with author.

20. I have taken the liberty of amalgamating two interviews with Frederic Mullally here: the first is with the journalist Steve Silver in 'No Regrets – Frederic Mullally Recalls his Fight against Mosley', March 1998, and the second is my own interview with Mullally.

21. Frederic Mullally, interview with author.

22. Silver, 'No Regrets'.

23. Jeffrey Hamm, *The Battle of Ridley Road* (Raven Books, 1947), p. 2.

24. Silver, 'No Regrets'.

25. HO 45/24470.

26. *Sunday Pictorial*, 24 August 1947.

27. HO 45/24470.

28. Philip Evans, interview with author.

29. Michael Mullally, interview with author. (Michael is Frederic Mullally's son.)

30. *Daily Worker*, 25 August 1947.

31. With statistics like this, one must remember just how bad the police were at distinguishing between Jewish and non-Jewish anti-fascists.

32. HO 45/24470.

33. West, 'Heil Hamm', p. 40.

34. Alexander Baron, *With Hope, Farewell* (Cape, 1952), p. 232.

35. West, 'Heil Hamm', pp. 42–3.

36. Ibid, p. 43.

37. *On Guard*, October 1947.

38. HO 45/24470.

39. Ibid.

40. They had managed to avoid detection by coming to the area from Hyde Park in small groups.

41. *On Guard*, October 1947.

42. Ibid., November 1947.

43. This piece of information was revealed by Wimborne at one of the Group's final reunions. Ivor Benjamin recalled that Wimborne came from a very well-off family and drove a sports car, something unheard-of in those days.

44. *On Guard*, February 1949; Ibid., April 1949.

45. *Evening Standard*, 10 October 1947.

46. Ibid., 18 October 1947.

47. *On Guard*, November 1947.

48. *Hackney Gazette*, 8 October 1947.

49. *On Guard*, October 1947, p. 1.

50. Rose, Survey of Open-Air Meetings; *Daily Express*, 13 October 1947; *Hackney Gazette*, 15 October 1947; *Hackney Gazette*, 22 October 1947.

51. *On Guard*, November 1947.

52. Hamm, *Battle of Ridley Road*, p. 8.

53. *Evening Standard*, 29 September 1947.

54. *On Guard*, October 1947.

55. This only really began to change following the victory of the Jews in Israel 1948–49. Kushner, *Persistence of Prejudice*, p. 126.

56. Renton, *This Rough Game*, p. 180.

7 Mosley Returns

1. *On Guard*, October 1947.

2. Ibid.

3. HO 45/24470; *Jewish Chronicle*, 29 August 1947.

4. *On Guard*, August 1947.

5. Rose, 'Survey of Open-Air Meetings'.

6. Moran was not just popular among British fascists. Mussolini himself recorded a tribute to Moran, in which he called him 'a fine man', to be played at Moran's funeral.

7. Poole, 'Oswald Mosley and the Union Movement', p. 60.

8. Beckman, *The 43 Group*, p. 67; *On Guard*, July 1947.

9. *Manchester Guardian*, 23 June 1948; HO 45/24469/2.

10. HO 45/24470.

11. Ibid.

12. HO 45/24470; *On Guard*, December 194[?].

13. HO 45/24470.

14. Ibid.

15. Grundy, *Memoir of a Fascist Childhood*, p. 25.

16. *On Guard*, October 1948.

17. KV 2/890 543.

18. *Daily Worker*, 28 March 1947.

19. HO 45/25395.

20. KV 2/906.

21. Oswald Mosley, *The Alternative* (Mosley Publications, 1947), p. 7.

22. Poole, 'Oswald Mosley and the Union Movement', p. 69.

23. Ibid., p. 74; see also Deborah Lipstadt, *Denying the Holocaust: The Growing Assault on Truth and Memory* (Free Press, 2012), pp. 50–1.

24. Mosley, *The Alternative*, p. 209.

25. Ibid., p. 211. Mosley was also one of the first revisionists to question the fairness of Nuremberg. Poole, 'Oswald Mosley and the Union Movement', p. 74.

26. Mosley, *The Alternative*, p. 211.

27. Ibid., p. 206.

28. Macklin, *Very Deeply Dyed*, p. 55.

29. Mosley, *The Alternative*, p. 281.

30. Ibid., p. 285.

31. Mosley had done a lot of reading in prison, including Goethe's *Faust*, on which he mused, considering 'the dilemma of how "evil" could be used in the service of the community'. This was, in the words of historian Richard Thurlow, 'heroic wishful thinking on a vast scale'. Richard C. Thurlow, 'The Guardian of the "Sacred Flame": The Failed Political Resurrection of Sir Oswald Mosley after 1945', *Journal of Contemporary History*, 1 April 1998: 248–9.

32. Mosley, *The Alternative*, p. 285.

33. *On Guard*, October 1947; HO 45/25395.

34. HO 45/25395.

35. KV 2/892 667a.

36. Macklin, *Very Deeply Dyed*, p. 54.
37. *On Guard*, December 1948.
38. Ibid., January 1949.
39. Ibid., March 1949.
40. Ibid., October 1947.
41. Ibid., February 1949.
42. Ibid., April 1949.
43. Ibid.
44. Ibid., May 1949.
45. Ibid., November 1948,.
46. Macklin, 'The Jewish Defence Committee'.
47. *On Guard*, December 1947.
48. Ibid., May 1949.
49. Ibid., July 1949.
50. *Daily Worker*, 16 November 1947.
51. *On Guard*, July 1949.
52. Hann, *Physical Resistance*, p. 177.
53. Rolnick, *That's What's in It for Me*, p. 185.
54. Philip Evans, interview with author.
55. Jules Konopinski, interview with author.
56. BOD DCR 1658/9/1/11/7/2.
57. BOD DCR 1658/9/1/11/7/10.
58. BOD DCR 1658/9/1/11/7/14; Philip Evans, interview with author.
59. *The Times*, 17 November 1947.
60. *Mosley Newsletter*, December 1947.

8 Behind Bars

1. *Daily Worker*, 28 November 1947.
2. *Hackney Gazette*, 20 November 1947; Beckman, *The 43 Group*, pp. 97–8.
3. Beckman, *The 43 Group*, p. 97.
4. Myerovitch had brought a counter-summons against Roberts for striking him in the face, but this was dismissed by the magistrate who declared himself satisfied that the accusations were unfounded. *Daily Worker*, 13 December 1947; *Hackney Gazette*, 20 November 1947.

5. *On Guard*, August 1948.

6. Text of press conference taken from Rose, *Fascism in Britain*, February 1948.

7. *Daily Worker*, 5 December 1947.

8. Ibid., 2 December 1947.

9. *A Rage in Dalston*, BBC Radio 4.

10. Grundy, *Memoir of a Fascist Childhood*, p. 34.

11. Beckman, *The 43 Group*, p. 54.

12. This quote was included in *On Guard*, which responded with a mocking verse recalling the Scarlett Pimpernel. *On Guard*, December 1947.

13. *On Guard*, November 1947.

14. Beckman, *The 43 Group*, p. 58.

15. Ibid., p. 57.

16. Ibid, p. 106.

17. 43 Group Bulletin No. 1.

18. Ibid., p. 45.

19. *On Guard*, August 1947.

20. Ibid., January/February 1948; MEPO 3/2866.

21. The government refused to stop German POWs held near Victoria Park from attending local fascist meetings. Consequently, a few former Nazis became involved with the home-grown fascists (*Daily Worker*, 9 July 1947). The details of the confrontation with Shultz come from Gerry Gable, interview with the author.

22. MEPO 3/2866.

23. Ibid.

24. Ibid.

25. *The 43 Group – Danger: Fascists at Work*, a pamphlet probably published between December 1947 and February 1948.

26. He would later serve as home secretary and lord high chancellor.

27. *Daily Express*, 16 January 1948.

28. Author's interview with Harold Melzack, who was assisting his older brother Maurice in court that day.

29. MEPO 3/2866.

30. Rolnick, *That's What's in It for Me*, p. 177.

31. *Daily Express*, 16 January 1948.
32. Jonny Goodman, interview with author.
33. *On Guard*, March 1948.
34. This figure is much in dispute, and numbers between 1,000 and 2,000 have been offered. As there was never an official membership list, these can only ever be estimates.
35. Details from Hann, *Physical Resistance*, p. 192; Beckman, *The Hatemongers*, p. 87; Beckman, *The 43 Group*, p. 200.
36. Murray Podro, interview with author.
37. *On Guard*, July 1949.
38. Ibid.
39. *Searchlight* Archives, Northampton University.
40. Turner used her real name undercover but in the Group was given the code name Helen Winick. For decades this was the name many Group members knew her by.
41. Rolnick, *That's What's in It for Me*, p. 1.
42. Konopinski, interview with author.
43. *Jewish Chronicle*, 1 September 1978.
44. Rolnick, *That's What's in It for Me*.
45. Ibid., p. 308.

9 Fun Days Out

1. Beckman, *The 43 Group*, p. 105.
2. Grundy, *Memoir of a Fascist Childhood*, p. 30.
3. A matter that was of course debated in Parliament a few days later.
4. BOD DCR 1658/1/1/3/168.
5. Renton, *This Rough Game*, p. 174; *On Guard*, March 1948.
6. Grundy, *Memoir of a Fascist Childhood*, pp. 29–33; BOD DCR 1658/9/1/12/54; *Manchester Guardian*, 8 February 1948; *Manchester Guardian*, 13 February 1948.
7. Harry Kaufman, interview with author.
8. HO 45/25395.
9. Martin Block, interview with author.
10. The 43 Group, 'A Guide to Branches', *Searchlight* Archives,

Northampton University; Beckman, *The 43 Group*, p. 176.

11. Murray Podro, interview with author.

12. Gerry Abrahams, interview with author.

13. Martin Block, interview with author.

14. Morris Beckman referred to them as the Group's commando unit. Again, this term is disputed, but Murray Podro agrees that the Group had 'special units of men'. Podro, interview with author.

15. Philip Evans, interview with author.

16. Author interviews with Jonny Goodman and Davina Bensusan. Davina was the wife of Roy Bensusan, one of Barry's best friends.

17. Rolnick, *That's What's in It for Me*, pp. 140–2.

18. These stories were told to Morris Beckman by Bernerd around the time Beckman was writing *The 43 Group*. As per Bernerd's wishes, Beckman did not include them. However, when ten years later he came to write *The Hatemongers*, he thought that as the vast majority of the participants, including Bernerd, were dead, enough time had passed and he decided to include them. *The Hatemongers* was never published, but Morris was kind enough to show me a draft.

19. Beckman, *The Hatemongers*, p. 87.

20. *On Guard*, January 1949.

21. Beckman, *The 43 Group*, p. 59.

22. LSE Coll Misc 1068; Tape 202, Jewish Museum Collection.

23. Martin Block, interview with author.

24. Gerry Lewis, interview with author.

25. Nigel Copsey, 'Anti-semitism and the Jewish community of Newcastle-upon-Tyne', *Immigrants and Minorities*, 11 (3), 2002: 63.

26. Ibid.

27. Hann, *Physical Resistance*, p. 179.

28. Hann, *Physical Resistance*, pp. 180–1.

29. BOD DCR 1658/1/2/4/121a, b.

30. MEPO 3/3093.

31. Hamm, *Action Replay*, p. 129.

32. Mosley later expressed annoyance at the size of the audience the police had left him. *On Guard*, May–June 1948.

33. Ibid.

34. Beckman, *The 43 Group*, p. 134.

35. Jonny Goodman, interview with author.

36. *On Guard*, May–June 1948.

37. BOD DCR 1658/9/1/11/5/126.

38. Jules Konopinski, interview with author.

39. Jonny Goodman, interview with author.

40. BOD DCR 1658/9/1/11/5/119.

41. Subsequently all three men were tried. Bidney and Sheppard were bound over and Smith received a month's imprisonment. *Hackney Gazette*, 26 May 1948.

42. Wendehorst, *British Jewry*, p. 263.

43. Renton, *Fascism, Anti-Fascism*, p. 39.

44. *A Rage in Dalston*, BBC Radio 4.

45. Gerry Abrahams, interview with author.

46. Hann, *Physical Resistance*, p. 183.

47. *A Rage in Dalston*, BBC Radio 4.

48. Jules Konopinski, interview with author.

49. This and many other details are from Beckman's account in *The 43 Group*, pp. 124–8.

50. Gerry Abrahams, interview with author.

10 Things Fall Apart

1. Dorril, *Blackshirt*, p. 579.

2. Thurlow, *Fascism in Britain*, p. 246.

3. Ibid., p. 64; Jules Konopinski, interview with author.

4. Beckman, *The 43 Group*, pp. 81, 91; Gerry Abrahams, interview with author.

5. MEPO 2/8659.

6. Rolnick, *That's What's in It for Me*, p. 136.

7. Harry Kaufman, interview with author.

8. Rolnick, *That's What's in It for Me*, p. 136.

9. Harry Kaufman, interview with author.

10. Macklin, *Very Deeply Dyed*, p. 53.

11. MEPO 2/8659.

12. Jules Konopinski, interview with author.

13. Beckman, *The 43 Group*, p. 46.
14. Harry Kaufman, interview with author.
15. Rolnick, *That's What's in It for Me*, pp. 137–8.
16. KV 2/894 760b.
17. *On Guard*, May–June 1948.
18. *Manchester Guardian*, 30 July 1948; *Jewish Chronicle*, 6 August 1948; *On Guard*, August 1948; *On Guard*, September 1948.
19. Morris Beckman, interview with author.
20. *On Guard*, August 1948.
21. BOD DCR 1658/4/2/1/83; 1658/3/1c/7/2/80; 1658/10/23/2/3/169.
22. *On Guard*, August 1948; BOD DCR 1658/3/1c/7/2/87; *Jewish Chronicle*, 16 July 1948; Beckman, *The 43 Group*, pp. 146–7.
23. *On Guard*, August 1948. Maclean subsequently returned to Birmingham where he formed the National Anti-Fascist League.
24. KV 2/894 772a.
25. Hann, *Physical Resistance*, pp. 191–3.
26. Beckman, *Hatemongers*, p. 88.
27. BOD DCR 1658/10/9/2/1/65.
28. MEPO 2/8659.
29. Ibid.
30. *On Guard*, August 1948.
31. KV 3/51 99a.
32. Beckman, *The 43 Group*, p. 122.
33. *On Guard*, October 1947.
34. Ibid., August 1948.
35. Ibid., July 1948.
36. KV 6/6 555a.
37. Hamm, *Action Replay*, p. 130.
38. Murray Podro, interview with author.
39. Hamm, *Action Replay*, p. 131.
40. KV 6/6 555a.
41. *Union*, 18 September 1948.
42. Murray Podro, interview with author.
43. KV 6/6 558.
44. KV 6/6 557.

45. Podro was fined 20 shillings for using insulting words likely to cause a breach of the peace. BOD DCR 1658/9/1/11/7/85.
46. Martin Block, interview with author.
47. KV2/895 870a.
48. Dorril, *Blackshirt*, p. 579.
49. KV 3/52 51b.
50. *On Guard*, November 1948.
51. Dorril, *Blackshirt*, p. 579.
52. *Jewish Chronicle*, 17 September 1948.
53. Ibid., 8 October 1948.
54. BOD DCR 1658/10/23/2/2/140.
55. *Jewish Chronicle*, 8 October 1948.
56. BOD DCR 1658/4/2/31/1.
57. *Jewish Chronicle*, 17 September 1948.
58. Ibid., 24 September 1948.
59. Ibid., 8 October 1948.
60. Jonny Goodman, interview with author.
61. Gerry Abrahams, interview with author.
62. BOD DCR 1658/1/2/4/189.
63. Martin Block, interview with author.
64. Harry Kaufman, interview with author.
65. *On Guard*, January 1949.
66. Ibid.
67. BOD DCR 1658/3/1c/7/2/140.

11 Cornered Animals

1. Hartog, *Born to Sing*, p. 77.
2. Harry Kaufman, interview with author.
3. KV 2/895 854, 868.
4. KV 3/52 56.
5. *On Guard*, February 1949.
6. Ibid.
7. BOD DCR 1658/6/10/1/41; *Manchester Guardian*, 1 February 1949; *Jewish Chronicle*, 4 February 1949.
8. Martin White, interview with author.

9. Gerry Abrahams, interview with author.

10. *Jewish Chronicle*, 18 February 1949.

11. BOD DCR 1658/6/10/1/43.

12. BOD DCR 1658/6/10/1/48.

13. *'43 Group Bulletin*, February 1949.

14. *On Guard* put the number of marchers at 150 and claimed there were just as many policemen protecting the marchers as there were marchers. *On Guard*, March 1949.

15. BOD DCR 1658/6/10/1/48; *Manchester Guardian*, 14 February 1949.

16. Macklin, *Very Deeply Dyed*, p. 55.

17. 43 *Group Bulletin*, February 1949. LSE Coll. Misc. 1068.

18. Rolnick, *That's What's in It for Me*, p. 212.

19. Ibid., p. 213.

20. BOD DCR 1658/1/1/3/319; 1/6/5. HC Deb, 21 March 1949, vol. 463 cc37-44 37; *Manchester Guardian,* 22 March 1949, 2 April 1949; KV3/52 60.

21. Harry Kaufman, interview with author.

22. *Jewish Chronicle*, 15 April 1949.

23. *On Guard*, May 1949.

24. Author's interview with Barbara Lambert, Flamberg's daughter.

25. *Jewish Chronicle*, 25 March 1949.

26. BOD DCR 1658/1/2/4/202.

27. *On Guard*, December 1948.

28. *On Guard*, April 1949.

29. HC Deb, 10 February 1949, vol. 461, c84W 84W.

30. At the same meeting, the UM was also banned from using it. *On Guard*, March 1949.

31. Ibid.

32. BOD DCR 1658/1/2/4/227.

33. BOD DCR 1658/3/1c/7/2/186.

34. BOD DCR 1658/10/23/2/4/31.

35. Beckman, *The 43 Group*, pp. 186–7.

36. One of these attacks was on the playwright Harold Pinter. 'Police Failed Harold Pinter', *BBC History*, 5 (9) (September 2004), p. 9.

37. BOD DCR 1658/1/2/4/227.

38. *Jewish Chronicle*, 6 May 1949 .

39. *Jewish Chronicle*, 20 May 1949.

40. BOD DCR 1658/3/1c/7/2/195.

41. BOD DCR 1658/3/1c/7/2/198.

42. BOD DCR 1658/3/1c/7/2/209.

43. *Jewish Chronicle*, 16 September 1949.

44. The 43 Group, 'A Guide to Branches'. *Searchlight* Archives, North-ampton University.

45. BOD DCR 1658/3/1c/7/2/204.

46. Hartog, *Born to Sing*, p. 77.

47. Beckman, *The 43 Group*, p. 183.

48. BOD DCR 1658/3/1c/7/2/200.

49. *Jewish Chronicle*, 24 June 1949.

50. *On Guard*, May 1949.

51. For comparison, in 1937 the BUF's forty-nine candidates received 27,409 votes. Macklin, *Very Deeply Dyed*, pp. 56–7.

52. BOD DCR 1658/1/1/3/339.

53. Macklin, *Very Deeply Dyed*, p. 56.

54. Dorril, *Blackshirt*, p. 580.

55. KV 6/6 559b.

56. KV 3/52 66a.

57. Macklin, *Very Deeply Dyed*, p. 58.

58. Ibid., p. 160–76.

59. BOD DCR 1658/1/1/3/348.

60. BOD DCR 1658/3/2/1/289.

61. KV 3/52 68a.

62. This info comes from a Home Office report and there is no indica-tion of whether the anti-fascists were 43 Group or not. KV 3/52 66a; *On Guard*, September 1949.

63. KV 2/986 947d.

64. Dorril, *Blackshirt*, pp. 581–2.

65. KV 2/896 951.

66. Dorril, *Blackshirt*, pp. 571–5; Macklin, *Very Deeply Dyed*, pp. 57–8.

67. OMD/8/4/1.

68. Macklin, *Very Deeply Dyed*, p. 58.

69. KV 2/1353.

70. *Jewish Chronicle* 16 September 1949; *The Times*, 12 September 1949.
71. Jules Konopinski, interview with author.
72. *A Rage in Dalston*, BBC Radio 4.
73. Harry Kaufman, interview with author.
74. *Jewish Chronicle*, 16 September 1949; *The Times*, 12 September 1949.
75. KV 3/52 74a.
76. BOD DCR 1658/1/2/4/249.
77. KV 3/52 74a.
78. OMD/2/3/5.
79. KV 3/52 74b.
80. *Jewish Chronicle*, 16 December 1949.
81. BOD DCR 1658/1/2/4/249.

12 Into Memory

1. *On Guard*, December 1949.
2. BOD DCR 1658/6/14/1.
3. BOD DCR 1658/10/4/4/1/140.
4. BOD DCR 1658/1/3/2/94.
5. KV 2/896 987.
6. MEPO 2/8894.
7. *Sydney Morning Herald*, 6 February 1950.
8. KV 3/52 79a.
9. KV 3/52 80a.
10. MEPO 2/8895.
11. *Jewish Chronicle*, 16 December 1949.
12. BOD JDC 1658/1/1/3/463.
13. *Jewish Clarion*, July 1950.
14. This might seem like a strange characterisation, but one of the 43 Group's founding objectives had been 'to advocate the immediate passing of legislation to make Fascist and Anti-Semitic Organisations illegal', and this had not been achieved. True, it was probably impossible and certainly could not have been achieved by the 43 Group, but still, technically Jules had a point.
15. Jules Konopinski, interview with author.
16. Harry Kaufman, interview with author.

17. Martin Block, interview with author.

18. Thurlow, *Fascism in Britain*, p. 249.

19. M. Testa, *Militant Anti-Fascism* (AK Press, 2015), pp. 161–2.

20. Later, this British National Party would become the infamous National Front.

21. *Searchlight Magazine*, September 1984.

22. Jordan and Tyndall spent much of this period in prison, with Jordan serving time for setting up a secret paramilitary organisation called Spearhead.

23. Details on 62 Group and interview with 43 Group veterans from Steve Silver, 'The Fighting Sixties', *Searchlight Magazine*, July 2002.

24. *Independent*, 24 September 2005.

25. Peter Underwood, *Haunted London* (Amberley Publishing, 2009).

26. *Jewish Chronicle*, 19 December 1986.

27. *Searchlight Magazine*, September 1984.

28. The headed paper had been kept by Stanley Marks, who stored a fair bit of 43 Group documentation which he subsequently donated to the Jewish Museum. On the letterhead is a quote from the Jewish hero Judah Maccabee: 'It is better for us to die in battle than to behold the calamities of our Nation and Sanctuary.'

29. *Jewish Chronicle*, 3 March 2006.

Index